MW01222325

teach yourself...
Freelance
Graphics 96

Jan Weingarten

with Katherine MacDonald

MIS:
PRESS

A Subsidiary of
Henry Holt and Co., Inc.

© 1996 by MIS:Press
a subsidiary of Henry Holt and Company, Inc.
115 West 18th Street
New York, NY 10011

Teach yourself® and the folded corner design are registered trademarks of MIS:Press.

All rights reserved. Reproduction or use of editorial or pictorial content in any manner is prohibited without express permission. No patent liability is assumed with respect to the use of the information contained herein. While every precaution has been taken in the preparation of this book, the publisher assumes no responsibility for errors or omissions. Neither is any liability assumed for damages resulting from the use of the information contained herein.

Throughout this book, trademarked names are used. Rather than put a trademark symbol after every occurrence of a trademarked name, we used the names in an editorial fashion only, and to the benefit of the trademark owner, with no intention of infringement of the trademark. Where such designations appear in this book, they have been printed with initial caps.

First Edition—1996

Printed in the United States of America.

Library of Congress Cataloging-in-Publication Data

Weingarten, Jan.
    Teach yourself... Freelance Graphics 96 / by Jan Weingarten with
Katherine MacDonald. —1st ed.
       p.   cm.
    ISBN 1-55828-389-7
    1. Computer graphics. 2. Freelance graphics for Windows.
I. MacDonald, Katherine. II. Title.
T385.W454   1996   95-53877
006.6'869—dc20   CIP

10 9 8 7 6 5 4 3 2 1

MIS:Press books are available at special discounts for bulk purchases for sales promotions, premiums, fund-raising, or educational use. Special editions or book excerpts can also be created to specification.

For details contact: Special Sales Director
                      MIS:Press
                      a subsidiary of Henry Holt and Company, Inc.
                      115 West 18th Street
                      New York, New York 10011

Associate Publisher: *Paul Farrell*

Managing Editor: *Cary Sullivan*	**Production Editor:** *Anne Incao*
Development Editor: *Judy Brief*	**Technical Editor:** *Kristy Clason*
Copy Edit Manager: *Shari Chappell*	**Copy Editor:** *Gwynne Jackson*

Co-Author Biography

Katherine MacDonald is owner of SebaCom, a technical documentation firm in Seattle, Washington. She is originally from New York City but came to Seattle by way of Bowling Green, Ohio, where she earned her M.A. in Technical Writing and M.Ed. in Career and Technology Education. She is currently working as a documentation specialist and World Wide Web page project manager for a specialty pre-press software firm in Everett, Washington. When she's not at the keyboard, she can be found enjoying the Pacific Northwest with her husband, Eric, and their three cats.

Acknowledgments

Kathy would like to thank her husband, Eric Beatty, for being patient and understanding when she went through the "book crazies" again.

Mucho thank yous to our crack technical editor, Kristy Clason.

My super-terrific editor at MIS:Press, Judy Brief. Judy and I have been through a lot together on several books—and she's still talking to me! Thanks, Judy, for your forbearance, professionalism, stamina, and friendship.

The rest of the MIS:Press team: Anne Incao, Shari Chappell, and Gwynne Jackson, who helped form our words into a book. Thanks for a terrific job, and your consistent dedication.

And as always, my agent, Matt Wagner, and the rest of his team at Waterside Productions. Just keep that work coming, Matt!

CONTENTS

CHAPTER 3: Working with SmartMasters 69

CHAPTER 4: The ABCs of Text. 93

CHAPTER 5: Text Properties—Making It All Look Pretty. . . 129

CHAPTER 1

Jumpstart

(Quick—I need to get a presentation together ASAP!)

This chapter is for all you type-A personalities who can't be bothered with a lot of details—"just give it to me straight." And that's exactly what you'll get here. No frills, no tricks, just the basics. By the end of this chapter, you'll know how to choose a presentation style and incorporate text, graphics, and charts into a simple presentation. In addition, you'll be able to print your presentation and open and close Freelance Graphics while running Windows 95.

Obviously, there's much more to mastering Freelance Graphics 96 (or they wouldn't have paid me to write this book), but it all builds on the basics of selecting a SmartMaster Look and page layouts, typing, saving, and printing. If you can do that, you can start to produce real presentations right away.

I'm not going to get into any shortcuts in this chapter. You'll have to stick with me a little longer to get those. (Yes, you're right—that *was* a blatant attempt to get you to keep reading.) I'm also not going to give you a lot of explanations

1

and tell you *why* things are the way they are. What you will get are bare-bones techniques to get you started until you learn all about neat stuff like SmartIcons, SmartMasters, and Page Views, all of which streamline the process of designing a presentation.

As we create the sample document, I'll point out *Roadmaps* along the way, directing you to areas of this book where you can get more information.

ROADMAP

Ready? Let's do it.

Starting Freelance Graphics

I'm assuming that you have both Windows 95 and Freelance Graphics 96 installed on your computer. Before you continue, make sure Windows 95 is running and that the taskbar is visible. All set? Let's open Freelance Graphics now.

Do It

To open Freelance Graphics 96:

1. Move your pointer to the Start button on the Windows 95 taskbar.
2. Click **Start** with your left mouse button. The Start menu opens.
3. Select **Programs** from the menu.
4. Choose **Lotus SmartSuite**. The Freelance Graphics menu opens.
5. Click **Freelance Graphics 96** as shown in Figure 1.1.

If you installed Freelance Graphics as part of SmartSuite, you will choose **Freelance Graphics 96** from the Lotus Applications menu instead of from the Freelance Graphics menu (this would replace steps 4 and 5 above). In addition, if the SmartCenter is visible, you can open Freelance Graphics simply by clicking its **Freelance Graphics** icon (this would replace steps 1–5 above).

NOTE

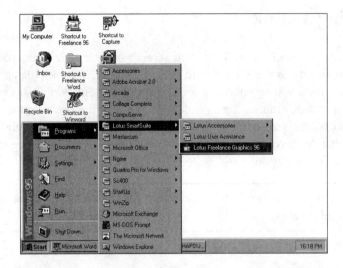

Figure 1.1 *The Start menu with* **Freelance Graphics 96** *selected.*

The software copyright information pops up on your screen, then the Lotus Freelance Graphics window opens. The Welcome to Lotus Freelance Graphics dialog box appears (see Figure 1.2).

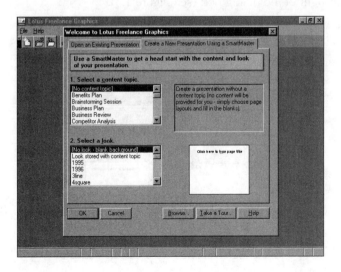

Figure 1.2 *The Welcome to Lotus Freelance Graphics dialog box.*

Selecting a Look

There's a whole bunch of stuff on your screen, but the only thing you have to deal with right now is the Welcome to Lotus Freelance Graphics dialog box. This dialog box allows you to choose a look for your presentation. You can select a SmartMaster that determines the overall appearance of the presentation, including background colors, page orientation, and text layout. You'll learn about all the choices available to you later in this book, but right now we're going to create a short, snazzy presentation.

ROADMAP

Go to Chapter 3, "Working with SmartMasters," for more detailed information.

Do It

Now, let's choose a SmartMaster for our presentation:

1. Click the **Create a New Presentation Using a SmartMaster** tab at the top right of the dialog box (see Figure 1.3).

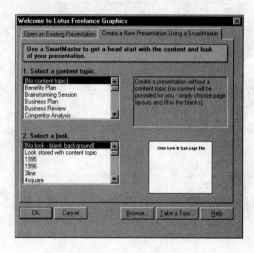

Figure 1.3 *The Create a New Presentation Using a SmartMaster tab.*

2. Select **No Content** from the "Select a content topic" list, if it isn't already highlighted.

3. Choose **Blocks** from the "Select a look" menu box.

4. Click **OK**. The New Page dialog box appears (see Figure 1.4).

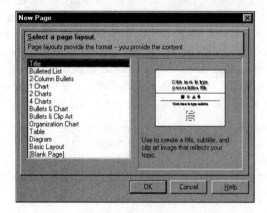

Figure 1.4 *The New Page dialog box.*

5. Click **Title** from the list.

6. Click **OK**. The title page of your presentation should look like Figure 1.5.

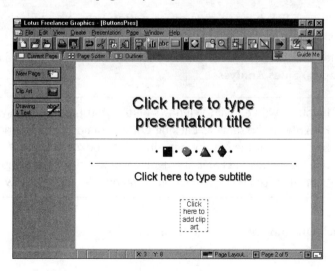

Figure 1.5 *The title page of your presentation.*

Creating a Title Page

Before you begin a presentation, it's important to plan it out in advance. We're going to create a two-page presentation titled *Sales Analysis for the 1995 Fiscal Year*. This presentation is for a company named Bountiful Buttons, a small, local manufacturing firm that makes—you guessed it—buttons. Bountiful Buttons' customers are national clothing manufacturers. These manufacturers are experiencing an increase in demand from clothing stores for their products, therefore the demand for Bountiful Buttons' products is also increasing. Sales exceeded the expectations of Bountiful Buttons' owner, Mike Taylor, at the end of the 1995 fiscal year. Mike plans on discussing this dramatic increase during the year-in-review meeting with the company's employees.

ROADMAP

"The ABCs of Text," Chapter 4, instructs you on how to make bullet lists, 2-bullet lists, mixed layouts, and even add your own text blocks.

Do It

Let's give our Bountiful Buttons presentation a title and subtitle now.

1. Click on **Click here to type presentation title**. A text block opens with a blinking cursor.

2. Enter the following text (mistakes and all, we'll fix them later in this chapter) **Sales Analysss**.

WARNING

If you've worked with Windows before, you probably know that pressing **Enter** is the same as clicking **OK** in a dialog box. The trick with text blocks is that they're not actually dialog boxes—they just look a little like them. Pressing **Enter** after typing text in a text block simply creates a blank line. To complete your presentation title, do the following steps.

3. Click **OK** to place your text on the page.

4. To add a subtitle, click on **Click here to type subtitle**.

5. Type **1995 Fiscal Yr.**.

6. Click **OK** to place your subtitle on the page.

7. Click anywhere outside of the text block to deselect the text. The title page of your presentation should now look like Figure 1.6.

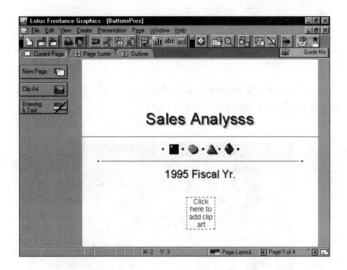

Figure 1.6 *The title page of your presentation.*

Adding a Graphic

You've probably noticed the box with the words "Click here to add clip art" appearing in it. Title pages usually provide a section on the page where you can add graphics. Freelance Graphics comes with more than 60 categories of clip art, mostly maps and common business objects, ready for you to include in your presentations. But you're not limited to the art that comes with Freelance Graphics—you can add your own art to an existing category or even create a new category.

Also, graphics aren't limited to clip art. You can add videos, sound, diagrams, bitmaps, and vector images to your presentation.

ROADMAP

To learn more about adding graphics to your presentations, see Chapters 7 through 10. Each chapter discusses a different type of graphic that you can include in your presentation.

Do It

Let's place a graphic on our title page.

1. Click on **Click here to add a graphic**. The Add Clip Art or Diagram to the Page dialog box pops up (see Figure 1.7).

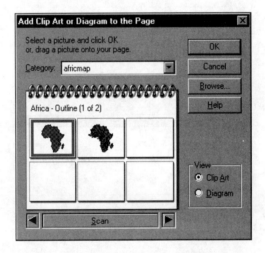

Figure 1.7 The Add Clip Art or Diagram to the Page dialog box.

2. Click the **Category** arrow to open the drop-down list.

3. Scroll down and select **Buttons** from the Clip art drop-down menu.

N O T E

Notice that the pictures change when you select **Buttons**. Every time you change a clip art category, the pictures change to show you what appears in that category.

4. Click the arrow to the right of the Scan button (located below the clip art images) twice. Your Add Clip Art or Diagram to the Page dialog box should look like Figure 1.8.

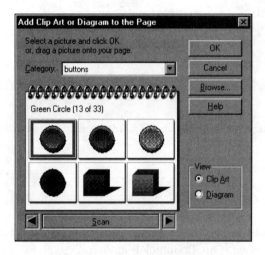

Figure 1.8 *Your Add Clip Art or Diagram to the Page dialog box.*

5. Click on the **Button** image (the one that looks like a shirt button on the lower left) icon to select the clip art.

6. Select **OK**. The Add Clip Art or Diagram to the Page dialog box closes and the title page of the presentation opens. The clip art now appears on your page, as shown in Figure 1.9.

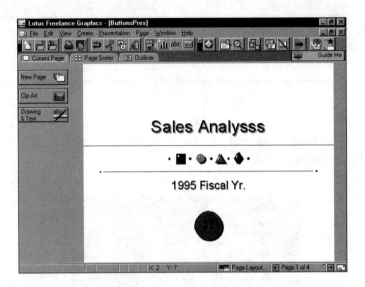

Figure 1.9 *The title page of your presentation with clip art.*

Adding Another Page

Presentations usually require more than one page to cover all the information that needs to be addressed. Our Bountiful Buttons presentation is no exception. We need to add several more pages to our presentation. Let's add a chart page next.

Do It

Here's how to add another page to a presentation:

1. Click the **New Page** button, which is located to the left of the title page. The New Page dialog box pops up asking you to select a page layout (see Figure 1.10).

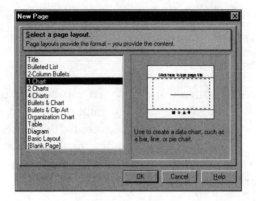

Figure 1.10 *The New Page dialog box.*

2. Select **1 Chart** from the menu box.

When you select a page layout, the thumbnail in the New Page dialog box changes to show what the selected page layout looks like.

N O T E

3. Click **OK**. The 1 Chart page appears, as shown in Figure 1.11.

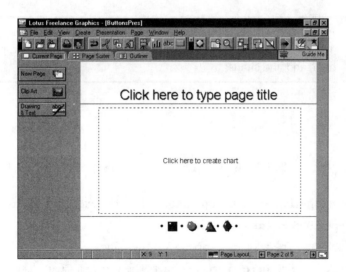

Figure 1.11 *The 1 Chart page.*

Next, we need to add a title to this page and create a chart.

Creating a Chart

Explaining data or information using only text can become unnecessarily complicated. Often, the message isn't clearly communicated and everyone ends up confused. A chart or diagram may make it easier for the audience to understand. Remember that old saying: a picture is worth a thousand words. When designing a presentation, it's a good idea to keep this in mind. Charts can make a big impact on an audience and, at the very least, help liven up a presentation when used appropriately.

In this section, we're going to create a bar chart showing the sales data for Bountiful Buttons' 1995 fiscal year. Bountiful Buttons' sales shot up dramatically in the past year. During the first quarter, the company sold barely 3 million buttons. The second and third quarters remained fairly constant, with 7 million and 10 million buttons sold per quarter respectively. The fourth quarter, however, showed a dramatic increase—almost 60 million buttons were sold. Mike Taylor, Bountiful Buttons' owner, wants to really impress his audience when he presents this information. He'd like to see this information presented in a chart that shows this dramatic, end-of-year increase. Let's convert this information into a bar chart so that the impact of these numbers can be clearly seen.

ROADMAP

In Chapter 7, "Charts for the Visual at Heart," charts are further discussed. You can learn how to create a variety of charts including bar, pie, scatter, area, and line charts.

Do It

Now that we've added another page, let's title this page and create a bar chart.

1. Click on **Click here to type page title**. The text block opens.
2. Type **1995 Fiscal Year Sales**.
3. Click **OK**. The text now appears on the page.
4. Click on **Click here to create chart**. The Create a Chart dialog box opens (see Figure 1.12).

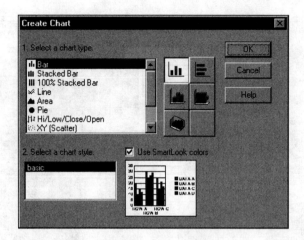

Figure 1.12 *The Create a Chart dialog box.*

5. Select **Bar** from the "Select a chart type" list.

Every time you click on a selection in the "Select a chart type" menu, the graphic in the dialog box changes to reflect your selection. This allows you to see the type of chart you're creating before you actually create it.

N O T E

6. Click **OK**. The Edit Data dialog box pops up (see Figure 1.13). Here's where we enter Bountiful Buttons' sales data.

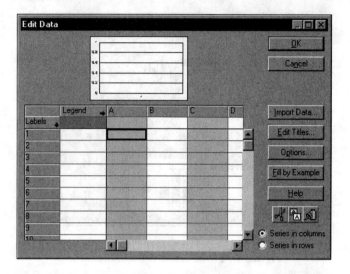

Figure 1.13 *The Edit Data dialog box.*

NOTE

The "boxes" in the Edit Data dialog box are called *cells*. These cells work like cells in spreadsheets such as Lotus 1-2-3, Excel, or QuattroPro; they can contain text or numerical data. Cells are organized into *rows* (going across the page) and *columns* (moving down the page).

❖ Using Figure 1.14 as your guide, enter the text and data I gave you in the introduction section of Creating a Chart. You can click in each cell to enter the data or use your directional arrows to move between cells. Don't worry about the Legend column. This is where you can add labels to the X-axis. While labels can help clarify a chart, our chart is fairly simple so it's not necessary to add a label here. In Chapter 7, "Charts for the Visual at Heart," I'll show you how to add labels to your chart.

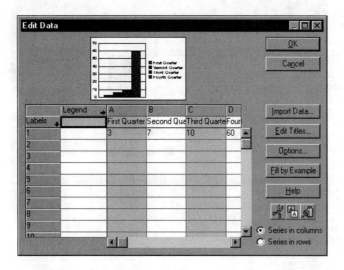

Figure 1.14 *Use this Edit Data dialog box as a guide to entering data.*

NOTE

As you enter the data into the cells, notice that the thumbnail chart in the Edit Data dialog box changes to reflect your entry. This allows you to double-check your entries visually and to preview the final chart.

7. Click **OK** to create your bar chart. The bar chart appears on page 2 of the presentation (see Figure 1.15).

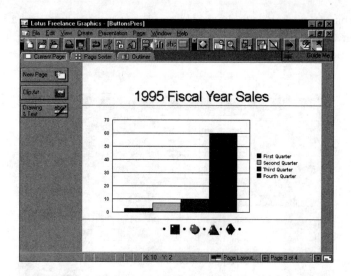

Figure 1.15 *Your bar chart.*

Creating a Bulleted List

Now that you know how to make a chart, it's time to move on. Your presentation would be pretty boring if it consisted of charts and nothing else. Presentations work best if there is a sprinkling of text, charts, tables, and graphics. You know how to create charts and title pages and how to add graphics, but what about a plain old page of text? In presentations, text is usually formatted into bullets, with each bullet representing an idea or specific point. Mike Taylor, our Bountiful Buttons owner, wants to present and discuss several key issues that he attributes to Bountiful Buttons' success in 1995. In this section, we'll create a bulleted list using these points.

Go to Chapter 4, "The ABCs of Text," to learn more about bulleted lists and text layouts in general.

ROADMAP

Do It

First we need to add another page and title it, then we can create our bulleted list. Let's review how to add a new page and then give it a title:

1. Click the **New Page** button. The New Page dialog box pops up.
2. Select **Bulleted List** from the menu.
3. Click **OK**. The new page pops up.
4. Click on **Click here to type page title**. The text block opens.
5. Type **1995 Sales Review**.
6. Click **OK**.

Next, let's create the bulleted list:

1. Click on **Click here to type bulleted list**. The text block opens with a bullet in place and the blinking cursor.
2. Type **Increased customer base**.
3. Press **Enter** to add a line.

NOTE
When you press **Enter**, Freelance Graphics automatically adds another bulleted line for you. The cursor is even located at the insertion point, so all you have to do is continue typing without worrying about bullets or tabs. Nice, huh?

4. Type **Widened product line** and press **Enter**.
5. Next, type **Hired more salespeople** and press **Enter** again.
6. Finally, type **Streamlined production**.
7. Click **OK** to finish entering your text.
8. Click anywhere outside the text block to deselect the text. The text appears on the page now, fully formatted as shown in Figure 1.16.

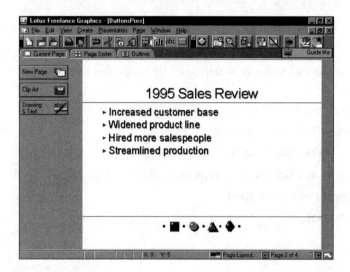

Figure 1.16 *Your bulleted list page.*

Adding a Table

Sometimes it's a good idea to present information for comparison. For example, in our Bountiful Buttons presentation, we'd like to compare 1995 sales data with 1996 sales goals. This way the audience can easily understand where we've been and where we want to go. The comparison could be shown in a chart, but in this case we'll use a table for both increased clarity and variety.

Mike Taylor wants to establish some sales goals for the 1996 fiscal year and challenge his salespeople. He wants to see them sell 10 million buttons during the first quarter (a traditionally slow period for the company), 20 million during the second and third quarters, and 70 million in the fourth quarter. While these numbers may sound incredible compared to 1995's data, these sales numbers are possible given predicted future trends in this industry.

ROADMAP

Go to Chapter 8, "Tables," to learn the details of creating tables.

Do It

Just like title pages and bulleted lists, Freelance Graphics has pages especially designed for tables. Here's how to select and title a table page:

1. Click the **New Page** button. The New Page dialog box pops up.
2. Select **Table** from the menu.
3. Click **OK**. The new page appears.
4. Click on **Click here to type page title**. The text block opens.
5. Type **1995 vs. 1996**.
6. Click **OK**.

Now, let's create a table:

1. Click on **Click here to create table**. The Table Gallery dialog box pops up (see Figure 1.17).

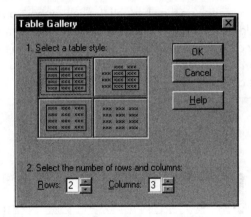

Figure 1.17 *The Table Gallery.*

2. Choose the second table in the first row from the Select a table style list.
3. Use the left and right arrows to enter **5** in the rows box and **3** in the columns box (see Figure 1.18).

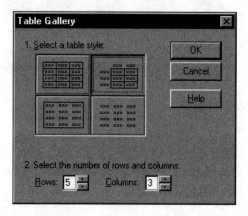

Figure 1.18 *Your chart settings.*

4.   Click **OK** to create the chart. The page appears with the chart highlighted.

5.   Click in the chart to add text. A thick line appears around the chart.

NOTE

When you click on the chart, all the cells appear on the page. Now you can add your data (text and numerical) to the table. You can move among cells by clicking in a cell, pressing the **Tab** key to move forward one cell or **Shift+Tab** to move backward, or using the directional arrows on your keyboard.

6.   Enter the data as shown in Figure 1.19.

	1995	1996
First Qtr	3	10
Second Qtr	7	20
Third Qtr	10	20
Fourth Qtr	60	70

Figure 1.19 *Data for the chart.*

7. Click anywhere on the page outside of the table. The table is unselected. The page now looks like Figure 1.20.

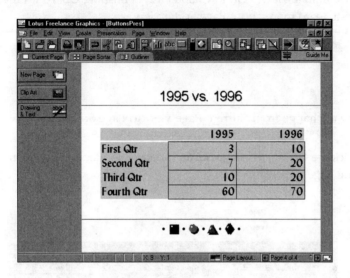

Figure 1.20 *The completed table page.*

Viewing Your Masterpiece

So far you've been working in Current Page view, which is Freelance Graphics' default. Current Page view allows you to change the design and text of your presentation and to access the "Click here" text blocks. Freelance Graphics has two additional views: Page Sorter and Outliner. Page Sorter's advantage is that you can see the entire presentation on one screen (shrunken down, of course). This allows you to check the presentation sequence and overall look for consistency. In Page Sorter view, you can alter the page sequence of the presentation just by clicking and dragging. Outliner view displays the text in your presentation as an outline. You can add or delete text, edit and spell check, and even move text around in Outliner view.

Our Bountiful Buttons presentation is four pages long now. Let's look at it using Page Sorter view and see if we need to move any pages around.

ROADMAP

For more information on Outliner view, go to Chapter 6, "Working in Outliner View." Go to Chapter 12, "Polishing Up Your Presentation," to learn more about Page Sorter view.

Do It

Here's how to change from Current Page view to Page Sorter view:

❖ Click the tab labeled **Page Sorter**, which is located just above the presentation page (see Figure 1.21).

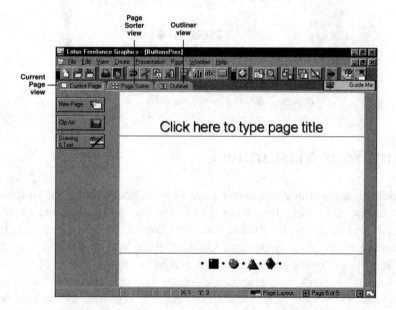

Figure 1.21 *The Page View tabs.*

The page view changes, and all four presentation pages appear as thumbnails (see Figure 1.22).

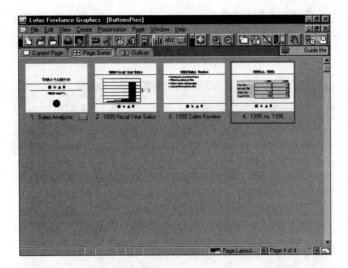

Figure 1.22 *The view from Page Sorter.*

After looking at the page sequence, page 2 really should be switched with page 3. Let's do it now:

1. Click on **2. 1995 Fiscal Year Sales** and hold the mouse button down.

When you click on a page and hold down the mouse button in Page Sorter view, the cursor turns into a small hand. This indicates that you have selected an item and can now move it.

NOTE

2. While holding the mouse button down, drag **2. 1995 Fiscal Year Sales** until it is on top of page 3, **3. 1995 Sales Review**.

You'll know that the page is positioned properly when a gray bar pops up to the right of the presentation page. When you see this bar, release the presentation page you are dragging.

NOTE

3. Release **2. 1995 Fiscal Year Sales** after you position it on top of page 3. Pages 2 and 3 are now switched, and the presentation should look like Figure 1.23.

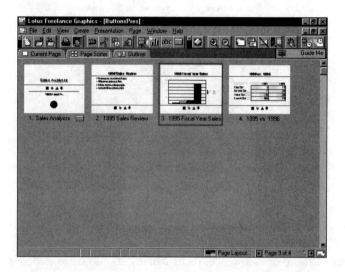

Figure 1.23 *Pages 2 and 3 are now switched.*

Creating Speaker Notes

Have you ever been to a presentation where the person presenting held a bunch of index cards in his hand? Those cards were the presenter's cheat sheets—little reminders of what to say and when. Now that you've created your presentation masterpiece, you'll probably want to accompany it with a thorough set of cheat sheets. You *could* use index cards, but there's a better way. Freelance Graphics has a feature called *Speaker Notes* (the same thing as a cheat sheet) that allows you to create notes for each page.

Let's add a speaker note to page 1 of our presentation. Dwayne is a salesman at Bountiful Buttons who was hired at the beginning of the second quarter. Throughout that quarter, he went through a rigorous training program. In the third quarter, he was sent out on his own sales calls, but he didn't get the sales. Finally, Dwayne decided that he needed to do something drastic. He removed the buttons from all of his shirts and suits and replaced them with buttons from

Bountiful Buttons' product lines. Instead of pulling out trays of buttons to show clothing manufacturers, he showed them the buttons on his own suits and shirts. This sales tactic was not only successful, but it enabled Dwayne to make 25% of the total sales for the fourth quarter. He was awarded the Quarterly Salesperson Award for his inventiveness and hard work. Mike Taylor wants to acknowledge Dwayne's work while giving this presentation. Let's add a speaker note to the Title page regarding Dwayne.

Go to Chapter 12, "Polishing Up Your Presentation," to learn more about Speaker Notes.

ROADMAP

Do It

I'm assuming that you're still in Page Sorter view. Here's how to add a Speaker Note:

1. Click on **1. Sales Analysss**. A gray box appears around the Title page.

2. Click the **Create Speaker Note** SmartIcon. The Speaker Note—Sales Analysss dialog box pops up (see Figure 1.24).

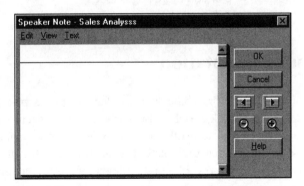

Figure 1.24 *The Speaker Note dialog box.*

3. Type the following text: **Dwayne's sales tactics were so original that maybe I should require all of our salespeople to wear only our buttons from now on**.

Janice—remind me to include that in our employee handbook for the coming year.

The result is shown in Figure 1.25.

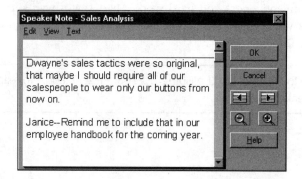

Figure 1.25 *Your Speaker Note for the Title page.*

4.   Click **OK** to save the Speaker Note.

After clicking **OK**, an index card icon appears beside the page title now. If you click on the icon, the Speaker Note pops up again. You can modify the Speaker Note or add more pages to it.

Saving Your Presentation

Saving should always be the first thing you do after creating a presentation. Until you save your document to disk, it only exists in the computer's temporary memory. If the power goes out or you turn off your computer without saving, all of your work will be lost. In fact, if your presentation is much longer than the one we just created, you should save it while you're in the middle of creating it, and then save it frequently while you're working. This is something I'll keep bugging you about throughout the book—saving presentations often is one of the best habits you can get into (unless you *really* like to work on the same stuff over and over).

Do It

To save your file:

1. Click on the word **File** on the menu line which is just below where it says Freelance Graphics (if you have SmartSuite installed, then it probably says Lotus SmartSuite 96—Lotus Freelance Graphics) at the very top of your screen, or press **Alt+F**. That opens the File menu (see Figure 1.26).

To press **Alt+F**, hold down the **Alt** key while you press the letter **F**, then release both keys. For any menu selection, the letter that's underlined is the one you press, either on its own or in combination with the **Alt** key.

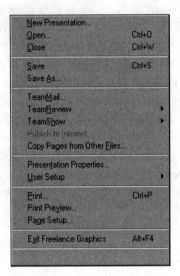

Figure 1.26 *The File menu.*

2. Click on **Save As** (or press the letter **A**). The Save As dialog box pops up, as shown in Figure 1.27.

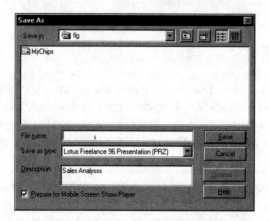

Figure 1.27 *The Save As dialog box.*

Any time a menu item has an ellipsis (...) after it, you'll see a *dialog box* when you choose that item. The dialog box is Freelance Graphics' way of saying it needs more information—in this case, it needs to know what name you want to give your file.

3. When the Save As dialog box opens, it looks like there are a lot of choices to make, but all you have to do is type a name for the document—the insertion point is already in the right place for you to just start typing. Type **ButtonsPres**.

4. Click on the **Save** button or press the **Enter** key. Notice that the **Save** button has a darker border around it than the other buttons. That indicates that it's the *default* button: its action will be executed if you press **Enter**. So, pressing **Enter** in this case is just like clicking on **Save**.

After you choose **Save**, the Save As dialog box disappears and you're back at the main Freelance Graphics screen.

Once you've saved a document, you can choose **Save** from the File menu at any time to save the document or press **Ctrl+S**. Freelance Graphics won't ask you any questions—it'll just do it. It's very fast, and it's a good idea to do this on a regular basis—any time you make major changes to your presentation or add a lot of text.

Go to Chapter 2, "Getting to Know Freelance Graphics," to learn more about saving documents.

ROADMAP

Spelling It Right

Once you've entered your text and saved the presentation, the next step is to make sure everything's spelled right. Wait—don't pull out your dictionary and start looking up every word. Freelance Graphics has a built-in feature that automatically checks your document. You might be wondering why we didn't spell check the document before saving it. That would've saved some time, right? Well, yeah, but there's a method here.

Any time you run a spell check or send a document to the printer (or do other complex things like running a slide show) there's a possibility that something could go wrong. Your computer could freeze up. If that happens before you save, you could lose all your work. I don't want to scare you; it's not going to happen often, but I'd rather be safe than sorry. (How's that for a tired but true cliché?)

Do It

Let's run a spell check:

1. With ButtonsPres on the screen, click on the **Edit** menu (or press **Alt+E**).

2. Click on **Check Spelling** (or press **Ctrl+F2**).

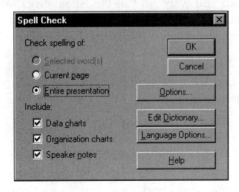

Figure 1.28 *Choose* **Check Spelling** *from the Edit menu (or press* **Ctrl+F2**).

3. Click **OK** to start the spell check. The Spell Check dialog box pops up. At this point you don't have to worry about all the Spell Check options. Spell Check automatically checks the whole document unless you specify something else.

ROADMAP

Go to Chapter 4, "The ABCs of Text," to learn about the different tasks you can perform with Spell Check.

4. When the Spell Checker stops on a word (in this case, **Analysss**), there are several choices you can make. Most of them are covered in Chapter 4—you just need to deal with a couple for now:

❖ If Spell Check stops on a word that's spelled correctly but isn't in Freelance Graphics' dictionary (a good example of this would be someone's name), you can choose **Skip Once** to skip over the word without making any changes (with **Skip Once**, the Spell Check stops the next time it sees the same word). Choose **Skip Always** to skip over the word every time the Spell Check sees it during the current spell check session.

❖ If the word really is misspelled, choose one of the words from the Alternatives box. If you see the correct spelling there, either click on that word or use your **Up Arrow** and **Down Arrow** keys to highlight the correct word. Then press **Enter** or click on **Replace** (**Replace** is the default selection in Spell Check).

ROADMAP

If the word you want isn't in the Alternatives list, you can edit the spelling manually. You'll know more about this after reading Chapter 4.

When Spell Check has finished checking the spelling, the Spelling Check Complete dialog box pops up.

5. Click **OK** to return to the presentation.

All the changes you made during the spell check are stored in the computer's temporary memory (RAM) until you save the document again. You should always save your work right after spell checking it by pressing **Ctrl+S**.

Editing Made Simple

What, you're not perfect? You mean there are still some problems with your presentation even after running the spell check? Well, join the club. Fortunately, Freelance

Graphics gives you a number of ways to clean up your work. For now, I'll give you a basic tool that will let you change a word or letter here and there.

The word *Yr.* on the first sentence should really be *Year.* Why didn't that get caught during the spell check? Okay, I'll give you the brief version of mini-lecture #3248 (which will be repeated at length in Chapter 4): *A spell checker does not take the place of proofreading your work.* Yr. is a commonly used abbreviation, and it's spelled correctly, even though it's not the word we meant to use. 'Nuff said for now.

Do It

You're probably still in Page Sorter view. To edit the page, let's return to Current Page view with the title page displayed. Here's how:

1. While in Page Sorter, click on the **1. Sales Analysis** page to select it.

2. Click the **Current Page** tab. Freelance changes view mode and the title page of the presentation appears in the window.

3. Double-click on the words **1995 Fiscal Yr**. The text block opens with a blinking cursor (see Figure 1.29).

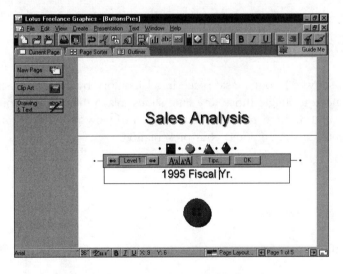

Figure 1.29 *The text block with blinking cursor.*

4. Move the mouse pointer (which is now a thin vertical line that looks like the capital letter "I") so that it's immediately before the abbreviation

Yr. and click the left mouse button. The *insertion point* (the flashing vertical line) is displayed at the point where you click the mouse.

5. Get rid of the abbreviation *Yr.* by pressing **Delete** or **Backspace** a total of three times. The key you press depends on where the insertion point is:

   ❖ If the insertion point is just after the letter you want to delete, press **Backspace**.

   ❖ If the insertion point is just in front of the letter you want to delete, press **Delete**.

6. Type **Year**. Until you learn more techniques for deleting and changing text, you can always delete one character at a time with **Backspace** or **Delete**, then type in whatever you want to replace it with.

7. Click **OK**, then click anywhere outside the text block to deselect it.

8. Don't forget to save again.

ROADMAP

You've probably already noticed that the mouse pointer changes shape depending on what's happening. Chapter 2, "Getting to Know Freelance Graphics," explains the different shapes and when they're used.

Creating a Slide Show

It's time to show off your masterpiece in all its glory by creating a slide show. You don't need to juggle those tiny little slides, place them in a carousel in the right order, and find the perfect wall or screen to view this slide show. All you need is Freelance Graphics and your presentation.

Do It

To create a slide show and run it:

1. With the presentation open, open the Presentation menu.

2. Choose **From Beginning** in the Run Screen Show menu. The Title page pops up on the entire screen.

NOTE

To navigate through the slide show, click the left mouse button to go forward a page; the right mouse button to move back a page.

3. Click the left mouse button to see how your presentation pages will appear. When you have looked through all the pages, the program automatically returns you to the Freelance Graphics window.

ROADMAP

To learn more about how slide shows work and the cool stuff you can do with them, turn to Chapter 14, "Creating a Screen Show."

Printing It Out

Finally, we can print our presentation! Again, no details here—just the basics so that you have the tools you need to print a document until you get a chance to delve into printing in more depth.

Do It

To print your file:

1. With the presentation on your screen, click on **File** (or press **Alt+F**).
2. Click on **Print** (or press **Ctrl+P**). The Print dialog box opens (see Figure 1.30).

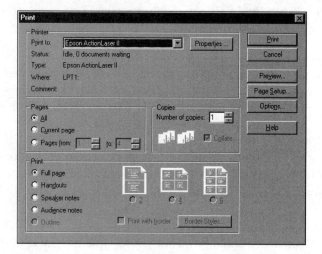

Figure 1.30 *The Print dialog box.*

N O T E

Notice the black dot next to **All Pages** in the Pages section of the Print dialog box. That means that Freelance Graphics will print the whole document unless you make another selection. For now, you don't have to worry about all the choices.

3. Press **Enter** or click **Print** to print.

ROADMAP

If Windows 95 and Freelance Graphics have been set up properly on your computer, you shouldn't have to worry about selecting a printer. But if you can't get the presentation to print, not to worry. It's probably just a matter of changing a couple of settings. Take a look at Chapter 13, "Printing the Presentation," to find out more.

Exiting Freelance Graphics

Let's pretend that presentation was the only thing you needed to do today (we can dream, can't we?), and it's time to get out of Freelance Graphics and turn off the computer for the day. So, without any further ado...

Do It

To exit Freelance Graphics:

1. Click on **File** (or press **Alt+F**).
2. Choose **Exit Freelance Graphics** from the File menu (or press the letter **X**).

If you haven't made any changes to your presentation since the last time you saved it, choosing **Exit Freelance Graphics** from the File menu takes you right out of Freelance Graphics and back to the desktop.

If any changes have been made, the Exit Freelance Graphics dialog box shown in Figure 1.31 pops up. If you want to save the changes, choose **Yes**. Otherwise, choose **No**. After choosing **Yes** or **No**, Freelance Graphics closes and returns you to the desktop.

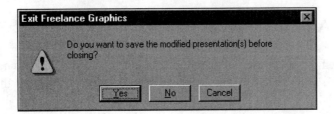

Figure 1.31 *If any changes have been made to your document, the Freelance Graphics dialog box is displayed when you try to exit Freelance Graphics.*

Exiting Windows 95

If you're really done for the day, you probably want to turn off your computer and go home (I know I do). There's only one more thing to do before you can hit that power switch: exit Windows 95.

Do It

Let's exit Windows 95:

1. Click the **Start** button on your taskbar. The Start menu opens.

2. Choose **Shutdown** from the Start menu. A dialog box is displayed asking if you really want to shut down the computer.

3. Click **OK** to exit Windows 95.

After you choose **OK**, you'll hear the computer churn and grind away a little bit. Several seconds later a note appears on your screen saying it is safe to turn off your computer.

Never turn off your computer without exiting Windows 95.

WARNING

Is That All There Is to It?

Give yourself a pat on the back. You got in and out of Freelance Graphics and Windows 95; you created a simple presentation, saved it, checked the spelling, made an editing change, and printed it. Whew! There's a lot more to learn, but you've got the basic ingredients. Everything else will build on the elements you learned in this chapter.

In the next chapter, "Getting to Know Freelance Graphics," I'll show you the techniques for using the mouse and keyboard. Then you'll learn how to recognize and work with different elements of the Freelance Graphics screen. I'll explain dialog boxes, scroll bars, pull-down menus, and much more.

CHAPTER 2

Getting to Know
Freelance Graphics 96

(and that Windows 95 thing everyone's talking about)

I attended a lecture series years ago where the guest speaker stood behind a podium in front of an audience of about 500. She droned on for a while and then, just to make the lecture a little more interesting, scribbled some notes on a whiteboard that had been wheeled out especially for the occasion. Of course, most of us couldn't see the notes because we were sitting too far away. Watching the speaker wrestle with a huge note pad on stage was worse but afforded us some amusement. People sitting in the back rows even placed bets on whether the note pad was going to win the match. Occasionally the lecturer would bring in slides and we would all sit in the dark for half an hour and doze off.

Does this sound familiar? As an audience member, I've had my fair share of these experiences, but not in recent years. Presentations have changed significantly in the last several years, because people have greater access to computers in the office and at home. Not only do people use computers more in their daily routine, but software companies saw a niche in the computer software market and decided to create and market programs that specialize in presentations. As an audience member, that means you'll probably be able to see the presentation and not be distracted by wrestling matches. As a presenter, that means you're able to create really cool presentations that won't make you feel like you're inflicting torture on your audience. And—most importantly—you'll get your point across. So, whether you're a businessperson or a student, you can make professional presentations that look sharp.

If you read and followed the tutorials in Chapter 1, "Jumpstart," you know the basics of how Freelance Graphics 96 for Windows 95 works. But that's just the basics. Freelance Graphics is a powerful presentation tool that allows you to create simple presentations or complex multimedia shows—and everything in between. Here are some of the powerful features you'll be able to use after working through this book:

❖ Select from more than a hundred SmartMasters to create a uniform, professionally designed presentation.

❖ Choose from more than ten preformatted pages to create title pages, bulleted lists, charts, tables, and diagrams.

❖ Select from more than ten predesigned typical business presentations that you can customize.

❖ Create automated screen shows with timed transitions.

❖ Create professionally designed speaker notes to use as "cheat sheets."

If you're hooked up to a network, Freelance Graphics allows you to share your presentations with other network users. Freelance Graphics' network capabilities are beyond the scope of this book, but I'll point out some of the network features available where appropriate.

Before we dive in, I'd like to go over the basics of how Windows 95 and the Freelance Graphics windows work.

A New Breed of Animal—Windows 95

Wait! Don't turn the page yet. I can hear you thinking, "I didn't buy this book to learn about Windows 95. I'll just skip right over to the Freelance Graphics stuff." Well, hold on a minute. I'm only going to talk about "Windows 95 stuff" that you need to know in order to use Freelance Graphics. In fact, I'll use Freelance Graphics as an example, so you can use this chapter to start getting familiar with the Freelance Graphics screen. So, stick with me for a little while (unless you're an old hand with Windows 95 and really don't need this introduction, in which case you have my permission to skip ahead).

Why Windows 95?

Okay, everyone's talking about Windows 95, and your best friend finally convinced you that you absolutely had to buy Windows 95 and Freelance Graphics 96 for Windows 95. So you did. But was it the right thing to do? The answer is an unequivocal *yes.* Why, you may ask? In a word: standardization.

What that means is that once you learn techniques for working with any Windows 95 program (in this case, Freelance Graphics), you have the basic tools for working in any other Windows 95 program. For example, you use the same method to save files and exit the program no matter which program you're using.

Windows 95's standardization extends to printing. Instead of having to set up a printer every time you install a new program, a Windows application *knows* what printer you have when you install it, by looking at your Windows setup. If you get a new printer, all you have to do is install and set it up in Windows 95, and all your Windows programs can automatically use it.

But why all the recent hoopla about Windows 95? Well, Windows 95 is a major improvement over Microsoft's Windows 3.1, the previous version of the operating system. Actually, Windows 3.1 wasn't quite an operating system because it ran on top of DOS. You had to open DOS, a clunky, behind-the-scenes operating system that required you to use an arcane language, before accessing anything else. This slowed things down, depending on what you were doing on the system. When you opened Freelance Graphics, for example, you could easily create your file because you were interacting only with Windows, but when you saved your file, Freelance was interacting with Windows and DOS. What does all this have to do with you? Well, with Windows 95, DOS and Windows are woven together; therefore—unless you really want to—you don't need to work in DOS at all. Windows 95 handles resources better and allows you to perform multiple tasks more easily.

There are more advantages to Windows 95, which you'll discover as you delve further into it. For now, just be aware that a lot of what you learn in this book will apply to the next Windows 95 program you decide to master.

If You're New to Windows 95

I'm going to assume that Windows 95 is already installed on your computer (if you're smart, you got that friend who talked you into buying it to install it or you). If it's not, refer to the booklet *Introducing Windows 95* that came with your software.

Using a Mouse

Before we go any further, I have one question. Do you have a mouse? A mouse is very important (if not crucial) to Windows 95 and Windows applications. You can use Windows and Freelance Graphics without a mouse, but you won't be able to take advantage of a lot of nifty shortcuts, and some things will be down-right cumbersome to accomplish.

Got your mouse now? Good. Let's go. Just rest your hand lightly on that little critter with your index finger over the left button and your middle finger over the right button. The left button is the one you'll use most of the time. A lot of Windows programs don't even use the right mouse button, but Freelance Graphics and Windows 95 use it to get to some shortcut features. If your mouse has three buttons, ignore the middle one—you won't use it at all in Freelance Graphics 96 for Windows 95.

N O T E

Lefties unite! For all you lefties out there, don't fret. Microsoft thought of you when they designed Windows 95. You can swap the left and right mouse buttons to make it easier to operate the mouse. To learn how, look up *switching mouse buttons* in your online Help Index. If you've swapped the mouse buttons, you'll have to mentally reverse any instructions I give for using the mouse. When I write "click the left mouse button," you'll click the right one.

Click, Click, Click... What a Drag

Click and drag. There, you just learned most of the mouse lingo you need to know. What's the rest? Pointing. That's all there is to it. You point, you click, or you drag. There are some fancy combinations, like double-clicking, quadruple-clicking, and dragging and dropping, but they're just extensions of the basic techniques.

❖ **Point.** This means that you move the mouse pointer (the little arrow that moves around on your screen when you move the mouse) to a particular spot. If I write "point to the **Save** button," move the mouse until the arrow is on the Save button.

❖ **Click.** If I write "click on the **File** menu," point to the File menu, press down on the mouse button (in this case it would be the left button), and then let go. It's called *clicking* because with most mice you'll hear a little click when you let go of the button.

❖ **Double-click.** Double-clicking is something you'll be doing a lot. All it means is that you point at the item in question and click the left mouse button (press and let go) twice in fairly rapid succession. This action might seem awkward at first, but with a little practice you'll be double-clicking with the best of them.

❖ **Drag.** This is a technique in which you point at the item and hold down the left mouse button while you move the mouse to a new location. When the object you're dragging is where you want it, release the mouse button.

The mouse pointer is a tricky little devil—it actually changes shape depending on what you're doing. The three shapes you'll see most of the time are an arrow (or some variation of an arrow), an hourglass, and an I-beam (sort of like a capital letter I). A regular arrow means that you can make a selection from a menu or dialog box; the arrow changes to a double-arrow to let you know you can change the size of a window or dialog box. The hourglass indicates that the computer is performing an action and is busy. In general, you'll probably see an hourglass most often when opening a file. The I-beam indicates you're in an area where text can be entered. Throughout this book, I'll use the term *mouse pointer* when I tell you to do something with the mouse, and I'll explain what's happening to the shape when it's important.

Using the Keyboard

There isn't much I need to tell you about the keyboard. When you're entering text, you can type the same way you would on a typewriter. But I do want to point out a few added attractions.

Special Keys

Your computer keyboard contains special keys that Freelance Graphics uses for different purposes at different times. How's that for a vague statement? All it means is that Freelance Graphics takes advantage of all the extra keys to give you shortcut methods for accomplishing tasks.

I emphasize mouse use in this book, since in most cases the mouse is the easiest way to do things. But I'll give you keyboard alternatives for most procedures and let you know when the keyboard method is actually a shortcut. Sometimes using the keyboard can save you time. As you become more familiar with Freelance Graphics, experiment with the mouse and the keyboard in various situations. The whole idea is to use whichever method feels most comfortable and efficient to you.

I'll point out specific keyboard alternatives as we go along. For now, here are the basics:

❖ **Function keys.** These are the odd-numbered keys labeled F1 through F12 (your keyboard might only go up to F10). Depending on what kind of keyboard you have, these keys are either at the top of your keyboard or in a lock to the left of the main typing area. As the name implies, function keys are assigned specific functions. For example, you can press **F7** to add a new page to your presentation.

❖ **Ctrl, Alt, and Shift.** These keys are used in combination with other keys to extend a key's power or to change what the key does. For example, pressing **F7** by itself creates a new presentation page, but **Alt+F7** is used to duplicate a page. If I write "press **Alt+F7**," hold down the **Alt** key while you press the **F7** key, then release both keys at the same time.

Don't worry if using these combination keystrokes seems awkward at first; it takes practice, and you'll get plenty of that throughout this book.

❖ **Esc.** This is the cancel key. If you open a menu or dialog box by mistake, just press **Esc** to back out of it.

❖ **Other special keys.** As we work through Freelance Graphics' features, I'll point out other keys that can be used as mouse alternatives (and, in some cases, shortcuts). The Home, End, Page Up, and Page Down keys make it easy to move around in a document or dialog box. You'll use the Delete key to delete text and other objects and the Insert key to change your typing mode.

Starting Windows 95 and Freelance Graphics

If you haven't started Windows 95 yet, go ahead. Windows 95 usually starts automatically when you turn on your computer. If your computer is set up differently (for example, someone might have set you up so that a menu appears on your screen when you start your computer), check with the person who installed Windows 95 and set up your system for instructions on starting Windows 95. Figure 2.1 shows the desktop with Windows 95 open.

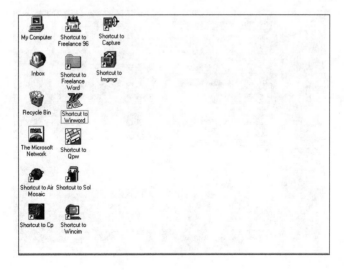

Figure 2.1 *Windows 95.*

Your screen probably doesn't look quite look this. One of the neat (and initially confusing) things about Windows 95 is that you can change just about everything, including the arrangement of the screen. But even if your screen has a different number of *icons* (the little pictures that look like a recycle bin or a computer) or they're arranged differently, you still have access to the same features and you use them the same way.

The screen that you see when you start Windows 95 is called the *desktop*. This is your starting point for getting anywhere in Windows 95. Let's open Freelance Graphics 96 now.

Do It

Here's how to open Freelance Graphics 96:

1. Click the **Start** button on the taskbar.

2. Choose **Freelance Graphics** (or **Lotus Applications**, if you have SmartSuite) from the Programs menu.

3. Select **Freelance Graphics 96**. The Freelance Graphics window with the Welcome to Lotus Freelance Graphics dialog box opens (see Figure 2.2).

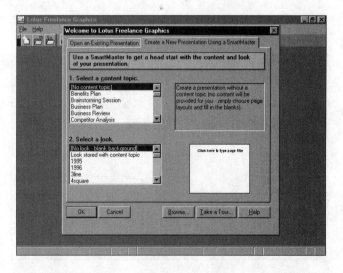

Figure 2.2 *Welcome to Lotus Freelance Graphics.*

4. Choose the **Create a New Presentation Using SmartMaster** tab.

5. Click **OK**. The Choose Page Layout dialog box pops up.

6. Click **OK** again. Don't worry about what the presentation page looks like right now. I only want to familiarize you with the Freelance Graphics window and some of its features at this point.

Anatomy 101—The Freelance Graphics Screen

Get used to looking at this screen; it's the starting point for almost everything you'll do in Freelance Graphics. Let's get acquainted with it by going over the elements shown in Figure 2.3.

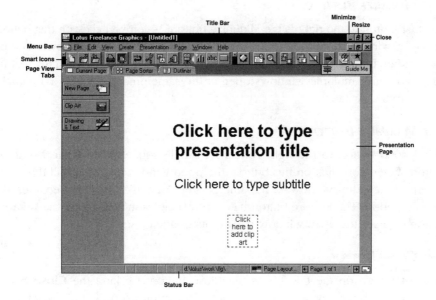

Figure 2.3 *The Freelance Graphics window.*

From here on out, I'm going to refer to Freelance Graphics as Freelance and trust you know what I'm referring to.

NOTE

The Title Bar

The *title bar* is the highlighted strip at the top of the window. Unless you've changed your screen colors, the title bar is dark blue when the window is active. When the window is inactive, the title bar is dimmed out and appears dark gray. After you save a document, the document name is displayed in the title bar. Keep an eye on this bar. As you move your mouse pointer around the screen or select items, you'll see Help Prompts that explain what will happen when you click on a button or give you hints about how to use a feature.

On the right of the title bar, there are three buttons: the minimize, maximize, and close buttons. You'll probably use these buttons often as you switch between programs and when you exit from the program.

THE MINIMIZE BUTTON

The first button to the right is the Minimize button. When you click on this button, the open window is sent down to the taskbar. To reopen the window, click on the taskbar button that contains the window's name. This is a useful feature when you have multiple windows open at the same time and you don't want to clutter up the desktop.

THE MAXIMIZE BUTTON

The second button to the right contains a single square. This is the Maximize button. When you click on this button, the open window resizes to fill the entire screen. When the window is maximized, the Maximize button becomes the Restore button. The Restore button has two rectangles in it. Clicking the **Restore** button changes the open window back to its original size.

THE CLOSE BUTTON

The last button on the title bar is the Close button. Clicking the **Close** button closes the open window and exits you out of the application. If you haven't saved your work yet, a dialog box pops up asking if you want to save the presentation.

You've probably noticed that there are two sets of Minimize, Maximize, and Close buttons. The buttons located on the title bar control the entire Freelance Graphics window. For example, if you clicked the **Close** button on the title bar, Freelance Graphics closes and you are returned to the desktop. The second set of buttons controls the presentation window. If you clicked the second **Close** button, for example, the presentation in the Freelance Graphics window closes but Freelance Graphics remains open. The difference is that the first set controls the entire program, and the second set controls the file.

The Menu Bar

The *menu bar* is right under the title bar. You open a menu by clicking on its name or by typing keystrokes. Menus work a little different in Windows 95 than they did in Windows 3.1. You may open a menu and decide that this isn't the one you need. To open another menu, you can drag the pointer to a different menu title or use the **Right Arrow** or **Left Arrow** key. The menus open automatically. The selected menu won't close until you make a selection from the menu, open a different menu, or click somewhere else on the screen.

To open a menu with the keyboard, press the **Alt** key to activate the menu bar. Use the **Left Arrow** or **Right Arrow** key to highlight your menu choice. Then press **Enter**. You can also open a menu by holding down the **Alt** key while you press the underlined letter for the item you want.

In Figure 2.4, I clicked on **Presentation** to pull down (or open) the Presentation menu. Once you've opened a menu, you can choose an item by either clicking on it or typing the underlined letter for the item. You can also use the **Up Arrow** and **Down Arrow** keys to highlight the item you want, and then press **Enter**.

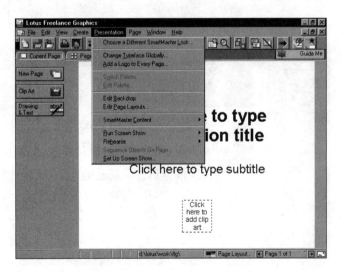

Figure 2.4 *The Presentation menu.*

For now, don't worry about what the features actually *do*. In this chapter we're concentrating on *how* the menus and dialog boxes work. We'll get to all the specific features later.

You will notice that some of the menu items have three little dots after them, and some of them have right-pointing triangles. Why? The symbols tell you what will happen if you choose that item.

❖ An ellipsis (...) signifies that choosing the item opens a dialog box. The dialog box gives you options or asks for more information before it executes the command. I'll talk about dialog boxes in a separate section in this chapter.

❖ A right-pointing triangle lets you know that choosing the item opens a *cascading menu*, which gives you another set of commands to choose from. In Figure 2.5, I clicked on **Rehearse** from the Presentation menu. This gave me a cascading menu with choices that are all related to practicing a screen show. Notice that there is an ellipsis after one of the items on the cascading menu. A dialog box is displayed when you choose an item followed by an ellipsis, whether it is on the main menu or a cascading one.

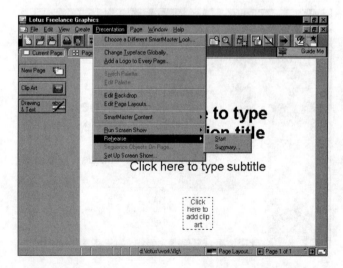

Figure 2.5 *The cascading Rehearse menu.*

❖ If a menu item is displayed without an ellipsis or triangle, choosing the item causes an action to happen. For example, choosing **Start** from the cascading Rehearse menu shown in Figure 2.5 changes an open document into a screen show presentation without any further input from you.

❖ Have you noticed the key combinations listed next to some of the menu items? Those are keystroke alternatives or shortcuts that you can use instead of choosing the item from a menu. For example, I could press **Ctrl+P** to print the presentation instead of choosing **Print** from the File menu.

In addition to ellipses, triangles, and shortcut keys, there are two more items you might see on menus.

❖ **Check marks.** When you see a check mark next to an item, the menu item is a *toggle*—you choose the same item to turn the feature on and off. A check mark next to it means that it's turned on, or activated. For example, click on **View** to open the View menu. In Figure 2.6, checks appear beside **Zoom to Full Page**, **Display in Color**, and **Show SmartIcons**. This indicates that these features are turned on. You can turn off one or all of these features by clicking on the item again. The check mark disappears and the feature is turned off.

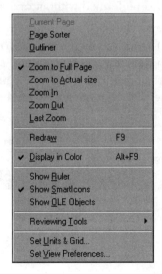

Figure 2.6 *Check marks next to activated items.*

❖ **Dimmed items.** If a menu item is dimmed, the command is not currently available. For example, in Figure 2.6, Current Page is dimmed. I cannot select this item.

CLOSING A MENU

You can close a menu by clicking anywhere outside the menu. (You can also close a menu by clicking on the menu's name, but the entire screen is a much bigger target.)

To close a menu with the keyboard, press **Esc** twice. Pressing **Esc** the first time closes the menu, but the menu bar is still active. You have to press **Esc** again to move your insertion point back into the document area.

SmartIcons

SmartIcons are a group of buttons arranged horizontally along the top of your screen (see Figure 2.3). When you install Freelance Graphics, SmartIcons are displayed by default, but you can hide them or move them if you choose. (I'll explain how you can customize your SmartIcons in Chapter 16.) SmartIcons are mouse shortcuts that represent actions, commands, or scripts. Press the button and the action or command is performed without opening a single menu.

SmartIcons are handy and can save you time, but how do you know what each SmartIcon does? If you move the mouse pointer to any of the buttons (don't click—just point) and hold it there for a moment, you'll see a help bubble that tells you what the button does. The SmartIcons shown in Figure 2.7 are standard, unless you change them. Every time you open or create a presentation, they'll appear.

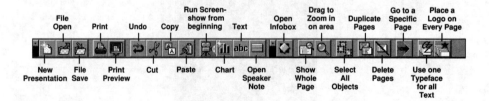

Figure 2.7 *SmartIcons.*

Buttons

In addition to SmartIcons, Freelance provides you with some special buttons that you can use as shortcuts. Just like SmartIcons, these buttons change depending on what you are working on. In Figure 2.8, the New Page, Clip Art, and Drawing and Text buttons help you design your presentation in Current Page view. When you open Page Sorter or Outliner view, however, these three buttons disappear. Freelance provides you with button shortcuts that I'll point out while we work on our presentation.

Figure 2.8 *Current Page buttons.*

The Insertion Point

If you click on text, you will see a blinking vertical line. This is the *insertion point*. It is where text will appear when you start typing. Go ahead, try it. Just type a word or two and notice that the insertion point moves to reflect the new text location. Always make sure your insertion point is where you want it to be before you type.

Scroll Bars

Because your computer screen is smaller than a standard piece of paper and your presentation is probably more than one page, parts of your presentation may be hidden from view when you're in Page Sorter or Outliner view modes. The vertical and horizontal scroll bars make it easy to view different parts of your document. I'll use the vertical scroll bar for the following examples. (The horizontal scroll bar does the same thing, except it moves you left and right instead of up and down.) In Current Page view, you probably don't have a scroll bar. That's okay. Click on the **Outliner** tab. A page changes to show a yellow note pad with a vertical scroll bar to the right of the page, as shown in Figure 2.9.

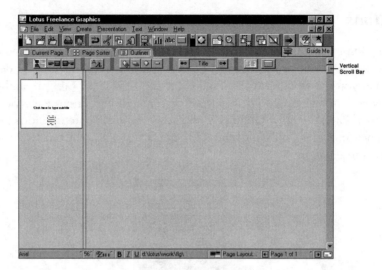

Figure 2.9 *Outliner view.*

❖ Click on the black **Up** or **Down Arrow** at the top and bottom of the vertical scroll bar respectively to move up or down a line at a time. Hold the arrow down to move continuously.

❖ The *scroll box* reflects your location in the document. For example, when the scroll box is at the top of the scroll bar, you're at the beginning of the document. If the scroll box is in the middle, you're somewhere in the middle of the document. To scroll to an approximate position in your document, just drag the scroll box up or down.

The Status Bar

The *status bar* (at the bottom of the document window) is a handy feature that provides you with alternatives to menus and SmartIcons. The blank buttons to the left on the status bar offer different options depending on what item is highlighted on the page. For example, if you still have the sample title page on your screen that we selected when we opened Freelance, click on **Click here to type presentation title.** Notice that the buttons on the status bar change and allow you to access fonts, point size, color, and text attributes (see Figure 2.10). Clicking the buttons on the right of the status bar makes things happen.

Figure 2.10 *The status bar.*

❖   The wide button in the center of the status bar is a three-way toggle button that indicates where the document is stored on the hard disk. Clicking it once shows the date and time. Clicking the button a second time shows your location on the page in inches. Another click and the button indicates again where on the hard disk your presentation is located.

❖   The next button on the right is the **Color/Black and White** toggle. Freelance's default is set to show your presentation pages in color. Click this button to see what your presentation looks like in black and white. Simply click the **Color/Black and White** toggle again to see the pages in color.

❖   Press the button labeled **Page Layout** to change how the page looks. The Choose Page Layout dialog box pops up and you can select a different page layout from the one currently on your screen. For example, you may decide that you want a title page instead of a bulleted list page. You can quickly change the bulleted page list into a title page by clicking the **Page Layout** button and selecting **Title** from the list.

❖   To navigate between pages, you can use the **Page Number** box. Click the button to see the titles of all the presentation pages. Select the title of the page you want and that page immediately opens. Or you can move between pages by clicking the **Previous Page** arrow or the **Next Page** arrow.

The last button on the right side of the status bar is the **TeamMail** button. If you're on a network, you can click this to send e-mail to your coworkers on the network and attach the presentation or pages from the presentation as a file.

Dialog Boxes

Choosing a menu command that's followed by an ellipsis opens a dialog box. Dialog boxes are the meat and potatoes of Freelance: except for some very basic commands, almost everything you do in Freelance happens through a dialog box. As you'll see throughout this book, dialog boxes come in many guises and can contain all sorts of different options. In this section, I'll use a few representative dialog boxes to show some of the common elements that you'll encounter. Figure 2.11 shows the Properties for: Text dialog box. I opened it by highlighting some text on the page, then choosing **Text Properties** from the Text menu.

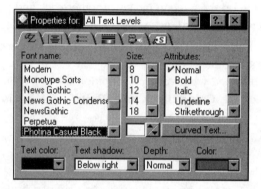

Figure 2.11 *The Properties for: Text dialog box.*

TAB DIALOG BOXES

The first thing you notice about the dialog box in Figure 2.11 are tabs that look like index tabs in a binder. Many of the dialog boxes you'll encounter in Freelance have tabs. Each tab represents a properties page within the dialog box. If you click on the first tab of the dialog box in Figure 2.11 (the one with "AZ" on it), you can access text features such as font, size, color, and attributes. If you click on the second tab (with the bullets and dashed lines), you can alter the appearance of bullets within text. To move between dialog box properties pages, click on the tabs.

Click on the **AZ** tab in the Properties for: Text dialog box and I'll show you some common features that you'll encounter.

List Boxes

A *list box* is just a box that has a bunch of choices. In the Properties for: dialog box, there are list boxes for Font name, Size, and Attributes. You choose an item from a list box by clicking on it or by using your **Up Arrow** and **Down Arrow** keys to highlight the item. If all of the choices don't fit in the list box, there are scroll bars that let you move through the list.

Drop-Down Lists

The down arrow next to Text color indicates a *drop-down list*. When you click on the arrow, you get a list of choices—in this case, colors. The drop-down list stays on the screen when you press and release the mouse button. Figure 2.12 shows the Text color drop-down list.

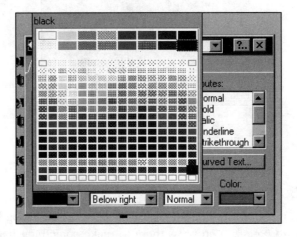

Figure 2.12 *The Text color drop-down list.*

Increment Buttons

The up and down arrows to the left of the Curved text button (that rectangular button to the right in the Text properties page) are examples of *increment buttons*. These buttons are often displayed next to text boxes where you're supposed to type in a number. Increment buttons have a line between the up and down arrows to indicate that you can select a number above or below the current selection.

They are an alternative to typing a number in the text box. You can click on the **Up Arrow** to increase the number or on the **Down Arrow** to decrease the number. If the number is already as high as it can go for that option, you'll hear a little click and the number won't change.

Let's look at another page within this dialog box for a few more examples. Open the Properties for: drop-down list and select **All Text Levels**. Notice that there are now more tabs in this dialog box. Click on the tab with a colorful **S** on it, which stands for Style. Figure 2.13 shows the Style properties page of the Text for: dialog box.

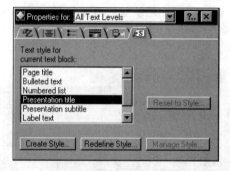

Figure 2.13 The Style properties page.

COMMAND BUTTONS

Look at the buttons on the bottom and right sides of the dialog box. These are called *command buttons*; you press them to make something happen. If there's an ellipsis after the name in the command button, choosing it opens another dialog box with more options.

Most dialog boxes have OK, Cancel, and Help command buttons. Choose **OK** to execute your commands after you've entered all the required information or made whatever choices you want to make in the dialog box. Choose **Cancel** to close the dialog box without executing any commands. Choose **Help** to open a Help window for the feature you're using (you'll learn all about using Help later in this chapter). Other command buttons, such as the buttons you see here, are specific to the dialog box you're using. Command buttons can be located anywhere in the dialog box.

TEXT BOXES

Click on the **Create Style** button on the Style properties page. The Create Text Style dialog box pops up (see Figure 2.14). A *text box* is an area where you can type specific information in a dialog box. In the Create Text Style dialog box, there's a text box in the middle-left corner. A blinking cursor appears in this text box, so all you need to do is type a name for the style you're creating (we're not really creating a style here so you don't need to do anything). Sometimes there is text already in a text box. The text inside the box is usually highlighted, or *selected*. Just start typing to enter the information. When text is in a text box, it's automatically deleted as soon as something else is typed. You'll see text boxes in dialog boxes where you need to enter specific information, such as a number or the name of a file. Since we're not making any changes right now, click **Cancel** to exit the Create Text Style dialog box.

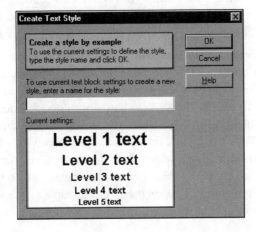

Figure 2.14 *The Create Text Style dialog box.*

CHECK BOXES

Since we're still in the Properties for: All Text Levels dialog box, click on the **Alignment** tab (the one with the straight black horizontal lines with two purple vertical lines). The alignment dialog box properties page pops up (see Figure 2.15). Notice that there is a check next to **Wrap Text**. Check boxes are toggles—you select a check box item by clicking on it, and clicking on the same item again deselects it. If you have several check box choices, you can select as many check boxes as you want.

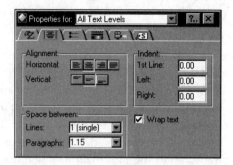

Figure 2.15 *The Alignment properties page.*

RADIO BUTTONS

There's one more dialog box button we haven't talked about yet. Take a look at the Alignment section of the Alignment tab in Figure 2.15. Those little square buttons look like check boxes, except there are lines in them already.

The buttons next to the **Horizontal** and **Vertical** choices in the Alignment section are called *radio buttons*. These radio buttons are square, but round ones are the norm. If you select the tab with the movie camera on it, you can see an example of round radio buttons. You can only choose one radio button at a time. Think of it like the buttons on your car radio—you can only tune in one station at a time. When you click on a choice to select a radio button, the previous choice is automatically deselected. Even though you can only select one radio button in each group, a dialog box can contain more than one group of radio buttons. When there is more than one group of radio buttons, you can select one radio button from each group.

Moving Dialog Boxes

Dialog boxes can sometimes pop up where you don't want them to. They might end up hiding text that you need to see. No problem. Did you notice that dialog boxes all have title bars, just like the Freelance window? You can move a dialog box anywhere on your screen by positioning your mouse pointer over the title bar and dragging the box. As you drag, a dotted outline of the box is displayed and moves with you. When the outline is where you want the box to be, release the mouse button.

N O T E

You can work with several presentations at one time, and you can change the size of the presentation window to see more than one presentation on-screen. Simply use the minimize and maximize buttons that appear in the upper-right corner of your presentation pages. These buttons work the same way as they do in the Freelance window.

WYSIWHAT???

Windows 95 (and most Windows programs, including Freelance) uses what's called a WYSIWYG display. *WYSIWYG* stands for *what you see is what you get*, and it means that what you see on the screen is a close approximation of what you'll see on the printed page. For example, if you change the size of your type or add a graphic image, you'll see all of those elements on your screen. In a non-WYSIWYG environment, a graphics image might appear as an empty box, and your text always appears the same size, which makes it hard to tell how the document will look when it's printed.

Freelance has two full WYSIWYG displays: *Current Page* and *Page Sorter*. There are several differences between the views. Current Page view displays a selected page at approximately 50% of the actual size in the Freelance window (see Figure 2.16). You can see what the text, layout, and images look like on each page. Page Sorter view displays all the pages of a presentation as thumbnail sketches with the title of each page immediately below it, as shown in Figure 2.17. This page view allows you to view an entire presentation for continuity and logic.

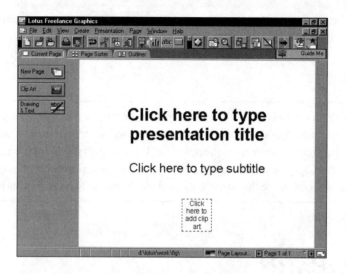

Figure 2.16 *Current Page view.*

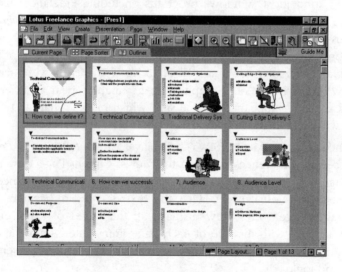

Figure 2.17 *Page Sorter view.*

Outliner view is a partial WYSIWYG display because it only shows what the text of the presentation looks like while the presentation page appears as a thumbnail to the left. Outliner view provides an outline of the presentation text—complete with that canary yellow pad look (see Figure 2.18). Thumbnails of each of the pages appear to the left of the text. You'll learn more about the different page views and what you can use them to do throughout this book.

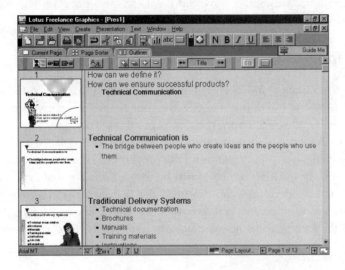

Figure 2.18 *Outliner view.*

Changing the View

To change between Current Page, Page Sorter, and Outliner views, simply click on the tab of your choice. You can also open the View menu by clicking on **View** or by pressing **Alt+V**. Then choose **Current Page**, **Page Sorter**, or **Outliner**.

Current Page view is the default, which means that your presentation automatically appears in this view unless you choose another one. I've used Current Page view most often in this book, but I'll show pages in Page Sorter and Outliner views where appropriate.

Online Help

I'd like to think that there's an answer to every question you may have somewhere in this book; however, that's unlikely. But if I don't have the answer, you won't be out on a limb. Freelance provides several forms of online Help features to assist you. You've already seen how the bubble help works and you know how that can help with SmartIcons, but Freelance also provides far more sophisticated forms of help.

Take a Tour

When you first installed and opened Freelance, you may have encountered a mini-tour of the program, but you can access the tour again any time you like. Click on the **Help** menu and select **Tour**. The first page of the Tour opens up, as shown in Figure 2.19. This Tour guides you through the basics of Freelance and shows you some of the things you can create using the program. You decide what you want to learn about first by clicking on the **Menu** button in the lower-right corner. A menu of available topics opens and you can press the button next to the menu item that you want to see. Click on the **Left Arrow** or the **Right Arrow** to page through the Tour. Press the **Exit** button when you want to return to the Freelance window.

Figure 2.19 *The Freelance Graphics 96 Tour.*

Taking the Tour is a way of understanding the basics of Freelance but it is limiting. When you're stuck and aren't sure what to do next, Guide Me is a helpful tool.

Guide Me

If you're unsure of what to do at any point while you're creating your presentation, click the **Guide Me** button in the upper right, just above the presentation area and below the SmartIcon bar (or you can open the Help menu and select **Guide Me**). A Guide Me dialog box pops up, as shown in Figure 2.20, asking what you want to do. Click on the appropriate button. The Guide Me dialog box prompts you to answer its questions until it narrows the search down and finds the help document that will answer your question. You can go back a page by clicking the **Back** button at any point, or you can access Help Topics by clicking the button labeled **Help Topics** at the bottom of the dialog box.

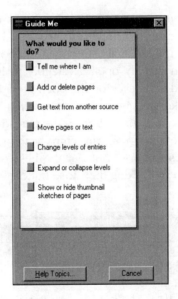

Figure 2.20 *The Guide Me dialog box.*

If you don't do anything to your presentation for awhile, a Guide Me prompt pops up suggesting you click the **Guide Me** button for assistance. You can close the Guide Me prompt by clicking **OK**. If you're searching for answers that Guide Me can't give you, the next step is to open Help Topics.

Help Topics

You'll probably visit Help Topics the most when you need assistance because this is where you can access in-depth help. Help Topics gives you in-depth assistance using three familiar methods of organization: Contents, Index, and Find. To get to the Help Topics dialog box, click on the **Help** menu and select **Help Topics**. Notice that this is a tab dialog box, so you have three ways of accessing help here. Your Help Topics dialog box may not look exactly like mine but that's probably because we have different tabs selected. Click on the **Contents** tab and I'll show you how it works.

CONTENTS

The Contents section of the Help Topics dialog box works just like the table of contents in a book. You can use Contents to help you look for help on a specific topic. Broad categories appear in the Contents list box. By double-clicking on each book icon, you can quickly open a category to locate subtopics. To close that subtopic's category, double-click on the open book icon. When you reach the icons with question marks, this means you've reached an actual help document. To open the help document, double-click on the **Question Mark** icon. The document pops up (see Figure 2.21). You can return to the Help Topics dialog box by clicking the **Help Topics** button, print out the help document by pressing the **Print** button, or exit help by clicking the **Close** button on the title bar.

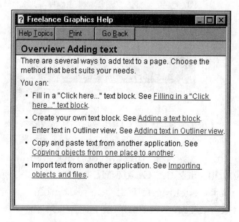

Figure 2.21 Actual help documents.

INDEX

Index is the next tab in the Help Topics dialog box. Using the Index allows you to search for help using a specific word. The Index is organized just like a book—in alphabetical order with all the available topics listed, as shown in Figure 2.22. Type the first couple of letters of the topic you're searching for in the **Type the first few letters** text box. As you type, the index automatically scrolls down to the nearest match to the letters you typed. You may have to scroll up or down to find an exact match but when you do, double-click the **Index** item. The help document opens. You can print this help document by pressing **Print** and following the prompts, exit the document by clicking the **Close** button on the title bar, or return to the Help Topics dialog box by selecting the **Help Topics** button.

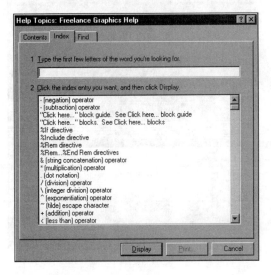

Figure 2.22 *The Index tab.*

FIND

Find allows you to search help using key words or phrases, so this is probably the most helpful if you don't know the exact terminology. Click the **Find** tab to open the Find page, as shown in Figure 2.23. To search for a topic, type the word or word you're searching for in the **Type the word(s)** text box. Then press the **Find Now** button. A word or list of words usually appears in the Select some matching words list box. To narrow your search, select a word from this list box. The search results appear in the Click a Topic list box. Double-click the topic you're interested in reading and the help document pops up. You can move through the box just like you can when you open the Contents and Index help documents.

There are several command buttons on the Find page in the Help Topics dialog box that you should know about too. Clicking the **Clear** button clears the word(s) you typed in the Type the word(s) list box. Clicking the **Options** button allows you to open the Options dialog box, where you can change search criteria. Pressing the **Rebuild** button re-creates the list of help topics. You don't need to press this every time you conduct a Find search.

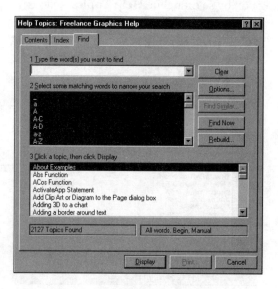

Figure 2.23 *The Find tab.*

Some help documents contain icons or highlighted (usually colored) text that can give you further assistance. The highlighted text provides a shortcut to another help document that gives you detailed information. To access this information, all you have to do is click on the colored text. In addition, you'll see icons labeled *See details, See related topics,* or *Go to procedure* at the bottom of the help document. These are shortcuts too, and clicking on the button icon takes you to the help document. But what do you do if you can't find the help you need here? Well, then it's time to contact Freelance Graphics support. You can find these telephone numbers in the documents that came with the software.

Exiting Freelance Graphics

Close Freelance Graphics by clicking on the **Close** button (the **X** on the far right in the title bar). If you haven't saved your work yet, an Exit Freelance dialog box pops up. Click **OK** to save your document, **No** to immediately exit, or **Cancel** to keep Freelance Graphics open. If you've never saved the file before and you click **OK**, the Save As dialog box pops up. Enter the document name in the File name text box, then click **OK**. Freelance Graphics closes and you're returned to the Windows 95 desktop.

From Here...

Now you know how to start up and shut down Freelance; you know the basics about the menus, SmartIcons, and dialog boxes; and you know how Windows 95 works.

Did you notice that I rushed you through the dialog boxes that open when you open Freelance Graphics? It's not that these dialog boxes are unimportant—quite the contrary. These dialog boxes are so important that an entire chapter is devoted to them. In the next chapter, I'll show you how to select and edit an overall look for your presentation and how to add a title page.

CHAPTER 3

Working with SmartMasters

(Sometimes looks do count!)

"How'd they do that?" Did you ever leave a presentation wondering that? Several artists must have worked on it day and night for weeks. How else could the fonts and headings be so uniform, or the charts and graphs look so perfect? And that colorful background—it must have taken days to create just for that presentation! In the old days, if you wanted your presentation to look that professional you hired an expensive artist to create it for you. Then you used those same presentation materials as often as you could to get your money's worth.

Creating a presentation is very different now. You don't need a background in design or art and five weeks of preparation time. All you need is a computer, a software program designed to create presentations, and a day or two. And what you get are the same quality presentations that you saw and wondered how to create way back then. Freelance is one of those presentation software programs that can help you create a sharp presentation that will make your audience wonder how you did it. To help you create that overall look that people notice first, Freelance uses a feature called SmartMasters. In this chapter, you'll learn exactly what *SmartMasters* are and how to work with them to create that perfect look for your presentation.

Defining SmartMasters

You've probably walked past a department store window and noticed the mannequins sporting the latest fashions and accessories at some point in your life. But did you ever take a really close look at the mannequin itself? Each mannequin physically looks the same, yet they look different too. That's because each mannequin has a different style wig; some heads are tilted upwards, some down, and some straight ahead; the cosmetics on their faces highlight different features, and each wears different pieces of clothing. These little customizations help make the mannequin look different from all the others in the window. SmartMasters are very similar to mannequins; they have the same basic features—a unique color backdrop, and page layouts and content topics. The difference is that you're the window dresser and you get to dress up your SmartMaster with your own message.

Each SmartMaster has its own unique look. This look, called a *SmartMaster Look*, consists of the background colors and images that appear throughout your presentation. Also, each look comes with its own set of page layouts that are unique to that look. These page layouts incorporate the background look into the page layout and provide you with different formats so that you can add your own text, graphics, charts, titles, diagrams and other elements. Content Topics give you an even bigger head start because they provide you with templates to create typical business presentations such as a business plan, a team meeting, a brainstorming session, a project update, or a proposal, to name a few. They even contain actual sample text that you can use or edit. SmartMasters control everything from the background colors down to the text fonts and sizes. Consider a SmartMaster the fundamental building block upon which you create your presentation. As you read through this chapter, I'll tell you more about the specific features and how to access them.

Introducing… Major Chips

Before we dive right into SmartMasters, I want to tell you about a company that I'll be referring to throughout this book. Every example I use in this chapter and in the rest of the book directly relates to a presentation that I'm creating for them. Okay, I'm not really creating this presentation for them. But by using this presentation as an example, I can show you how to do all the things you need to do in order to create a sharp presentation yourself.

The company is called Major Chips. Major Chips is a privately owned company that manufactures computer chips and potato chips. Odd combination, huh? The company is owned by Bob Refose and Ellen Nacey. Bob established a potato chip manufacturing company ten years ago, while Ellen has been manufacturing computer chips for over fifteen years. When Bob and Ellen married eight years ago, they decided to merge their businesses into one company with two separate divisions. The company employs over 400 people altogether. During the first year of the company merger Major Chips reported losses, but profits rebounded the following year and have increased gradually in the last six years.

There is a new development within the company. Bob and Ellen have decided to conquer the last major chip industry by entering the chocolate chip market. Ellen had the research department thoroughly research the chocolate chip marketplace over a one year period. Based upon the results, Bob and Ellen decided there was room for Major Chips to expand. Food researchers were hired to modify a chocolate recipe that Ellen's grandmother brought to the US. when she emigrated from Germany so that it can have a long shelf-life when packaged. Bob and Ellen are happy with the research results and are now ready to begin production of their chocolate products. A third division within the company has been created, the equipment is in place, and employees have been hired. Based upon market research, Bob and Ellen have decided to target the food industry before they introduce their chips to the general public. This means they need to target restaurants and companies that sell prepared foods using chocolate in their products. Sales people are planning to attend meetings at large food corporations and food industry trade shows where Major Chips and its product will be introduced to the chocolate industry. The Communication Services Department have been given the task of creating a sharp presentation that the salespeople can take with them to these meetings. Together, you and I are going to create pieces of the presentation throughout this book.

So where do we begin? The best place to begin is at the beginning. In this chapter, you'll learn how to select a SmartMaster Look and select the first page of the presentation—the title page.

Selecting a Simple SmartMaster Look

The background appearance of your presentation is almost as important as what you say. Your audience will notice how your presentation looks before it listens to your message; therefore, you need to choose your background carefully when considering your audience. Every SmartMaster comes with a look (or palette) that incorporates color into the background and text, or a look that appears in black and white. You can choose between the color or B/W (black and white) palettes or change the color palette (see Chapter 13 for more information).

Now it's time to start creating the foundation for the presentation we will be working with for the rest of this book. One of Major Chip's owners, Ellen Nacey, will be presenting the Major Chips chocolate chip launch presentation using over-heads, in a room of approximately 50 people. With these facts in mind, let's select a SmartMaster Look. Open Freelance Graphics now if it isn't already on your screen. The Welcome to Lotus Freelance Graphics dialog box (the dialog box that immediately opens when you select Freelance) should appear on your screen.

Do It:

In the Welcome to Lotus Freelance Graphics dialog box, select the **Create a New Presentation Using a SmartMaster** tab if it isn't already selected (see Figure 3.1).

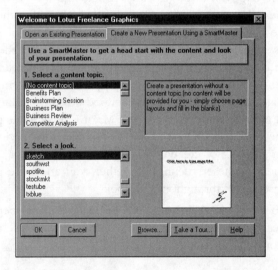

Figure 3.1 *Create a New Presentation Using a SmartMaster properties page.*

Follow these steps to select a SmartMaster Look:

1. Select **[No Content]** from the "Select a content topic" list box.

NOTE

Freelance lets you select a look for presentations. You can choose from a variety of styles and colors but, depending upon the type of presentation you're preparing, some backgrounds may work better than others. Here are some tips to make your selection a little easier:

❖ **Overheads**. Since overheads are usually presented in a well- or partially-lit room, they work best if you select a SmartMaster look with dark text on a light or white background.

❖ **Slides.** Slides are usually shown in a darkened room; therefore, a SmartMaster look with a dark background and light or white text is an excellent choice.

❖ **Monitors**. Computer and video monitors are often being used as presentation mediums now. Like slides, they're usually presented in a darkened room, so a SmartMaster look with white or light text and a dark background is appropriate.

❖ Screen Shows. Screen shows usually incorporate sound and/or movies and pictures into presentations and are displayed in a variety of situations. Screen shows can be displayed on monitors or displayed on a screen in a lightened or darkened room. When creating a screen show, think carefully of where and how it'll be presented and then choose an appropriate SmartMaster look that'll show the presentation off.

2. Scroll down the "Select a look" list box and highlight **spotlite**.

KEYBOARD

Highlight the **Select a look** list box by clicking anywhere within it. Then, press the letter **S** on your keyboard. The first SmartMaster look that begins with the letter **S** pops up in the list box window. Scroll down until you find spotlite, then highlight it.

❖ If you'd prefer to select your SmartMaster Look using the Directory dialog box, then highlight the **Select a look** list box by clicking in it and select the **Browse** button. The Directory dialog box opens with a list of all the SmartMaster documents saved in the Master folder. You can move between folders on your hard drive by changing the folder in the Look In drop down list box. This is particularly helpful if you have customized Looks or other items such as graphics that you want to incorporate into your presentation.

❖ Clicking the **Help** button opens an actual help document titled "Creating a new presentation using a content topic." This document can help guide you when you begin to create your presentation. If you need additional help, click the **Help Topics** button and the Help Topics: Freelance Graphics Help dialog box pops up.

3. Click **OK**. The New Page dialog box pops up (see Figure 3.2).

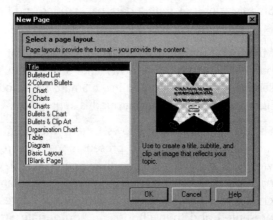

Figure 3.2 *The New Page dialog box.*

Excellent, you've just selected the SmartMaster look for the presentation. The next time you create a presentation, your last SmartMaster Look will be highlighted but you can make another selection if you prefer. Now it's time to select the title page.

Selecting the Title Page Layout

Have you noticed that the bulleted lists in this book are all precisely indented the same way, and that the paragraph following a heading always begins without an indent but the following paragraphs are indented? These features are a part of the page layout and they are standard elements throughout this book. How the page looks (where the text and other elements appear on the page) is called the **page layout**.

Each SmartMaster comes with the following standard page layouts:

- ❖ Title
- ❖ Bulleted List
- ❖ 2-Column Bullets
- ❖ 1 Chart
- ❖ 2 Charts
- ❖ 4 Charts
- ❖ Bullets & Chart
- ❖ Bullets & Clip Art
- ❖ Organization Chart
- ❖ Table
- ❖ Diagram
- ❖ Basic Layout
- ❖ Blank Page

To maintain a consistent appearance between pages, each page layout incorporates the background of the SmartMaster Look that was selected (except the Blank Page page layout) and contains "Click here" boxes that prompt you to enter information. For instance, when you select the Bulleted list page layout, there are two prompts: a "Click here to type page title" prompt and a "Click here to type bulleted list" prompt. We'll begin entering text into these "Click here" boxes starting in Chapter 4.

You begin your presentation by selecting a page layout. While there aren't any rules about where to start a presentation, I like to begin at the beginning—with the title page. If I decide the title page is all wrong, I can go back and change it later but a title page is a good place to begin focusing your creative energy. So let's select the title page layout for the Major Chips chocolate chip launch presentation.

Do It:

Make sure the Choose Page Layout dialog box shown in Figure 3.2 is still open.

1. Select **Title** from the Select a page layout list box.

To the left of the list box is a thumbnail of the SmartMaster Look that you selected. As you highlight the different page layouts available to you, notice that the thumbnail changes to reflect the page layout selected. You can refer to the thumbnail to decide if this really is the page layout that you want.

2. Click **OK** to select the title page. The title page of the spotlite SmartMaster Look pops up, as shown in Figure 3.3.

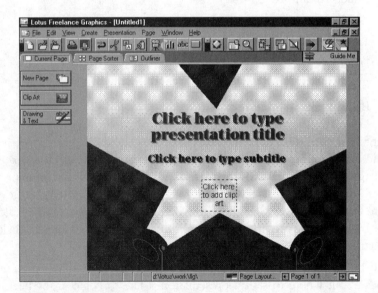

Figure 3.3 *The title page.*

Now that we've started to create our presentation, let's save it.

Saving the Presentation for the First Time

Saving your work is an important part of creating a presentation—you don't want to keep recreating the same pages over and over again, do you? And that's exactly what you might have to do if there is a power surge, or your computer freezes up, or someone accidentally turns off your computer and you hadn't saved your changes. You should save your work every time you make a change. I'm going to continue building on this presentation throughout the book, so now is the best time to begin saving your work. I'll continue to remind you to save, but let's go through the steps you need to follow to save your work for the very first time.

Do It:

Here's how to save a presentation for the first time:

1. With the presentation open, choose **Save As** from the File menu. A dialog box pops up telling you that the file you're saving has only one page (see Figure 3.4).

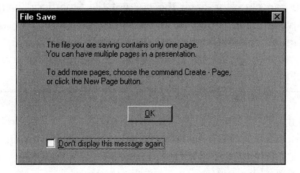

Figure 3.4 *The File Save dialog box.*

Click in the box marked "Don't display this message again" if you'd prefer not to have this dialog box pop up again when you save a file with one page.

N O T E

2. Click **OK** to continue saving your file. The Save As dialog box pops up, as shown in Figure 3.5. Notice that the cursor is blinking in the File name text box.

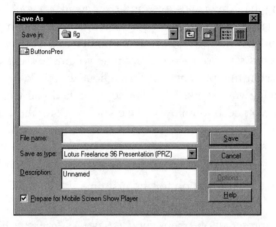

Figure 3.5 *The Save As dialog box.*

SHORTCUT

You can click the **Save the current file** SmartIcon or press **Ctrl-S** to save your file. If the file has previously been saved, either of these methods will automatically save any changes you've made without any further input from you. If this is the first time you're saving the file, then the Save As dialog box opens.

3. Select the Folder in which you want to save your file from the Save in drop down list. Freelance automatically saves your files to a folder called "flg" which is located within the Work folder located in the Freelance folder, unless you choose otherwise.

   The radio buttons to the right of the Save in drop down list box are a Windows 95 feature that allows you to move through your folders, create a new folder, and view your documents as a list (complete with icons) or as a list with details about the file size, type and date modified.

4. Type **MjrChips** in the File Name text box.

5. Next, select **Lotus Freelance 96 Presentation [PRZ]**, if it doesn't already appear in the Save as type drop down list. This is the default setting unless you change it.

   ❖ Optionally, you can add a short description of the presentation's purpose in the Description text box. Select **Unnamed** and begin typing a brief explanation of the presentation. For instance, for the Major Chips presentation we can add **Product launch presentation aimed at industry chocolate consumers** to this box.

   ❖ Check to make sure that the Prepare for Mobile Screen Show check box is selected, if you plan on showing your presentation on a computer but you're unsure if it is equipped with Freelance Graphics. Prepare for Mobile Screen Show allows you to show your presentation as a screen show even if Freelance is unavailable.

6. Click **OK** to save your presentation. When the file has been saved, the Save As dialog box closes automatically.

Good, now you've saved your presentation. Saving it will be easier next time—simply press **Ctrl-S** or click the **File Save** SmartIcon. The pointer turns into an hourglass while your presentation is being updated. We're not going to use the presentation again for this chapter so let's close it.

Closing a File

If you're working on multiple presentations and you've finished working with one presentation and want to open another, you don't need to exit Freelance entirely. Here's how to close a presentation while leaving Freelance open.

Do It:

To close a file:

1. Open the File menu.
2. Select **Close**.

An even quicker way to close a file is to click on the presentation window **X** button. Next, let me show you another feature of SmartMasters that you may want to use.

Selecting a SmartMaster Using a Content Topic

Sometimes you may need a little more of a head start than what you get when you select a simple SmartMaster. After all, do you know what is typically found in a business plan, a corporate overview or a project proposal? I know I don't and, unless you create these types of presentations all the time, you probably don't know everything that should be included either. And that's okay because Freelance has a handy feature called *Content Topics* that can help you design a specialized presentation such as a business proposal.

Freelance provides you with Content Topics for a number of typical business presentations, and they can help make creating a presentation a little easier. Not only do Content Topics provide you with a SmartMaster Look, but they also include actual text and graphics. Content Topics also give you a head start with presentation tips that can help you customize your pages.

In this section, I'll show you how to select a Content Topic and change its Look. While I'm not planning on using this for our Major Chips presentation (we just closed the file that we'll be using in the book), I'll use our Major Chips chocolate chip launch as the example. Let's select a SmartMaster using a Content Topic now.

Do It:

When you open Freelance, the Welcome to Lotus Freelance Graphics window pops up. Select the Create a **New Presentation Using a SmartMaster** tab as shown in Figure 3.6.

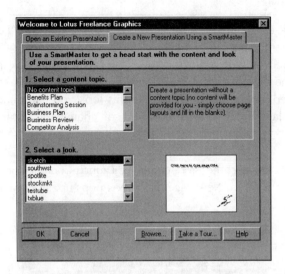

Figure 3.6 *The Create a New Presentation Using a SmartMaster tab.*

Here's how to select a Content Topic:

N O T E

If Freelance is already open, click on the **Create a new file** SmartIcon and the New Presentation dialog box appears. This dialog box has all the same features as the Create a New Presentation Using a SmartMaster tab. The only difference between the dialog boxes is that the dialog box in Figure 3.6 is accessed when *starting* Freelance and the New Presentation dialog box is opened when you're in Freelance. You'll have no problem following the rest of this tutorial if you have the New Presentation dialog box opened.

1. Select **Product/Service Launch** from the Select a content topic list box.

N O T E   Look at the Select a look list box. Notice that the "Look stored with content topic" is highlighted. This is because each Content Topic is associated with a specific look. You can see that look in the thumbnail to the right of the list boxes. Just remember that you're not stuck with a stored look so if you don't like this look you can change it. I'll show you later in this chapter how you can change the Content Topic look.

2. Click **OK** to select the Product/Service Launch Content Topic using the look stored with it. The New Page dialog box pops up, as shown in Figure 3.7

Figure 3.7 *The New Page dialog box.*

When you selected a simple SmartMaster earlier in this book, you also selected the title page for your presentation. When the New Page dialog box opens, you have the opportunity to select your title page layout for your Content Topic too. Keep the New Page dialog box open and in the next section I'll show you how to select your presentation title page layout.

Selecting the Title Page Layout for the Content Topic

As I wrote earlier, Content Topics are a special Freelance feature because they supply you with actual text and graphics. But what I didn't mention was that Content Topics also provide you with entire page templates for each Content Topic available. These page templates are listed in the logical order that they would appear in a typical business presentation. This means that you can select from a number of pages, called *content pages*, that are especially designed for that Content Topic. Content pages have titles such as Agenda, Primary Target Market, Key Messages, Share Goals, or Launch Timeline. They still provide you with "Click here" prompts but these prompts are more task specific. For instance, instead of seeing "Click here to type bulleted list," you'll see a task-specific prompt such as "Type here to describe your primary target market." Let's choose the title page layout for the Product/Service Launch Content Topic.

Do It:

Now that you've selected a Content Topic and clicked **OK**, you're faced with the prospect of selecting a page layout from the New Page dialog box (see Figure 3.7). With the New Page dialog box on your screen:

1. Select the **Content Pages** tab.
2. Choose **Product/Service Launch title page** from the "Content topic: Product/Service Launch" list box.
3. Click **OK** to select the title page. The Product/Service Launch title page opens, as shown in Figure 3.8.

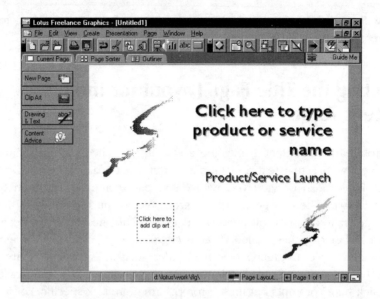

Figure 3.8 *The Product/Service Launch title page.*

N O T E

Click the **Content Advice** button to the left of the page. This button gives you suggestions about what is normally included on each page in a typical presentation. For instance, when you select the Content **Advice** button with the Product/Service Launch title page open, a Content Advice for Current Page dialog box pops up telling you what this Content Topic is used for and what you should include in the presentation. Click **OK** to exit the Content Advice dialog box.

When the New Page dialog box is open and the Content Pages tab is selected, Freelance gives you the opportunity to select more that one page at a time using the **Choose Multiple Pages** button. Follow along and I'll show you how to use this button.

Choosing Multiple Pages for a Content Topic Presentation

Instead of choosing one page at a time like you do with standard page layouts, when you begin setting up a SmartMaster using a Content Topic you may want to choose more than one page. This is a helpful feature when you want to select the pages you plan on using for your presentation and get right down to work. Here's how to select more than one page of your presentation when you're using a Content Topic.

Do It:

After you select a Content Topic and click **OK**, the New Page dialog box pops up with the Content Pages tab selected. When you first create your presentation, you can select page layout sections or even all the pages when the Content Pages tab is open. For our example, we've selected the Product/Service Launch Content Topic and the title page, now let's add the entire Product/Service Overview-Section content pages to the presentation next. Here's how:

1. Click on the **New Page** button. The New Page dialog box opens.

2. Click the **Choose Multiple Content Pages** button. The New Page-Choose Multiple Content Pages dialog box pops up, as shown in Figure 3.9.

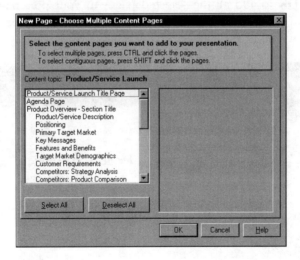

Figure 3.9 *The New Page-Choose Multiple Content Pages dialog box.*

3. Select **Product Overview-Section Title** and drag down to **Suppliers**. All the pages between these two titles should be highlighted (see Figure 3.10).

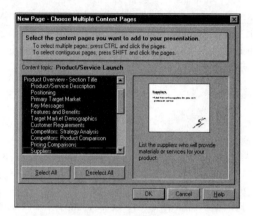

Figure 3.10 *The Product/Service Overview section.*

❖ Optionally, you can click **Select All** to select all the page layouts listed in the Content topic: Product/Service Launch dialog box. Click **Deselect All** if you change your mind and decide not to add all the page layouts to your presentation.

4. Click **OK** to add all the selected pages to your presentation. The first page of the pages you've just added appears in your Freelance window, as shown in Figure 3.11.

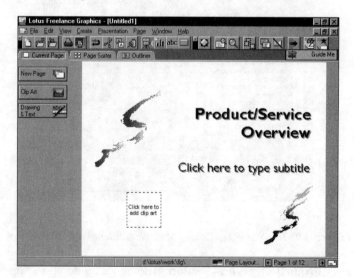

Figure 3.11 *The Product/Service Overview section title page layout.*

You've just added eleven pages to your presentation. Now you know how to create a presentation using a Content Topic, select the title page layout or add multiple page layouts to your presentation. Next you need to know how to select a standard page layout when you're setting up a presentation using a Content Topic.

Selecting a Standard Page Layout for a Content Topic Presentation

When you first begin setting up your SmartMaster using a Content Topic, you may not want to use a Content Page immediately or you may want to add a standard page layout later in your presentation. Well, Freelance allows you to easily do it. Here's how:

Do It:

Let's add a bulleted list page to our Product/Service Launch presentation.

1. Click on the **New Page** button.
2. Select the **Page Layouts** tab. The Page Layouts properties page opens as shown in Figure 3.12.

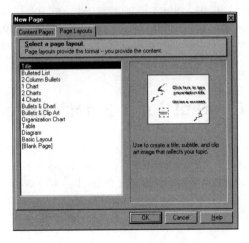

Figure 3.12 *The Page Layouts properties page.*

3.   Select **Bulleted List** in the Select a page layout list box.

4.   Click **OK** to add the page to the presentation. The Bulleted List page opens in your Freelance window as shown in Figure 3.13.

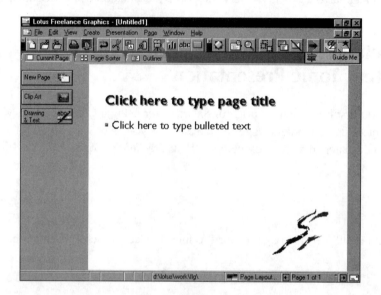

Figure 3.13   *The Bulleted List page.*

Very good. Now you can add multiple pages to a Content Topic or standard page layouts to your presentation. In the next section I'll show you what to do if you really like the Content Topic you selected but absolutely hate the stored Look that comes with it.

Changing a Content Topic SmartMaster Look

You really want to use the Brainstorming Content Topic but you don't like the SmartMaster Look that is stored with it? You may decide as soon as you select the Brainstorming Content Topic that the Look has to go. I'll show you how to change that Look right now. Brainstorming is stored with a Look called **buttons**. Let's change the look to **ship** instead.

Do It:

When Freelance Graphics is opened, you're greeted by the Welcome to Lotus Freelance Graphics dialog box. Select the **Create a New Presentation Using a SmartMaster** tab. Here's how to change the Look of a Content Topic when you first select it:

1. With the Create a New Presentation Using a SmartMaster tab selected, choose **Brainstorming Session** from the Select a content topic list box (see Figure 3.14). The thumbnail appears in the lower right corner.

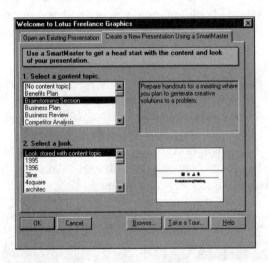

Figure 3.14 *The Brainstorming Session Content Topic.*

2. Next, select **ship** from the Select a look list box. Notice that the thumb-nail changes to show the "ship" look selected.

3. Click **OK** to select the Brainstorming Content Topic with the "ship" SmartMaster Look. The New Page dialog box with Content Pages selected pops up.

Now you can select the pages for your Brainstorming Content Topic presentation as I showed you earlier in this chapter. Changing a Look for a Content Topic is that simple, but what happens if you start to dislike the SmartMaster Look once you've been working with it for a while? You could start your presentation all over from scratch—but that's a drastic measure. Instead, Freelance allows you to change your SmartMaster Look anytime you want. In the next section I'll show you how.

Changing a Selected SmartMaster Look

You may decide that you don't like your SmartMaster Look after all, or the media by which the presentation is being displayed may change. If that's the case, you don't have to start a new presentation from scratch. Freelance allows you to change your SmartMaster Look any time you want; it automatically updates your customizations to the new page layouts.

Do It:

It's important to remember that you're not locked into a SmartMaster Look once you've selected it. Here's how to change it:

1. With the presentation open, select **Choose a Different SmartMaster Look** from the Presentation menu. The Choose a Look for Your Presentation dialog box pops up, as shown in Figure 3.15.

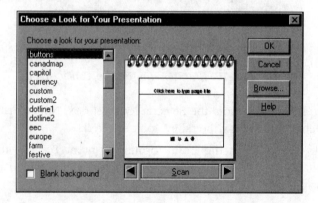

Figure 3.15 *The Choose a Look for Your Presentation dialog box.*

2. If you're unsure which SmartMaster Look you want to select, click the **Scan** button. The Scan button turns into the Stop Scan button and the

thumbnail begins to change as the different Looks are highlighted in the Choose a Look for your presentation list box.

N O T E

If you know the name of the SmartMaster Look you want, click in the Choose a look for your presentation list box and press the first letter of the name of the Look. For instance, if you want to change the presentation SmartMaster Look from spotlite to bluegray, type the letter "B." The first look beginning with the letter **B** pops up. Scroll down the list box until you see Bluegray, then select it.

❖ Alternatively, if you don't want to use a Look, click in the **Blank background** check box.

❖ If you've created your own Look that you would prefer to use, then click the **Browse** button. The Browse dialog box pops up, as shown in Figure 3.16. To select the file, type the name of the file in the File Name text box or click its icon in the dialog box window. Click **Open**. The Browse dialog box closes and your Look pops up in the thumbnail.

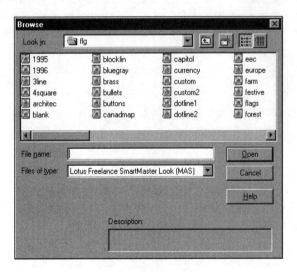

Figure 3.16 *The Browse dialog box.*

WARNING

When you create your own look, the file must be saved as a SmartMaster Look for you to be able to use it. More about creating and using your own SmartMaster Look can be found in Chapter 15.

3. When you have selected your new SmartMaster Look, click **OK**. The Choose a Different Look dialog box closes and your presentation has a new look. Your text, graphics, charts and clip art page layouts are all automatically updated to reflect the new look.

Changing a look is simple and you can change it as often as you like.

From Here…

After working through this chapter, you now know how to select a SmartMaster Look, choose a title page layout, save your presentation, select a SmartMaster Content Topic and a lot more. You've gotten the hang of opening Freelance and creating a new presentation. Up until now, however, you still haven't added your own text to the presentaton. In the next chapter I'll show you how to customize those "Click here" prompts that keep popping up on your pages. In addition, I'll show you how to open a previously created presentation, and add page layouts to your work in progress.

CHAPTER 4

The ABCs of Text

(Adding text to your presentation)

Ready to learn your A-B-Cs? We've just finished choosing a SmartMaster Look and adding a title page to the Major Chips presentation that we're creating. Now we need to customize the title page by replacing the "click here" prompts with our own text. And in the process of completing the presentation, we'll start adding additional pages.

There is at least one "Click here" prompt on every page layout. "Click here" guides are one of the most important and basic features you'll be using in Freelance. They are there to guide you when entering text or chart data, diagrams and clip art. There are really two types of prompts: "Click here" text blocks that allow you to enter text, and "Click here" graphics blocks that allow you to create charts, diagrams, tables, add clip art and organization charts. Either way, the information you add in a "Click here" block is automatically formatted based upon the SmartMaster Look you selected, so you don't have to mess with the formatting unless you really want to (we'll get into that in the next chapter). In this chapter, I'll show you how to work with the "Click here" text blocks so that you can add your own text to the presentation.

Before we begin adding text, I'd like to give you a few composition tips for your presentation. You'll be adding most of the text to your presentation in this chapter, so now is a good time to discuss some of the elements of a good presentation.

❖ First, consider your audience and use language that is appropriate for them. You don't want to use language that is too technical or advanced. If you're addressing an audience that has little or no knowledge of your business and the jargon used, avoid using that jargon and provide them with the knowledge that they need to follow your presentation.

❖ Second, you want to use strong, action verbs in your writing. There's a difference between "I received a gold medal" versus "I earned a gold medal." Received is a passive verb, while earned is action-oriented. Earned, increased, plummeted, introduced, resulted, rose—these are all good action-oriented words.

❖ Third, as a general rule, use phrases instead of full sentences. For example, "Reported 1995 earnings increased 80%" works better than "It was reported that earnings increased by 80% in 1995."

In this chapter, I'll show you how to add pages to the presentation and add your own text to each page. I'll also show you how to perform some basic text maneuvers like copy, edit, move, paste and how to use that all important Spell Checker. Since this chapter's about text, I'm not going to mess with any of the other types of "Click here" blocks right now. But don't worry—you'll learn about all of them before you finish this book.

Just in case you took a break after the last chapter and your presentation's no longer on-screen, let me show you how to get back to your work in progress. Even if your presentation is already open, read this section for future reference.

Opening a File

While working on your presentation, you will undoubtedly open and close your file several times. You already know how to close your file, but you may not know how to open an existing Freelance presentation. Let me show you how.

Do It:

When Freelance opens, the Welcome to Lotus Freelance Graphics dialog box pops up. This is the same dialog box we used to select a SmartMaster but notice that this time the **Open an existing presentation** tab is selected. Here's how to open the MjrChips file:

If you're already in Freelance but you want to open a file, click on the **Open an existing file** SmartIcon. The Open dialog box pops up. Locate the file you want to open and select it. Click the **Open** button. The presentation appears in the Freelance window.

1. With the **Open an existing presentation** tab selected, select **MjrChips** in the Select one of these presentations list box.

When you select a presentation name listed in the Select one of these presentations list box, a thumbnail of the first page in your presentation pops up to the right of the list. If you can't recognize the presentation by name, you may be able to identify it by its SmartMaster Look.

2. Click **OK** to open MjrChips. The presentation opens and the first page appears in the Freelance window (see Figure 4.1).

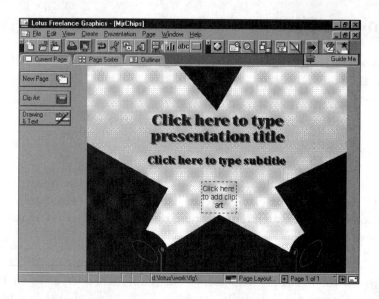

Figure 4.1 *The title page of Mjr Chips.*

Once we have the MjrChips presentation open we can start replacing the "Click here" prompts with our own text.

Adding Your Own Text to the Title Page

We already selected the title page layout in the previous chapter. Let's begin replacing "Click here" prompts with your own text. The presentation title should clearly state the overall presentation topic. The title on each subsequent page should state the topic for that specific page. We're preparing a presentation for one of the owners of Major Chips to introduce the company's new product line: chocolate chips. They're already in the computer chip and potato chip markets and they're branching into the chocolate industry. Let's title this presentation *Introducing Major Chips' Chocolate Chips.* Also, the company slogan is, "We're guaranteed to have a chip to suit your needs;" let's use that as the subtitle.

Do It:

Adding your own text to "Click here" prompts is a simple matter of clicking and typing. Let's add a title and subtitle to this presentation now.

1. Click on the **Click here to type presentation title** prompt. The text block opens, as shown in Figure 4.2.

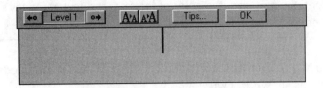

Figure 4.2 *A text block.*

SHORTCUT

To begin adding your text, you can start typing without opening the text block. Freelance enters the text you type into the highest text level that appears on the page.

2. Type **Introducing Major Chips' Chocolate Chips** in the text block.

N O T E

The buttons and symbols at the top of the text box help you format text. I'll show you how to work with these features in the next chapter when I show you how to change text formatting.

3. Click **OK** to place the text on the page.

SHORTCUT

To close the text block, you can click anywhere on the page outside the text block or click the next **"Click here"** prompt to enter text in another text block. You can also use your up and down arrows to move between text blocks when the text block is open. For instance, press the **down arrow** to move from the "Click here to type the presentation title" text block to the "Click here to type subtitle" text block. Press the **up arrow** to return to the "Click here to type the presentation title" text block.

4. Click the **Click here to type subtitle** prompt to enter a subtitle on the title page. The subtitle text block opens with the cursor blinking in the center of the block.

N O T E Look at the status bar at the bottom of the Freelance window. Information about the text appears to the left on the status bar. You can easily see the font, the font size, the color of the text, and text attributes such as bold, underline and italics.

5. Type **We're guaranteed to have a chip to suit your needs** in the text block, as shown in Figure 4.3.

Figure 4.3 *A text block with text.*

6. Click **OK** to close the subtitle text block. Figure 4.4 shows how your title page should look now.

Figure 4.4 *The title page.*

NOTE After clicking the **OK** button, the text is still selected. You need to click anywhere on the page outside of the text block to deselect it. Throughout the rest of this chapter, and the book, I'm going to assume that you know this and not remind you constantly.

That wasn't so bad, was it? Adding your own text to a page is really very easy. You're not done yet, though—you still need to add the meat of the presentation.

Bulleted Lists

The meat of the presentation—all that information you want to give your audience—is usually presented in bulleted lists. There's a good reason for this: bulleted lists enable the audience to focus on your message more easily. It's difficult to read text when it's smushed together and dumped on a page. Instead, break your message down into the key points you want to make and assign each point to a bullet. You'll obviously be using lots of bulleted lists, in different formats, throughout your presentation.

Another tip to remember when creating your bulleted lists is parallel syntax. Using parallel syntax is just a fancy way of saying that you should begin all your bulleted items on a page with the same grammatical structure, such as all verbs, nouns or adverbs. For example, here's a list of steps to take when caring for a cut or minor wound:

❖   Wash the cut with soap and warm water

❖   Dry the area thoroughly

❖   Apply an antibacterial ointment to the area

❖   Cover the area with a bandage

While this may seem like an odd example, take a look at the first word in each bullet. They are all verbs and that is what parallel syntax is all about. You could also begin each of the bullets above with nouns and create parallel syntax again. For example:

❖   Soap and warm water should be used to clean the wound

❖   The area needs to be thoroughly dried

❖   An antibacterial ointment can be spread on the area

❖   A bandage should be placed on the wound

While both examples work, notice that the first bulleted list has more punch to it, because it uses active verbs.

Of course you should continue to use phrases instead of full sentences in your bulleted lists. Each bullet should represent a main point and there should be only a couple of points per page so that the information is easy to follow. The time to give details and examples is when you're speaking to the audience. If the visual presentation includes *everything* you want to say, then what's the point? You want them to be interested in what you have to say. If your presentation is designed to stand alone (in other words, it won't be accompanied by a live presenter) you should elaborate on each point. For instance, you're not going to be there to expand upon the bulleted lists if you're publishing to the internet so you should give more information in each bulleted item than normal. But be careful when you expand on information. Rather than trying to cram everything onto one page, try to layer the information or create additional lists. For example, introduce some key points on one page, then make each key point the title of a subsequent page. You can elaborate on each point that way and still make everything look nice.

Let's start adding pages and text now. In the next section, you'll learn how to add a bulleted page to your presentation and then add your own bulleted list items to the page.

Adding a Bulleted List Page

Presentations can vary in length but it's safe to assume that your presentation will be more than one page and probably less than 50 pages (unless you want to put your audience to sleep). So one of the most basic steps you'll take when creating your presentation is to add pages. Freelance is pretty user friendly, so adding another page won't be any more difficult than it was to add your own text to the title page. You'll probably have the steps down pat in no time. Now, let's add a bulleted page.

Do It:

The first page we're adding to our presentation is a Bulleted List page layout. With the presentation open, here's how:

1. Click the **New Page** button. The New Page dialog box pops up, as shown in Figure 4.5.

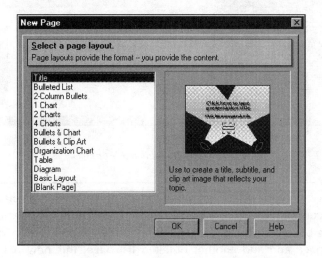

Figure 4.5 *The New Page dialog box.*

You can also open the New Page dialog box by pressing **F7**.

2. Select **Bulleted List** from the Select a page layout list box. Notice that the thumbnail changes to reflect the page layout for a bulleted list. Underneath the thumbnail is a brief description of a bulleted list page.

3. Click **OK** to add a bulleted list page to the Major Chips presentation. The bulleted list page appears, as shown in Figure 4.6.

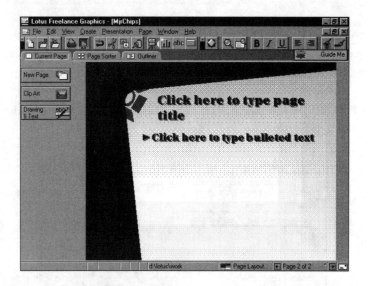

Figure 4.6 *The bulleted list page.*

NOTE

When you add a page, it's automatically placed immediately after the current page. For instance, right now I have a title page (page 1) and a bulleted list page (page 2) in my presentation. If I go back to the title page and add another bulleted list page, this new page would be page 2 and the original bulleted list page would become page 3.

While we have this page open, let's add a title and some text.

Adding Text to a Bulleted List

Karen Margolis, the Director of Marketing at Major Chips, wants me to include a brief introduction about the company. I need to inform my audience that Major Chips has been in business for eight years and is a leader in both the computer chip and potato chip markets. The idea here is to build credibility and show that Major Chips, no matter what product it produces, lives up to high standards of excellence. The purpose of my first bulleted list is to begin paving the way for this credibility. On this page, I plan on introducing these facts about the company. Later in the presentation I'll introduce some statistics in the form of charts. (You'll learn more about charts in Chapter 7). Follow along with me while I create my bulleted list.

Do It:

"Click here to type bulleted list" prompts work similar to the "Click here to type presentation title" blocks, but there are some subtle differences. Here's how to title the page and create a bulleted list:

1. Click on the **Click here to type page title** prompt to open the text block.

2. Type **Introducing Major Chips**.

If you misspell a word, use your **backspace** key to delete the misspelling and continue typing.

N O T E

3. Click the **Click here to type bulleted list** to begin entering text. Notice that a bullet automatically appears to the left of the insertion point.

4. Type **Eight years in business** as the first bulleted item.

5. Press **Enter** to add a second bullet and start a new line of text, as shown in Figure 4.7.

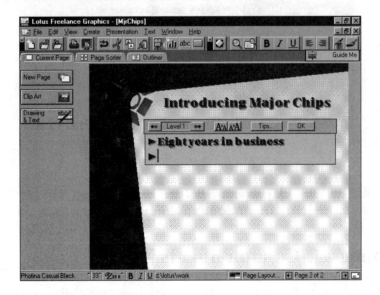

Figure 4.7 *A second bullet.*

NOTE When you press **Enter** after typing the first line of bulleted text, a bullet appears at the beginning of the next line and the cursor is positioned where the text will appear when you start typing.

6. Next, type **Major Manufacturer of computer chips in the U.S.** on the second line.

7. Press **Enter** again.

8. Type **Leader in the potato chip market**.

9. Click outside the text block to close the text block. Your bulleted page should look like Figure 4.8.

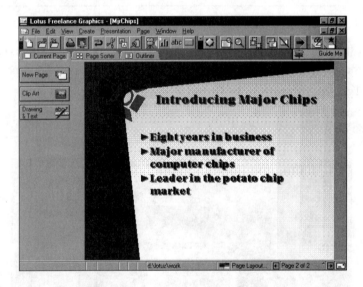

Figure 4.8 *The customized bulleted page.*

Congratulations! You've just created a bulleted list page. Don't forget to save your presentation by pressing **Ctrl-S**. Next let's add some more pages to the presentation.

Creating a 2-Column Bullets Page

It's a good idea to vary your page layouts to liven up a presentation. Since you'll be working with a lot of bulleted lists, Freelance gives you several ways to work with them using different page layouts. You just learned how to add a Bulleted List page, but regular bulleted list pages have only one column of text. Another page layout is the 2-Column Bullets page which you can use to make comparisons between bullets. For instance, you can create an "Our Company vs. The Competition" type comparison. Or you can use a 2-Column Bullets page just as a change of pace. I'll show you how to add and customize a 2-Column Bullets page in this section.

Adding a 2-Column Bullets Page

Adding a 2-column bullets page is a matter of clicking and selecting.

Do It:

To add a 2-Column Bullets page layout to the presentation:

1. Click the **New Page** button. The New Page dialog box pops up.
2. Select **2-Column Bullets** in the Select a page layout list box.
3. Click **OK** to add a 2-Column Bullets page to your presentation. The 2-Column Bullets page appears in the Freelance window, as shown in Figure 4.9.

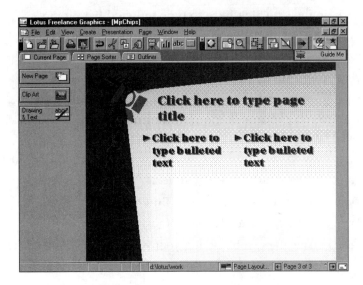

Figure 4.9 *2-Column Bullets page.*

Now let's add text to our 2-Column page.

Adding Text to a 2-Column Bullets Page

Major Chips administered more than 1000 surveys to professionals in the food industry. Results indicated that an overwhelming majority wanted several changes made to the chocolates on the market. Major Chips, when refining their chocolate recipes, incorporated these changes into their chocolates and wants to impress this fact upon the audience. Let's use this page to let the audience know about Major Chips' chocolates.

Do It:

With the 2-bullets page open, here's what you do:

1. Click on the **Click here to type page title** prompt. The text box opens.

2. Type **Incorporating Your "Musts" into Our Products** in the text box. When this text is placed on the page, it overlaps the other "Click here" prompts on the page. Don't worry about it—I'll show you how to correct this later.

3. Click on the left **Click here to type bulleted list** prompt.

4. Type **Dark, Milk, Bittersweet and "White" chocolate sold**.

5. Press **Return** to start a new line of bulleted text.

6. Type **Available in 10 sizes to suit YOUR needs**.

7. Click the right **Click here to type bulleted list** prompt. The text you just entered appears on the page and now the right text block is open (see Figure 4.10).

8. Type **Easy to use** as the first bulleted item in the right text block.

9. Press **Enter** to start a new line of text.

10. Type **Smooth Texture** and press **Enter** again.

11. Type **Great taste** as the last line of text.

12. Click outside the text block and your page should look like Figure 4.11.

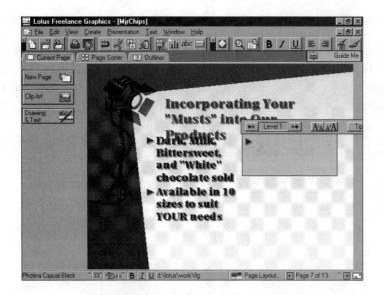

Figure 4.10 *The right text block.*

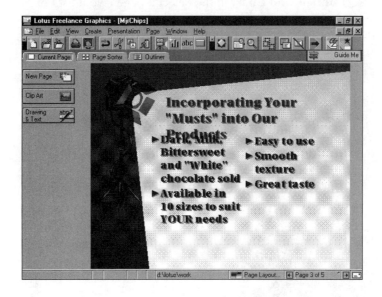

Figure 4.11 *2-Column Bullets page with text added.*

Hmmm, I already see something I don't like about this page. I'll show you how to make changes to a page later in this chapter. But for now, let's continue adding pages. I'm going to add a Bullets and Chart page next. A Bullets and Chart page is usually used to present information in chart form and point out specifics of the chart using the bullets section. And that's exactly what we're going to do. We're going to enter the text in this chapter and create the chart in a later chapter.

Adding a Bullets & Chart Page

Adding a Bullets & Chart page is as simple as adding any other type of page to your presentation.

Do It:

To add a Bullets & Chart page:

1. Click the **New Page** button. The New Page dialog box pops up.
2. Select **Bullets and Chart** in the Select a page layout list box.
3. Click **OK** to add a bullets and chart page to your presentation. The Bullets and Chart page appears in the Freelance window, as shown in Figure 4.12.

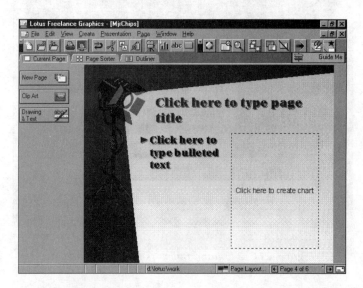

Figure 4.12 *The Bullets and Chart page.*

Now let's customize this page. Before we do, let me explain my plan.

Adding Text to a Bullets & Chart Page

When I was asked to create this presentation, Karen wanted me to address the survey results that were gathered over the two year period and stress how these results were incorporated into Major Chips' chocolate products. I want to use this page as an introduction to the survey results. For the bullets section, I'm including the top three or four responses and in the chart, I'll show these responses in a stacked bar chart or pie chart, perhaps. We'll take care of the chart later. Let's add the text to this page.

Do It:

With the Bullets & Chart page open in the Freelance window, here's how to customize the page:

1. Click on the **Click here to type page title** prompt to open the text block.
2. Type **The Resulting Answers** in the text block.
3. Click on the prompt titled **Click here to type bulleted text**.
4. Type **Smoother texture** next to the first bullet.
5. Press **Enter** to begin a new line of text.
6. Type **Easier to handle** as the second line of text and press **Enter** to begin a third line.
7. Type **Richer flavor** next to the third bullet and press **Enter** again to start a fourth line.
8. Type **Lower prices** as your final line of text. Your Bullets & Chart page should look like Figure 4.13.

Now you've completed entering text for the Bullets & Chart page. Don't worry about the Chart section of the page. I'll show you how to create your own charts in Chapter 7. If you must know right now, skip to Chapter 7 and come back when you're done. We still have a Bullets & Clip Art page to add to our presentation.

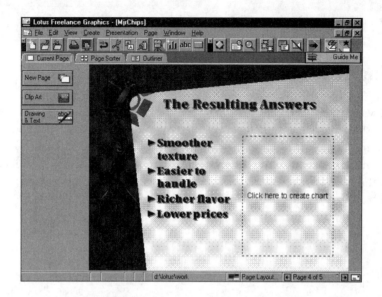

Figure 4.13 Your Bullets & Chart page.

Creating a Bullets & Clip Art Page

It's always good to add graphics or even humor to a presentation. It helps break up the monotony of reading endless pages of text and data. Freelance allows you to select a page layout that includes text and clip art. It looks similar to a Bullets & Chart page but instead of a chart, there is space for clip art. I'll show you how to add a Bullets & Clip Art page to your presentation.

Adding a Bullets & Clip Art Page

We need to add just one more page in this chapter—the Bullets & Clip Art page. This page is another variation on the bullets layout that I've showed you in this chapter.

Do It:

To add a Bullets & Clip art page:

1. Press the **New Page** button. The New Page dialog box pops up.

2. Select **Bullets & Clip Art** in the Select a page layout list box.

3. Click **OK** to add a Bullets and Clip Art page to your presentation. The Bullets & Clip Art page appears in your Freelance window, as shown in Figure 4.14.

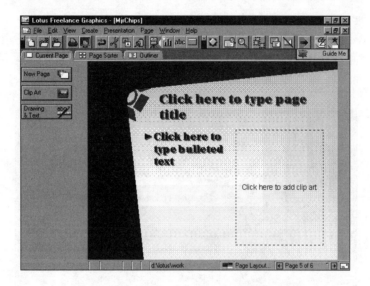

Figure 4.14 *The Bullets and Clip Art page.*

Adding pages to a presentation is really quite easy. In this chapter, we've added every page layout that uses text to our presentation. Let's add text to this page, and then I can show you how to edit and work with the text.

Adding Text to a Bullets & Clip Art Page

For this page, I want to inform the audience about Major Chips' key research points. Verbally, the presenter can explain to them how the research was actually conducted, who the subjects were and give examples of survey questions.

Do It:

To customize a Bullets & Clip Art page:

1. Click on the **Click here to type page title** prompt to open the text block.

2. Type **Researching the Market** in the text block.

3. Click on the **Click here to type bulleted text** prompt.

4. Type **Administered 1,000 surveys** as the first bulleted point.

5. Press **Enter** to start a second bulleted line.

6. Next, type **Created 22 recipes**.

7. Press **Enter** to start a third line.

8. Type **Conducted 2,500 taste tests** as your final line of text. Click anywhere outside the text block and the page appears as in Figure 4.15.

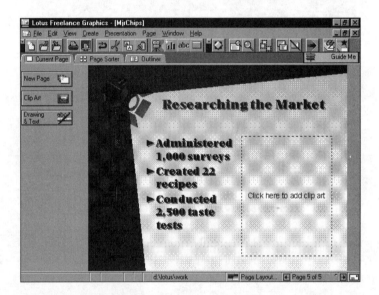

Figure 4.15 *The customized Bullets & Clip Art page.*

You've just added text to the bullets section of your Bullets and Clip Art page. Again, don't worry about the Clip Art section of the page. I'll show you everything you need to know about clip art in Chapter 10. We'll finish this page later. Don't forget to save your presentation by pressing **Ctrl-S**.

Changing a Page Layout

While looking over the presentation, you may decide that instead of a section for clip art, you'd rather have an area where you can add a chart instead or that Bulleted List page should really be a 2-Column Bullets page. In either case, you could delete the entire page, add a different page layout and type the text in all over again. But you can circumvent all that hassle by simply changing the page layout.

Do It:

Freelance lets you change everything about your presentation, including page layouts. With the Bullets & Clip Art page open, here's how to change the page layout to a Bulleted List page:

1. Click on the **Page Layout** button on the status bar. The Switch Page Layout dialog box opens, as shown in Figure 4.16.

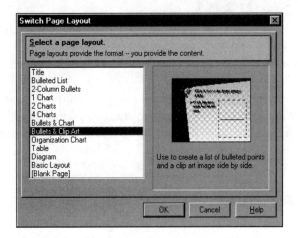

Figure 4.16 *The Switch Page Layout dialog box.*

2. Select **Bulleted List** from the Select a page layout list box.

3. Click **OK** to change the presentation page layout. The Researching the Market page appears as a Bulleted List page in the Freelance window, seen in Figure 4.17.

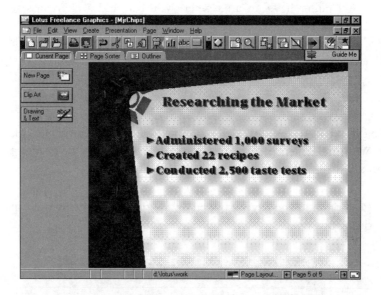

Figure 4.17 *The Researching the Market page as a bulleted list.*

We don't want this page to be a Bulleted List page in the presentation, so click on the **Undo** SmartIcon (it's the one with the two arrows on it) to change the layout back to a Bullets & Clip Art page. You'll find that Undo can be your best friend when designing presentations.

Deleting a Page in Current Page View

You may decide that you want to remove a page in your presentation. You don't like the topic, you don't like the way it looks or you accidentally selected the wrong type of page and now you want to remove it. In Current Page mode, you can remove a page with a couple of mouse clicks. Here's how:

Do It:

Let's remove the current page (don't worry, we won't really get rid of it). Here's how:

❖ With the current page in the Freelance window, choose **Delete Page** from the Page menu. The page is removed from your presentation and the page immediately following the deleted page appears in the window. If you decide not to delete the page, simply press the Undo SmartIcon.

Removing a page is just as easy as adding a page to your presentation. If you don't want to remove the page that's currently displayed, what do you do? Just move to the page you want to delete and follow the same step outlined above. (You can also delete pages from Page Sorter view.) I'll show you how to move between pages in the next section.

Moving Between Pages

We've just added five pages to the Introduction to Major Chips' Chocolate Chips presentation. This is a good time to look at the presentation thus far and really assess what we've done and what we want to change. Don't forget we're in Current Page view, so the Bullets & Clip Art page is still in the Freelance window. If I want to review my work page by page, I need to move between pages. Freelance gives you several ways to move between pages, and in this section I'll tell you how to use them.

Going to a Specific Page

Do you remember that 2-column bullets page that we created earlier? I've been thinking about it and I really don't like the way it looks. I want to make some changes. I remember titling it **Incorporating Your "Musts" into Our Product**. Let's go to that page now.

Do It:

To go to a page using a specific title:

1. Click the **Page Number Box** in the status bar. (It's the button between the left and right arrows at the far right end of the status bar.) A list of all the page numbers and their titles pops up, as shown in Figure 4.18. Notice that the title of the current page in the Freelance window is selected.

1. Introducing Major Chips' Chocolate Chips
2. Introducing Major Chips
3. Incorporating Your "Musts" into Our Products
4. The Resulting Answers
5. Researching the Market

Figure 4.18 *Page Number list box.*

2. Select **Incorporating Your "Musts" into Our Product** from the titles listed. That page appears in the Freelance window.

Click the **Go to a specific page** SmartIcon (the one that looks like an arrow pointing to the right). The Go to Page dialog box pops up. Select the title of the page you want to go to and click **OK**. The page appears in the Freelance window. You can also open the Go to Page dialog box by pressing **Ctrl-G**.

SHORTCUT

Moving Between Pages Consecutively

At some point during the creation of your presentation, you may want to look through it page by page and see how it all looks. Also, you may want to check to see what topics you've covered and what you haven't covered yet. Therefore, instead of going to one specific page, you want to view every page in order. Follow along with me and I'll show you how to do it.

The best way to really check the overall appearance of your presentation is by using the Page Sorter view. To learn how to work in Page Sorter, flip to Chapter 12, *Polishing Up Your Presentation.*

N O T E

Do It:

To move forward in a presentation, you need to click the **Right Arrow** in the Page Number Box on the Status Bar (or choose **Next Page** from the Page menu); to move backward in a presentation, click the **Left Arrow** (or choose

Previous Page from the Page menu). With the Bullets & Clip Art page in the Freelance window, let's move back to the 2-Column Bullets page. Here's how:

1. Click the **Left Arrow** in the Page Number Box on the Status Bar to go back a page. The Resulting Answers page created earlier is displayed.

2. Click the **Left Arrow** again. The Researching the Market 2-Column bullets page is displayed.

NOTE

If you continue pressing the left arrow, you will eventually return to your starting page. The reason is that when you come to the end of your presentation or the beginning of your presentation, Freelance loops back around. For instance, if you reach the last page in your presentation and you click the **Right Arrow** key, the first page is displayed. If you're at the title page, clicking the **Left Arrow** key takes you back to the last page.

Leave this page open so we can make some changes to it. Let's move on to the next section where I'll show you how to work with text.

Working with Text

We've finished adding text to five pages of the presentation. I already know of one page that has several items that need to be changed. We'll probably need to change some other items later on too, but let's work on the page in the Freelance window now. In this section, I'll show you how to edit, copy, paste, and move text and also how to use the Spell Checker. Let's start by editing some text.

Editing Text

Earlier in this chapter, I showed you how to fix typos using the backspace key. Well, I don't know about you, but my mistakes aren't limited to typos. Sometimes I type the wrong word or words and sometimes I like to rearrange sentences. This process is the same for presentations. You may want to change words and rearrange things. And that's the case with the presentation page titled **Incorporating Your "Musts" into Our Product.** In this section, I'll show you how to edit text using this page.

Replacing Text

I've decided to change the text in the left bulleted list. I think Ellen should verbally elaborate on the different types of chocolate available during the presentation, so we won't list them in the first bullet. Let's change the opening words in the first bullet so it reads "Four flavors of chocolate sold." In addition, I want to change the second bullet in that list to read "Ten industrial sizes available to suit YOUR needs."

Do It:

Here's how to replace text on a presentation page:

1. Double-click the **Bulleted list** on the left. The text block opens (see Figure 4.19).

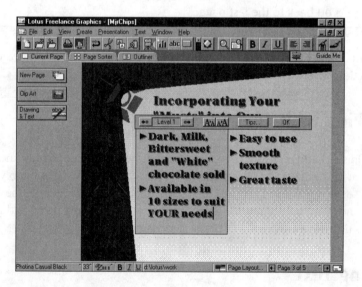

Figure 4.19 *The text block.*

2. Click and drag the cursor to select **Dark, Milk, Bittersweet and "White"** as shown in Figure 4.20.
3. Type **Four flavors of**. The text you enter automatically replaces the selected text.
4. Next, select the words **Available in 10 sizes**.

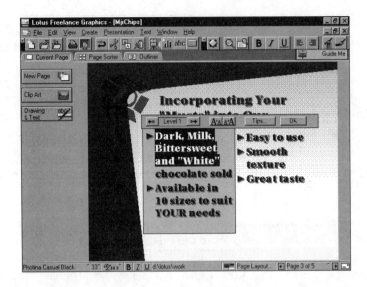

Figure 4.20 *Dark, Milk, Bittersweet and "White" selected.*

5. Type **Ten industrial sizes available**.

6. Click **OK** to close the text block. Your left bulleted list should look like Figure 4.21 now.

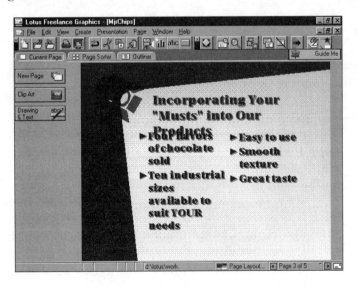

Figure 4.21 *The revised bulleted list.*

Don't forget that if you decide you don't like your changes after all, you can press **Ctrl-Z** or press the **Undo the last command or action** SmartIcon. These are both Undo commands.

N O T E

I think that looks much better now so let's save the changes. I also want to make a change to the right bulleted list. In the next section, I'll show you how to copy text.

Copying Text

Copy is a helpful feature when you want to move blocks of text or information to another area but you want to leave the original block where it is. Copying the items saves you time because you don't have to type it all over again. In the right bulleted list, notice that I don't have parallel syntax. The last bulleted item, "Great taste," should really read "Tastes great." Let's flip those two words around using Copy and Paste.

Do It:

To copy text:

1. Double-click the **bulleted list** on the right to open the text block.
2. Select **Great** by clicking and dragging the cursor over the word.
3. Next, click the **Copy to the clipboard** SmartIcon.

Instead of choosing the **Copy to the clipboard** SmartIcon, you can copy a selected item by pressing **Ctrl-C**. The clipboard is an area within the program where copied items are stored until you copy another item.

KEYBOARD

And that's it! Nothing changes in the window but you've just copied the word "Great" to the clipboard. It'll stay on the clipboard until you copy another item to the clipboard or you exit Freelance. In the next section, I'll show you how to paste an item from the clipboard into the file.

Pasting Text

Naturally, if you copy something to your clipboard, you'll probably want to paste it somewhere else. In this section, we'll paste "Great" back into the bulleted point after the word "taste."

Do It:

To paste an item from the clipboard:

1. Position the cursor after the word "taste" and click. The insertion point is now after the word "taste."

2. Type the letter **s** (we do want to add an "s" to the word "taste") then press the **Spacebar** once to put a space after the word "tastes."

3. Then click the **Paste the clipboard contents** SmartIcon. The word "Great" appears after the word "tastes," as shown in Figure 4.22.

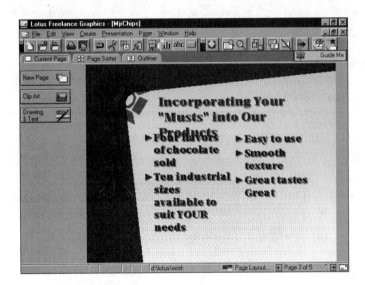

Figure 4.22 *"Great" is now after "tastes."*

Instead of choosing the **Paste the clipboard contents** SmartIcon, you can paste an item from the clipboard by pressing **Ctrl-V**.

KEYBOARD

We're almost finished, but we still need to get rid of the first "Great" from our bulleted item. If you want to entirely remove an item from one place and have it appear somewhere else, you can use the Cut feature instead.

Cutting Text

Cutting text removes the text from a location within your file and places it on the clipboard. The text remains on the clipboard until you copy or cut more text or you exit Freelance. To show you what I mean, let's cut the first "Great" out of the bulleted item we've been working on.

Do It:

To cut text or an object:

1. With the text block selected, double click on the word **Great** to select it.
2. Click the **Cut to the clipboard** SmartIcon. The selected word disappears.

KEYBOARD

Instead of clicking the **Cut to the clipboard** SmartIcon, you can press **Ctrl-X** to cut an item.

The word is now stored on your clipboard. Using your backspace key, remove the extra space in front of Tastes and then make the "G" in Great lowercase following the steps I outlined in Replacing Text. Your page should now look like Figure 4.23.

There are still several items we need to change on this page. First, notice that the title still has text overlapping the bulleted lists. It makes reading difficult and looks unattractive. In the next section, I'll show you how to move text blocks.

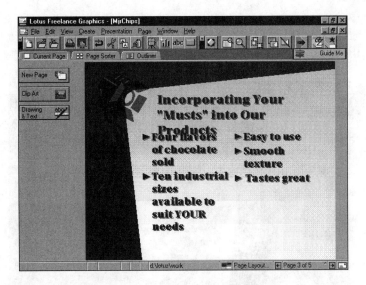

Figure 4.23 *The presentation page.*

Moving Text Blocks

We still have the Incorporating Your "Musts" into Our Products page open. The next thing I want to do is move the bulleted lists down so that the text in the title block doesn't overlap the left list. I could move just the left bulleted list (the one that is partially covered by the title) but then it won't be aligned with the right bulleted list. Instead, I want to move the bulleted lists down together. This will save you from spending valuable time trying to readjust the blocks so they line up again. The following section shows you how to move text blocks around.

Do It:

Sometimes you may want to move one (or more) text blocks to rearrange the layout or put more space between the text and the title like we are doing here. Here's how to do it:

1. Click on the left **Bulleted list** to select it.
2. While pressing the **Shift** key, click the right **Bulleted list**. Now both bulleted lists are selected.

3. Click on one of the selected text blocks and hold down the left mouse button. Notice that the pointer turns into a hand. Drag the text blocks to the new location (see Figure 4.24).

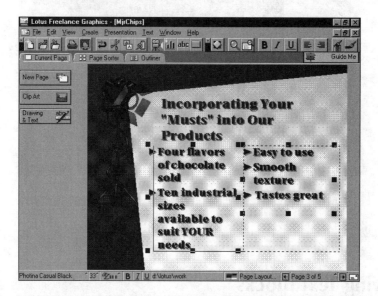

Figure 4.24 *Dragging the text block.*

If you're moving one text block, simply skip step two in the steps I've described above. This page looks much better now. The title and 2-column bullets aren't overlapping any longer. Before we spell check the file, I want to change one more thing.

Wrapping Text

Look at the left bulleted list again in the 2-Column Bullets page layout that we've been working on. The second bullet breaks oddly so that the words "sizes" and "needs" wrap around and each occupies one line. This makes it a little difficult to read. To change the way the text wraps, do the following:

Do It:

To change how the text wraps in the first bulleted list:

1. Click once on the left **Bulleted list** to select the list. Notice that eight little boxes appear around the text. These little boxes are called *handles*.

2. Move the pointer to the center handle on the left side. Notice that the pointer turns into a double-ended arrow.

N O T E   Grabbing a middle handle on the left or right edges only changes the width of the box. Grabbing a top or bottom center handle only changes the length of the box. Grabbing corner handles changes both the width and length of a text block. Experiment and see how they work. You can use the **Undo** command to revert back to the previous shape.

3. Drag the handle to the left slightly.

4. Release the handle. The text block is resized and the text wraps now so that the words "sizes" and "available" are on the same line of text, as shown in Figure 4.25.

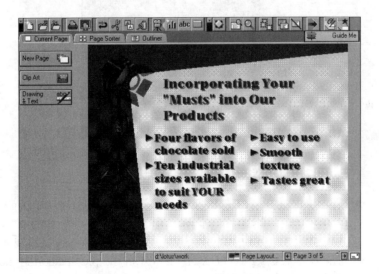

Figure 4.25 *The text block resized.*

We're going to change more items as we work on this presentation throughout the book, but I think that we've made a good start in the right direction. Now let's spell check the file.

Using the Spell Checker

Spell checkers are certainly helpful and they can find those commonly misspelled words we're all prone to using. While spell checkers will probably catch most of your spelling mistakes, don't rely upon them totally. Remember that a spell checker can't tell whether you really meant to use "your" or "you're," so it is important to look over your work too. I'm going to do a quick spell check and see if I've made any typos.

Do It:

To spell check your work:

1. Choose **Check Spelling** from the Edit menu. The Spell Check dialog box opens (see Figure 4.26).

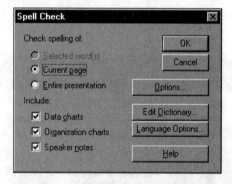

Figure 4.26 The Spell Check dialog box.

❖ The default is set to check the spelling of the current page only. If you want to check the spelling of the entire presentation, select the **Entire Presentation** radio button in the Check spelling of section.

❖ The default is set to check all the text in the presentation including text in Speaker Notes, Data Charts and Organization Charts. If you don't want to check the spelling of all these different elements in the presentation, then click the check boxes in the Include section to deactivate them.

❖ The default is also set to check for repeating words, words with numbers, and words that begin with capitals. Click the **Options** button to change these defaults.

❖ If your company uses specialized jargon frequently or a technical vocabulary that isn't normally found in spell checkers, you can customize your Freelance dictionary so that these commonly used words or letters aren't flagged constantly. Click **Edit Dictionary** and the Spell Check User's Dictionary dialog box pops up. Type the word you want to add in the New Word text box. Click **Add** and the word appears in the Current Words window. To delete the word, select it in the Current Words window and click **Delete**. The word is removed from the Current Words list. Click **OK** to exit the Edit Dictionary and save any changes you've made.

❖ While many people throughout the world speak English, we all speak different types of English. American English is different from Canadian English, and both are different than British English. Freelance recognizes these differences and gives you the option to change your dictionary. To change a language dictionary, click the **Language Options** button. The Spell Check dialog box pops up. Choose the language you want and click **OK**.

2. When you've completed any changes and are ready to begin your spell check, click **OK**. Another Spell Check dialog box pops up, as shown in Figure 4.27, with the first word the Spell Checker is questioning in the Replace with text box.

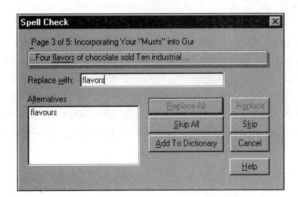

Figure 4.27 *The Spell Check dialog box.*

If you don't want to make any changes to your default settings, you can completely skip the first Spell Check dialog box by pressing **Ctrl-F2** to move directly to the Spell Check dialog box in Figure 4.27.

❖ Click **Skip All** to keep the spelling as it is and not select the word again.

❖ Click **Skip** to keep the spelling of the word as it is and move to the next word.

❖ To replace a word, select a word in the Alternatives List box. The spelling changes in the Replace with text box. Click **Replace** to substitute the misspelled word with the word in the Alternatives List box. Click **Replace All** to replace the word wherever it appears in the entire file or page (depending upon which option you choose) with the word in the Alternatives List box. If the correct word does not appear in the Alternatives list, simply type what you want in the Replace with text box before you click **Replace**.

❖ To add the word to the Freelance dictionary, press **Add to Dictionary**. Next time the Spell Checker finds the word in a file, it won't question it.

3. When the Spell Check is complete, the Spell Check Complete dialog box pops up. Click **OK** to close the dialog box.

You've just successfully worked through the Spell Checker. It's a good idea to use it periodically just to make sure no typos have cropped up.

From Here...

We've come a long way in this chapter. We began with a selected SmartMaster Look and a blank title page. Since then we've added several pages to the presentation; added text to each page, and even edited them using the Cut, Paste, and Copy tools; moved text boxes; changed text wrap; even used the Spell Checker. You've done a lot of work in this chapter and hopefully learned a lot.

In the next chapter you'll learn how to change styles, fonts, point size, colors, borders and a whole lot more.

CHAPTER 5

Text Properties— Making It All Look Pretty

(And still be meaningful)

In the last chapter, I showed you how to add several different bulleted list pages to the Major Chips presentation. You also learned how to add text to each of the bulleted list pages, how to move between pages, and how to edit, move, copy, paste and cut text on a page. Those are the text basics. After working through this chapter, however, you're going to be a real text connoisseur. In this chapter you'll learn how to do some really neat stuff with your text. It's all about making your text aesthetically pleasing beyond the basics that Freelance provides.

When you customized your presentation, you probably noticed that the text was automatically given a color that matched your presentation background, and that the bullets popped up in a certain shape, that the text was aligned to the

129

right or left or centered. You didn't have to tell Freelance to do any of this, it just happened like magic. All this stuff (and more) is a part of the SmartMaster Look you selected. Colors, alignment, fonts, point size—all of these things are called *text properties*—and these text properties are automatically assigned to the text that you enter. Even though they are standard items that come with the SmartMaster Look, you can change them if you want. And in this chapter, I'll show you how. Before we begin changing text properties though, I want to show you the tool you will probably use most often to make these changes. It's called the *Infobox*.

Accessing Properties

Every page, text block, chart, table, diagram, or object has a set of properties associated with it. To view or change these properties, you need to open an Infobox. Infoboxes are Freelance's way of organizing and packaging properties so that you can work with them more easily. Infoboxes are organized into properties pages. Each page contains the properties for a specific element. For example, there is a properties page for text. You'll find text properties such as font, size, color, and attributes on that page. There are pages for borders and lines, text, bullets, alignment and much more. Let's access the page properties by opening the Infobox (I'm assuming that you have your presentation open in the Freelance window). Let's get started and open the Infobox and view page properties now.

Viewing Page Properties

To access the properties for a presentation page, you need to open the Infobox. The page Infobox provides you with general information about the page that appears in the Freelance window. Let's open the Infobox for the title page of the presentation and you can see what it looks like.

Do It:

We're going to continue working on the Major Chips presentation, so open it if you haven't already done so. The title page of the Major Chips presentation is called *Introducing Major Chips' Chocolate Chips*. With the title page in the window and no items on the page selected, here's how to open the page's Infobox:

❖ Click the **Open Infobox** SmartIcon (it's the one with a yellow square tilted onto one corner). The page Infobox opens with the page properties displayed, as shown in Figure 5.1.

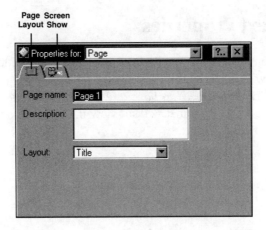

Figure 5.1 *The page properties.*

 You can also view properties by clicking your right mouse button once. The shortcut menu pops up. Then choose **Page Properties**. The same dialog box opens as in Figure 5.1.

N O T E

Notice that the word Page appears in the Properties for text box. This text box indicates what object the Infobox is displaying the properties for. Also, the Page Layout tab is selected. When you open the page Infobox, the Page Layout tab is the default. Behind the Page Layout tab is the Screen Show tab. This is a special properties page that you can use when you're creating a screen show. I'll show you how to create a screen show in Chapter 14, but be aware that the Screen Show tab appears in almost every Infobox that you open.

The Page Layout properties page contains text boxes. The Page name text box indicates the page number of the current page. You can add a brief description of the page in the Description text box by clicking in the box and typing. You can also change the layout of the current page by clicking the **Down Arrow** of the Layout drop-down list box. Select a different layout name from the drop-down list box and the page automatically changes to reflect the new page layout.

A page Infobox allows you to change the layout and set up a screen show. You can't work with the text or any objects that may appear on the page. To work with text, you need to open an Infobox for text.

Viewing Text Properties

The title page of the Major Chips' chocolate chip introduction is open in the Freelance window. The title of the presentation is *Major Chips' Chocolate Chips* and the subtitle is *We're guaranteed to have a chip to suit your needs*. In this section, we're opening the Infobox so that we can view the text properties for the subtitle of the presentation page.

Do It:

To open the text Infobox:

❖ Click on **We're guaranteed to have a chip that suits your needs** to select the text. The handles appear around the text box.

The Text properties page appears in the Infobox, as shown in Figure 5.2. The properties pages displayed in the Infobox automatically change when you click on different items.

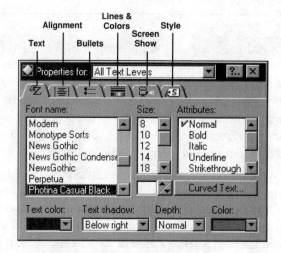

Figure 5.2 *The Text properties Infobox.*

NOTE

The Infobox always opens to the Text properties page, shown in Figure 5.2, when you have text selected.

SHORTCUT

Typing **Alt-T**, then the letter **F**, opens the Infobox with the Text tab selected. If you have the Infobox open so that you can see the page properties, you can switch to text properties by clicking on a text block. You don't need to open and close the Infobox each time you want to look at different properties. You really should keep the Infobox open throughout this chapter. If the Infobox gets in the way of these exercises, double-click on the title bar to collapse the box (you'll see only the title bar and tabs). When you want to view a properties page, double-click on the title page and the box expands, or simply click the tab.

If you read Chapter 2, you've seen this dialog box before. There are text boxes, drop-down lists, list boxes and buttons to help you change your text properties. Keep this dialog box open for the rest of the chapter. I'll show you how to use the Alignment, Bullets, Lines and Colors, Named Styles, and Text tabs. Since the Text tab is already selected, let's begin by changing the subtitle that is highlighted.

Changing Text Properties

Major Chips' slogan, "We're guaranteed to have a chip to suit your needs," appears on all the company's literature and official materials including presentations. The company's policy is that the slogan appears on all company materials in Arial, 24 point size, bold, in a dark purple color known as Eggplant with no shadow, and centered. The subtitle properties are currently Photina Casual Black, 36, normal, in the color Scarlet with a shadow. The way it appears now doesn't conform with Major Chips' policies. In the next sections I'll show you how to change the font, point size, attributes, color, shadows, and alignment.

Changing Fonts

Every SmartMaster Look has a typeface (or font) that is associated with it. The text you add to the presentation appears in that typeface because it's the default.

You may want to change the font for a portion of the presentation you're working on. When you installed Freelance, you automatically installed a number of fonts that came with the software so there are quite a few to choose from. Avoid using really fancy or unusual fonts because they're difficult to read. The default font for the Major Chips SmartMaster is Photina Casual Black. I need to change the subtitle text so that the typeface is Arial.

Do It:

The Infobox is still open and displaying the text properties for "We're guaranteed to have a chip to suit your needs." In the Font Name list box, notice that Photina Casual Black is selected. The selected text currently appears in this font. To change the typeface from Photina Casual Black to Arial:

❖ Use the scroll bar to choose **Arial** from the Font Name list box. The selected text immediately changes to reflect the new font selection. The subtitle appears in Arial now, as shown in Figure 5.3.

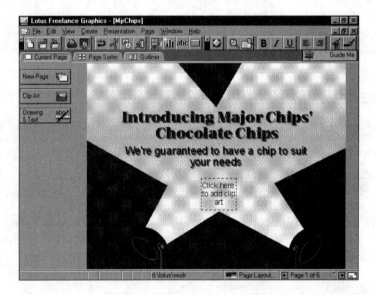

Figure 5.3 *The subtitle in Arial font.*

SHORTCUT

Instead of opening the Infobox to change fonts, you can use the **Font** button on the Status Bar. To change the subtitle font from Photina Casual Black to Arial, click the text to select it. The status bar buttons change to give you information about the text including the font, point size, color and attributes. Click the button marked **Photina Casual Black**. A list box opens. Select **Arial** from the list box. When you make a selection, the box automatically closes. Notice that the subtitle text is changed now.

N O T E

If you want to change the typeface for the entire presentation, Freelance has a different set of steps for you. Instead of changing each and every text block, you can open the Presentation menu (**Alt-P**) and then choose **Change Typeface Globally** (**T**). The Change Typeface Globally dialog box pops up. Select a typeface from the Choose a typeface list box. Click in the Data Charts, Tables or Organization charts check boxes if you want to change only the text that appears in a data chart, a table or an organization chart. Click **OK**. A Change Typeface Globally warning pops up telling you that all the text will be changed and it can't be undone. Click **OK** to change the typeface globally or **Cancel** to cancel your changes.

We still need to change some more properties. Next I'm going to change the point size of the text.

Changing Font Size

The size of text is usually referred to as the *point size* or *size*. Points are one of the smallest units of measurement in the print industry. Freelance takes care of the text size automatically. If you do decide to change sizes, however, remember to use at least 18 point text for overheads and slides. I'd recommend that you use even larger sizes, depending upon the size of the room. Otherwise your audience might be squinting to read the information on your overheads. Now, we need to change the subtitle point size to 24.

Do It:

To change the font size from 32 to 24:

❖ Use the scroll bar to select **24** from the Size list box in the Text properties page. The text automatically changes when you select a different size, as shown in Figure 5.4.

Figure 5.4 *Text in 24 point size.*

N O T E

To increase or decrease the point size in smaller increments than what is displayed in the Size list box, click the increment buttons immediately below the Size list box.

SHORTCUT

You can change the point size without opening the Infobox. To change the point size from 32 to 24, begin by selecting the subtitle text. Click the button labeled **32** on the Status Bar. A list box opens. Select **24** from the list box. The box automatically closes and the text is reduced in point size.

The font has now been changed and the point size has been reduced. Next I need to change the text attributes to conform to Major Chips' policies.

Changing Attributes

Bold, italic, underline, superscript, subscript, strikethrough, and normal are all text features called *attributes*. They indicate what the text looks like. The text default is set to *normal*. To select an attribute, follow the steps outlined below.

Do It:

With the subtitle still selected and the Text properties page displayed in the Infobox, here's how to change the text's attribute from normal to bold:

❖ Select **Bold** from the Attributes list box to change the text from normal to bold. The check mark in the attributes window now appears beside bold. The selected text on the presentation page is changed from normal to bold immediately.

You can select more than one attribute when changing text attributes. After selecting **bold**, you could click on **italic**, then scroll down and choose **underline**. Check marks appear beside all three attributes and the text now appears in bold, italics and underlined.

Instead of opening the Infobox, you can use the buttons on the Status Bar marked **B**, *I* and U or the bold, italic and underline SmartIcons. Whether you prefer the Status Bar or the SmartIcons, the buttons work the same.

Changing attributes is simple and can help you stress a point during your presentation. Bolding or italicizing one word in every bulleted item, however, can overdo it and your audience won't pay as much attention to the points you want to stress. Try to use attributes sparingly. Another item that you should use sparingly is color. I'll show you how to work with text colors in the next section.

Changing Font Colors

Every time you customize a "Click here" prompt, you're entering information that is automatically assigned a color. That holds true for your text too. When we entered text in the "Click here" prompts, the text was automatically assigned a color. The SmartMaster Look I'm using assigned the color scarlet to my text and it looks sharp with the background color scheme. But sometimes you may need to change a color. You may want to change a color to stress a point or conform with your company's policies about official images, as we're doing here. I need to change the subtitle text from scarlet to eggplant.

Do It:

Freelance gives you a color palette for your text. To open the color palette and change the text color:

1. Click the **Down Arrow** of the Text Color drop-down list box in the Text properties page. A color palette pops up, as shown in Figure 5.5.

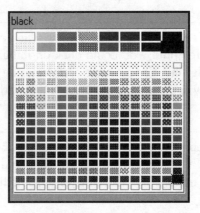

Figure 5.5 *The Text Color palette.*

SHORTCUT To open the Text Color palette, you can select the text on the page and then choose the button between the point size and bold buttons on the Status Bar (it has a row of colorful lines on it). When you click it, the Text Color palette pops up.

2. Select **Eggplant** from the color palette by clicking and dragging the pointer across the top column to the right. The text changes as soon as you select a different color.

N O T E

Your selection of colors appears as small boxes in the drop-down list window. When you click on a colored box and drag the pointer, notice that the name of the color you're pointing to appears at the top of the box. The colored boxes are small so that the names can help you differentiate between the numerous selections available to you.

As you can see, there are plenty of colors to choose from in the color palette. Try not to go overboard though, because too many colors can confuse and distract your audience. Use color sparingly. Also, don't use colors that are hard on the eye. Shadows are another feature that may make reading text difficult. The default is set to automatically create a shadow. In the next section, I'll show you how to turn off shadowing effects and change them.

Removing Text Shadows

Shadows can be a really cool effect or they can be a big pain. They're those gray or black images that usually appear behind and to the lower right of the text. Shadows can be altered so that they appear in different positions—above, below, right and left—of the text. You can even change shadow colors. Reading text with shadows can be difficult. The letters look fuzzy, especially when the shadow is shallow. Shadows work best when you use them sparingly and with small text blocks.

I want to remove the shadow of the subtitle text block we've been working on. Here's how:

Do It:

With the text selected and the Text properties page displayed, follow these steps to remove a shadow:

1. Click the **Down Arrow** of the Text shadow drop-down list box. The list opens, as shown in Figure 5.6.

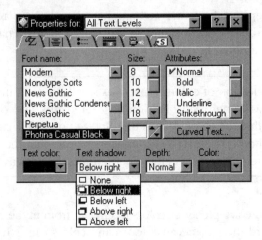

Figure 5.6 *The Text Shadow drop-down list box.*

2. Select **None** from the Text shadow drop-down list box to remove the selected text's shadow.

Removing a shadow is really a simple process. You may want to add a shadow, however, and that involves a few more selections. In the next section I'll show you how.

Adding Text Shadows

While shadows are a default for many of the SmartMaster Looks available in Freelance, there are some Looks where you may want to add a shadow to highlight the text or create a visual effect. I'll show you how to add a shadow to text.

Do It:

Let's add a shadow back to the subtitle. Here's how:

1. Open the **Text Shadow** drop-down list box.

2. Select **Above left** to create a shadow above and slightly to the left of the text.

   ❖ Freelance allows you to create one of four different shadows behind your text. Select **Below right** to create a shadow to the lower right of the text. Choose **Below left** to create a shadow appearing to the lower left of the text. Select **Above right** to create a shadow to the upper right of the text and choose **Above left** to create a shadow appearing to the upper left of the text.

3. Open the **Depth** drop-down list box to select how deep you want the shadow to appear.

4. Choose **Deep** so that this shadow is very noticeable.

   ❖ Select **Shallow** to create a very slight shadow, **Normal** to create a standard depth shadow (this is the default shadow setting) or **Deep** to cast a large shadow.

5. Next, open the **Color** drop-down list box. The color palette appears.

6. Choose **Red** by clicking and dragging the pointer along the top row of the color palette. The subtitle now looks like Figure 5.7.

Figure 5.7 *The subtitle with a shadow.*

You see what I mean? Shadows can be a pain. The subtitle is difficult to read with that shadow. Use your judgment and always keep the audience in mind when you're adding or removing shadows. What looks good to you on the computer screen may not to someone who's sitting in the fiftieth row and trying to read it. I'll remove the shadow I just created by following the steps in the "Removing a Shadow" section. I want to make two more changes to the subtitle before we move on to another page.

Aligning Text

Text alignment usually refers to how the lines of text appear on the page between the left and right margins. There are four types of alignment: left, right, centered, and justified.

❖ **Left** aligned text begins at the left margin and leaves a ragged right edge. A ragged right edge means that the text doesn't touch the right margin. Instead, Freelance tries to get as close to the right margin as it can and then wraps the characters it can't fit on the line down to the next line.

❖ **Right** aligned text aligns at the right margin and has a ragged left margin.

❖ **Centered** text begins in the middle of the page and is centered between the right and left margins. Usually centered text doesn't touch either the right or left margins.

❖ **Justified** alignment stretches or condenses the text as best it can to reach both margins. Freelance calls this *horizontal alignment* because you're changing how the lines appear horizontally between the right and left margins.

Freelance also allows you to change the vertical alignment of text. *Vertical alignment* determines text placement between the top and bottom margins. Your text can be closer to the top margin, the bottom margin, or even centered between the two margins. This is helpful when you have several text blocks on a page and you want to space out the text in each block so it doesn't look so crowded or you want to place the text in a specific area of an object.

For the subtitle, I want the text to be justified horizontally and centered vertically. Let me show you how to align text.

Do It:

With the text selected, here's how to align the subtitle text:

KEYBOARD

Instead of opening the Infobox to align your text, you can type **Alt-T**, then **G** to open the text menu and the alignment cascading menu. From the alignment cascading menu, you can type **Ctrl-L** to left justify, **Ctrl-E** to center, **Ctrl-R** to right justify, and **Ctrl-J** to full justify your text. This changes only the horizontal alignment.

1. Click the **Alignment** tab in the Infobox (that's the one with the straight lines centered between two purple lines). The Alignment properties page pops up, as shown in Figure 5.8.

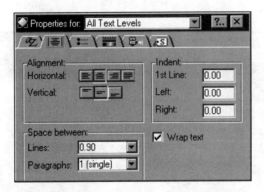

Figure 5.8 *The Alignment properties page.*

N O T E

Each square radio button in the alignment section has a picture of what the text looks like if that button is selected. Simply select the button that matches the picture of how you want the text to look.

2. Click the **Justified** radio button (that's the one where the lines are the same width) in the Horizontal line of the alignment section. The text immediately changes to reflect your selection.

3. Next, select the **Centered** radio button in the Vertical line of the alignment section to center the text between the top and bottom margin of the text block.

SHORTCUT

You can right, center or left justify your text by highlighting the text block, then choosing the **Align to the left** SmartIcon, Center SmartIcon, or the **Align to the right** SmartIcon.

You can use any or all types of alignment throughout your presentation. For instance, we've just justified and centered the text. But we could right justify and place the next piece of text at the top or the bottom of the text block. Your title page now looks like Figure 5.9. It looks a little odd still, doesn't it? The word "needs" is on a line of its own. We need to change this so that there is only one line of text.

Figure 5.9 *The text aligned.*

Wrapping Text

Freelance uses text wrapping by default. It creates a second line of text if it can't fit all the characters on one line. Depending upon the size of the text block, each line is capable of containing a certain number of characters. When you type one more characters than the line can hold, it automatically creates a second line. The word "needs" can't fit on the first line so it is knocked down to the second line.

We could reduce the point size or change the font to make it fit, but an easier way is to disable text wrapping. To disable (or enable) text wrapping, you need to access the Alignment properties page in the Infobox. The subtitle needs to be on one line, so let's try to disable text wrapping now.

Do It:

To disable text wrapping:

❖ With the alignment tab displayed, click in the **Text Wrap** check box. The check mark in the check box disappears. The text now occupies one line.

 Word wrap is used by default. If you turn text wrapping off and decide you want the text block to wrap after all, then click in the **Text Wrap** check box again. A check mark appears in the check box and text wrap is enabled.

Disabling text wrap works really well when you need to squeeze in just a word, maybe two. There are times, however, when disabling text wrap will cause the text to run off the page or you may have to move text blocks to make everything fit.

The Alignment properties page in the Infobox dialog box contains indenting and spacing features too. To show you how they work, I need to open a different page in the presentation. Do you remember that bulleted list we created in the last chapter? Well, I want to open that page again and make some additional changes. To open the bulleted list page again, click on the **Page Number box** on the status bar and select **Introducing Major Chips**. The bulleted list page appears in the Freelance window.

Spacing Text

The spacing between lines, sometimes referred to as *leading*, and the spacing between paragraphs are both controlled from the Alignment tab in the Infobox. Freelance uses a default of single spacing between lines and 1.15 lines for spacing between paragraphs. A block of text is considered a·paragraph when there is a carriage return (pressing **Enter**) after the text. To facilitate reading of the text, sometimes it's better to add more spacing between lines and/or paragraphs. The paragraphs on this presentation page may be too close together. Let's space them out and see how that looks. Let's also space out the lines slightly. Here's how to change the spacing defaults.

Spacing between Lines

Freelance allows you to choose from single, 1.15 (which is a little more than single), double and 2.15 for the space between lines. In this bulleted list, I want to change the spacing between lines from single spaced to 1.15.

Do It:

To change the spacing between lines:

1.   Select the bulleted list.

2.   Choose the **Alignment** tab from the Infobox.

3.   Click the **Lines** arrow to open the drop-down list box in the Spacing between section of the Alignment tab. The Spacing between Lines drop-down list box opens (see Figure 5.10).

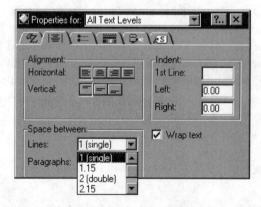

Figure 5.10   *The spacing between lines drop-down list box.*

4.   Choose **1.15** from the list. The text immediately changes to reflect the selection and the list box closes.

Next, let's change the spacing between paragraphs.

Spacing between Paragraphs

Besides making it look nice, adding space between paragraphs (or bullets) can help set your points apart. Freelance gives you the same choices between paragraphs as it does for line spacing. Next I'll add double spacing between my paragraphs.

Do It:

To add double spacing between paragraphs:

1. Select the bulleted list.

2. Select the **Alignment** tab.

3. Next, click the **Paragraphs** down arrow. The spacing between paragraphs drop-down list box pops up.

4. Choose **2 (double)** from the list box. The text changes to reflect the selection and the list box automatically closes. The presentation page now looks like Figure 5.11.

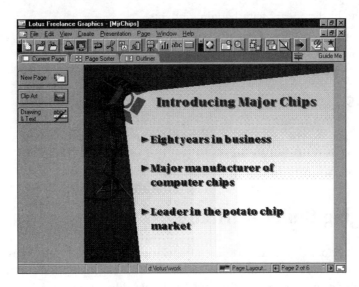

Figure 5.11 *The presentation page with the spacing altered.*

Adding space between lines and paragraphs can help your audience read your text and make the page format look nicer. I'm changing the spacing settings back to the defaults. The bulleted items look better that way.

Creating a Hanging Indent

Hanging indents are often used to make the beginning of a new paragraph obvious. You've probably seen them before: the first line of text juts out and the rest of the lines are indented.

Do It:

With the alignment properties page displayed, here's how to create a hanging indent:

1. Select the bulleted list.
2. Enter **.5** in the 1st Line: text box of the Indent section.
3. Enter **1** in the Left: text box. To create a hanging indent, remember that the value you place in this text box has to be greater that the value in the 1st Line: text box, otherwise it doesn't work.

The bulleted list appears with hanging indents.

Let's change the indentation back to the default by entering zero (**0**) in the 1st Line: and Left: text boxes.

Bullets

Freelance allows you to change the bullet style, color, size, shadows and the spacing between the bullets and text. You can also change bullets to numbers if you'd prefer to have a numbered list instead.

Changing Bullet Attributes

The bullet shape, color, and size are all included in the bullet attributes category. You can individualize your presentation a little by including special bullets unique to your company (see Chapter 10 about adding your own art to Clip Art) or you can choose from the selection that Freelance provides you. You can also use the bullet attributes section to change a bulleted list to a numbered list. I'll show you how to change bullet attributes to suit your preferences now.

Do It:

For this exercise, I'm going to change my arrow bullets to numbers. Here's how:

1. With the bulleted list selected, select the **Bullets** tab (that's the one with the blue bullets and dotted lines). The Bullets properties page pops up, as shown in Figure 5.12.

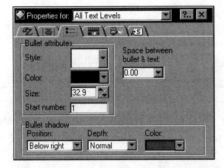

Figure 5.12   *The Bullets properties page.*

KEYBOARD

You can press **Alt-T**, then **B** to open the Infobox with the Bullets tab selected.

2. Click the Bullet attributes **Style** drop-down list button. The Style list box opens, as shown in Figure 5.13.

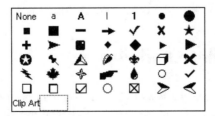

Figure 5.13   *The Style list box.*

3. Select the **1** bullet in the top row. This bullet represents a numbered list.

❖ To change the color of a bullet (or number), click the **Color** drop-down list box. The color palette pops up. Select the color you want. The color palette closes and the bullets change color immediately.

❖ You can also change the size of your bullets by clicking on the up or down **increment buttons** next to the Size text box. The size of numbers can't be altered using this box because numbered bullets are in equal proportion to the text. For instance, if you reduce the text size to 14, the numbers are reduced to 14 point size to match the text.

❖ The Start Number text box allows you to decide what number you want your list to start with. This is particularly useful when you continue a numbered list on another page.

N O T E

There are numerous styles of bullets that you can choose from. You can make any of the clip art items that Freelance provides you (or clip art you add) into bullets too. To change clip art into bullets, open the Style list box. Select **Clip Art** from the list. The Choose Clip Art for Bullet dialog box pops up. Use the right and left arrows to move through the clip art. When you find something that you want to use as a bullet, click on the picture and then click **OK**. The piece of clip art, in miniature, pops up in the Style window and the bullets are automatically updated to the clip art you select. The clip art bullet is now in your Style list box for you to select any time you want.

Changing bullet styles and attributes is really easy. You can get clever and use some neat bullets provided in the style drop-down list or Freelance's clip art. I'm changing my bullets back to the default by clicking the **Undo** SmartIcon.

Changing Bullet Shadows

Just like text, bullets have shadows too. So if you alter your text shadows, you can alter your bullet shadows to match. You can change the shadow's appearance by changing the color, depth and position. Here's how:

Do It:

Let's change our shadows from the lower right to the upper left, make the shadow deep, and change the color from Chartreuse to Flamingo. To alter bullet shadows:

1. With the bulleted list selected, and the Bullets properties page displayed, click the **Position** drop-down list box arrow. The drop-down list opens.

2. Select **Above left** to change the position of the shadow. The shadow position changes immediately.

3. Next, click the **Depth** drop-down list box arrow. The drop-down list opens.

4. Select **Deep** to change the depth of the shadow. The drop-down list closes upon making a selection.

5. Select the **Color** drop-down list box arrow. The color palette list appears.

6. Choose **flamingo** by clicking and dragging the mouse pointer across the color palette to the 13th Column from the left and the 5th row down.

Your bullet shadows look similar to Figure 5.14 now. Let's adjust the space between the bullets and text now.

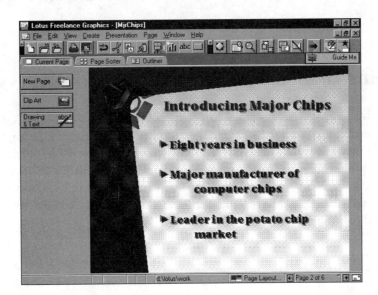

Figure 5.14 *The bullets with the shadows changed.*

Besides changing bullet shadows, Freelance also allows you to change the spacing between the bullets and text.

Spacing Between Bullets and Text

Adding space between your bullets and text can help make the text more noticeable. Freelance allows you to choose from several settings: single space, 1.15, double space, 2.15 and 3.00 too. Putting more space between bullets and text is a simple matter of making a couple of selections.

Do It:

Let's put a double space between the text and bullets. Here's how to change the spacing between bullets and text:

1. Select the bulleted list.
2. Click the **Space between bullet & text** drop-down list box arrow in the Bullets properties page to display the choices.
3. Choose **2 (double)** from the drop-down list. The text changes immediately.

Now, let's get our creative juices really flowing and have some fun reshaping text.

Curving and Rotating Text

Curving text into different shapes can help you create some unique logos and designs and add character to your pages. It also adds an artistic flavor to your text. You may not want to curve text too often, but when you do, Freelance has several options for you. You can curve text within a text block into circles, squares, s-shapes, ovals, straight lines, or you can contour your text to the shape of a selected object. Let's have some fun in this section and I'll show you how to curve text into different designs.

Curving Text

Freelance provides templates that curve the text into perfect circles, semi-circles, quarter circles, squares, S's, ovals, straight lines, and triangles. Let's change the text to an S-shape.

Do It:

Add a Bulleted List page to the presentation and enter **Having fun rotating text** in the "Click here to create title" prompt. Now let's turn it into an S-curve. Here's how:

1. Select **Having fun rotating text**.
2. Open the **Text** properties page in the Infobox.
3. Click the **Curved Text** button. The Curved Text dialog box pops up, as shown in Figure 5.15.

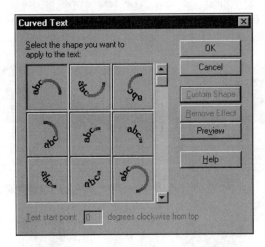

Figure 5.15 *The Curved Text dialog box.*

SHORTCUT

You can open the Curved Text dialog box by pressing **Alt-T**, then the letter **v**. The dialog box pops up.

4. Use the scroll bar to locate and select the **S-Shape** button.

    ❖   To preview your rotated text, click the **Preview** command button. The Preview dialog box pops up. Select **OK** to rotate your text and return to the presentation page, or choose **Change** to go back to the Curved Text dialog box.

SHORTCUT

If you want to preview your rotated text but don't want to deal with the Preview dialog box, click the **Preview** button and continue to hold the left mouse button down. The presentation page with the rotated text pops up in the window. Release the left mouse button and the Curved Text dialog box reappears.

5. Click **OK** to rotate the text. The text appears on the page similar to Figure 5.16. (I've dragged the text block to another area on the page so you can see it better.)

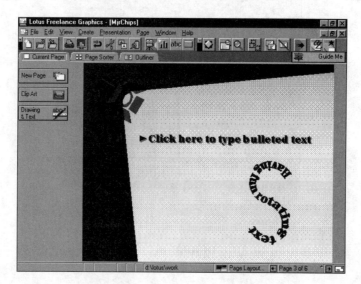

Figure 5.16 *S-shaped text.*

When curving text, be aware that all the text in the text block is curved when you select the **Curve Text** button. You can't pick and choose which pieces of text you want to change. Freelance also allows you to curve text around objects or shapes.

Curving Text Around Shapes

You may want to get a little imaginative on your own and have your text contour to shapes that you create. You can curve text to create some neat effects and still be able to read it. To really do this exercise, you need to know how to draw objects, which are covered in Chapter 9. If you'd like, skip over the section and come back to it when you know how to work with objects, or flip to Chapter 9 and learn how to do objects now, then come back.

Do It:

First off, you need to have a shape that you want to curve your text around. I'm not going to show you how to create a shape here (that comes in Chapter 9). But I will show you how to curve text around the shape. For this example, I've created a wavy line using the drawing tools and typed **Curving my text in a wave pattern** in the "Click here to type bulleted list" prompt. Now I'm going to curve the text to the contours of the wavy line. Here's how:

1. Select the object you want the text to wrap around, as shown in Figure 5.17.

2. While pressing the **Shift** key, select **Curving my text in a wave pattern**.

3. Select the **Curved Text** button from the Text properties page. The Curved Text dialog box pops up.

4. Choose the **Custom Shape** command button. The text curves immediately to the shape of the wavy line (see Figure 5.18).

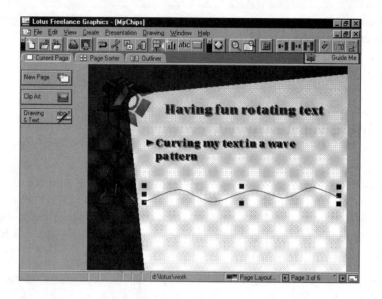

Figure 5.17 *An object selected.*

Figure 5.18 *Text in a custom curve.*

N O T E
If you choose, you can remove the line so that it isn't visible when you attach the text. Before selecting the text, highlight the object. Open the Infobox. The Lines and Colors properties page appears. Click the **Line Style** drop-down list box arrow. The Style drop-down list pops up. Select **None.** The line disappears but it's still there. Continue with steps 2 through 4 to curve the text to the line's contours. The text curves but you can't see the line anymore.

That's all there is to contouring text. Now I'm going to place a border around the text I just contoured into a wave.

Creating a Border

Borders are great for enhancing your titles, framing your text or surrounding an object. They're also good for designing charts and tables. Borders come with window dressing though—you can fill them with patterns and colors, you can choose the width and style of the lines, and you can even create shadows for your borders. Let's create a border around the text we just curved into a wavy line.

Do It:

Here's how to create a border around text.

1. Select the **Curving my text in a wave pattern** text block.

2. Choose the **Lines & Colors** tab (the one with lines and colors in the shape of a square) from the Infobox. The Lines & Colors properties page opens, as shown in Figure 5.19.

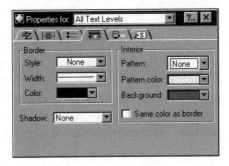

Figure 5.19 *The Lines & Colors properties page.*

3. Select the **Style** drop-down list box. The list box opens.

NOTE The Style drop-down list shows you different line patterns. Each pattern shows you how the line looks when selected. You can choose from a solid line, dashes, dashes and dots, or no visible line at all. The border is created even if you select **None** from the Style drop-down list box; you just can't see it.

4. Select the solid line.
5. Next, select the **Width** drop-down list box. The Width drop-down list opens with a selection of line widths to choose from.
6. Choose the thickest line.
7. Now, select the **Color** drop-down list box arrow. A color palette pops up.
8. Choose **Aztec Blue** in the second line. Your text is now surrounded by a border.

Let's fill the border in with a colored pattern now.

Filling a Border

You can add more interest to your border, if you fill the interior in with a pattern and a color. Some of the border interior patterns can get a little busy—especially from a distance—so consider your audience when you select the border fill-in pattern.

Do It:

For this border, let's select a graduated fill for the interior and add some color. Graduated patterns are dark at one end and gradually get lighter as the pattern moves through the border. Patterns (except solid patterns) have two colors: the pattern color and the background color. For this border, we're selecting scarlet for the pattern color and then parchment for the background color. To select an interior pattern:

1. Choose the **Pattern** drop-down list box arrow from the Lines & Colors properties page. The selection of patterns appears, as shown in Figure 5.20.

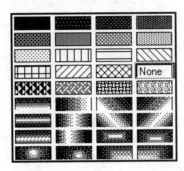

Figure 5.20 *The Pattern drop-down list box.*

2. Select a graduated fill from the Pattern drop-down list box.

3. Next, choose the **Pattern color** drop-down list box arrow to open the color palette.

4. Select **Scarlet** from the color palette. The pattern immediately turns scarlet. Except for solid patterns, patterns usually have a pattern color and a background color. Scarlet is the pattern color, so next we need to select a background color.

To make your pattern and border color the same, click in the **Same color as border** check box.

NOTE

5. Select the **Background** drop-down list box arrow. The color palette opens.

6. Choose **Parchment** from the color palette. The background of the pattern changes to parchment.

Everything I've showed you in this chapter so far has been about changing isolated blocks of text. For instance, I changed my bulleted list on the page titled *Introducing Major Chips* but if I add another bulleted list page, the changes I make don't appear in the new bulleted list. If I wanted to incorporate these changes into my new bulleted list, I would have to open the Infobox and make the same changes to the properties again. I could change each and every text block, or I could do it faster and easier by changing the style. Consistency is very important in a presentation. To maintain consistency, it's probably better to use the styles features.

Styles

Text properties such as the font, size, color, shadows, spacing between lines and paragraphs, the text color and attributes—in short, everything we've been working with thus far—can all be neatly boxed into a package called a *style*. A style is a collection of text properties that you can name, save and then apply to other text blocks throughout the presentation. When you selected a SmartMaster Look, you also selected a set of styles that came with the Look by default. These styles are called *Presentation title, Presentation subtitle, Page title, Bulleted text, Numbered list,* and *Label text.* When you enter text into a "Click here" prompt, you're automatically using the default named style. You can, however, modify the styles that came with the Look or you can create your own styles.

WARNING

If you create a presentation using the SmartMaster Look default styles and you change the SmartMaster Look, your presentation will incorporate all the new default styles. Therefore, any changes you made to a bulleted list or even the default style are lost when you switch Looks. If you create your own styles and use them throughout the presentation, they are saved as a part of the file. So if you switch presentation Looks, your created styles are incorporated into the new Look.

Go back to the Introducing Major Chips page and I'll show you how to work with styles. Just a note: follow these exercises when you actually want to work with styles, don't incorporate the changes I'm making into the Major Chips presentation that we're working on together. If you follow along and do make any changes, use the **Undo** command to change the presentation back.

Creating a Style

To create a style, you need to make changes to the text block first. Once you've made all the changes you want to incorporate into the text, then you can create the style. I'm going to create a style where bulleted lists appear with a double space between the arrow and text. I'll show you how now.

Do It:

Once the Introducing Major Chips page is open in the Freelance window:

1. Select the bulleted list.
2. Select the **Bullets** properties page in the Infobox.
3. Choose **2 (double)** from the Space between bullet and text drop-down list box. The space between the bullets and text widens.
4. Click on the **Style** tab (that's the one with an "S" on it). The Style properties page appears, as shown in Figure 5.21.

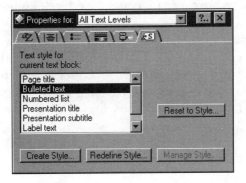

Figure 5.21 *The Style Properties page.*

5. Click the **Create style** button. The Create Text Style dialog box, shown in Figure 5.22, pops up.

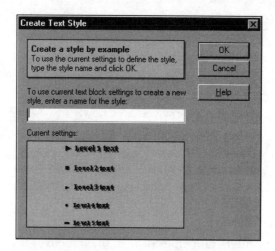

Figure 5.22 *The Create Text Style dialog box.*

6. Enter **Bulleted List** in the To use current text block settings text box.

7. Click **OK**. The Create Text Style dialog box closes and Bulleted List is selected in the Text style for current text block list box.

Congratulations, you've just created a style. To use the new Bulleted List style, you need to select each text block (that you want to reflect that style), open the Infobox, choose the **Style properties** page and select **Bulleted** List from the list box. There is a faster way of changing ALL the bulleted list text blocks and that's to redefine a style. Let me show you how.

Redefining a Style

What was the point of creating a style then, if only that text block is changed? Well, remember that when you create a style and use it in the presentation, it is saved as a part of the presentation. That means that you can change the SmartMaster Look twenty—or a hundred—times and each text block that incorporated the style you created will look exactly the same in each Look. When you redefine a style, however, you are changing the default style and every text block that uses the style will automatically change. This also means you lose all these properties changes if you change the Look. In addition, creating a style means that you can use it in any presentation you create by copying and pasting the text block into the presentation. If you redefine a style, you can only use it in that presentation. There are some subtle differences here that you need to be aware of before you start redefining text blocks. The most important thing to consider is whether you'll want to use the style again and again. Here's how to redefine a style.

Do It:

To show you how to redefine a style, I'm changing my Bulleted Text default style so that all the text in the bulleted list appears in the color green. Remember—don't follow along with these exercises until you really need or want to work with a style. Here's how to redefine a style:

1. With the bulleted list selected, choose **Green** from the Text color drop-down list box in the Text properties page. The text in the block turns green.

2. Display the **Style** properties page.

3. Choose the **Redefine Style** button. The Redefine Style dialog box pops up, as seen in Figure 5.23. Bulleted text appears in the Style name box.

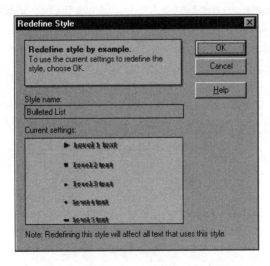

Figure 5.23 *The Redefine Style dialog box.*

4. Click **OK** to redefine the style.

That's a quick way of changing all the text blocks that use that named style to suit your preferences. Just remember though that you cannot carry these changes over if you decide to use a different SmartMaster Look. The color green!! Yuck! Select the **Undo** SmartIcon to change the text color back to black. I've also reapplied the Bulleted list style to the text block.

Resetting a Style

After making a ton of changes to your presentation, you may find that you don't like the way it looks now. How do you change it back? You could go back and reverse each and every change, or you could use the Reset a Style feature. I'm going to change the scarlet title page to blue and then use the reset button to change it back.

Do It:

With the Introducing Major Chips page open:

1. Select **Introducing Major Chips**.
2. Select **Blue** from the Text color drop-down list box in the Text properties page. The selected text immediately turns blue.
3. Display the **Styles** properties page.
4. Click **Reset to Style**. The Reset to Style dialog box pops up, as shown in Figure 5.24.

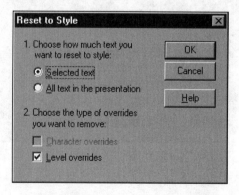

Figure 5.24 *The Reset to Style dialog box.*

5.   Choose **Selected Text** if it's not already selected.

6.   Click **OK** to change the text back to the default settings. The text color changes back to scarlet.

This is really helpful when you've made numerous changes to a text block. In the next section, I'll show you how to get rid of a created style.

Managing a Style

You can remove a style that you've created when you decide that it's not needed any more, it's causing too much confusion, or you want to create a new style with that name. Freelance euphemistically refers to deleting a style as "Managing a style." To remove a created style, obviously, you need to have created a style. So, remember that style I created earlier and titled Bulleted List? Well, let me show you how to delete it.

Do It:

With the presentation open, here's how to manage a style:

1.   Select **Introducing Major Chips**.

2.   Choose the **Styles** tab from the opened Infobox.

3.   Select **Manage Style**. The Manage Styles dialog box, seen in Figure 5.25, pops up.

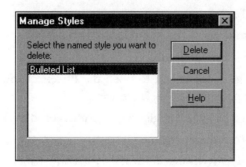

Figure 5.25   *The Manage Styles dialog box.*

4. Select **Bulleted List** in the Select the named style you want to delete list box.

5. Click **Delete** to delete the style. The Text Named Styles dialog box pops up warning you that if you delete the style, you cannot undo the command.

6. Click **OK** to continue deleting the style.

7. Click **OK** to exit the dialog box.

Bulleted List no longer appears in the Text style for current text block list box.

Using Fast Format

Instead of changing the formatting for the entire presentation, you may want to apply the formatting of a text block to only a few text blocks. You could change each text block individually, or you could use the Fast Format feature. Fast Format picks up all the attributes that are assigned to a text block and applies them to a different text block.

Do It:

To show you how it works, let's take the text block we changed in the Introducing Major Chips page and apply those formatting changes to the text block on the Researching the Market page. To use Fast Format:

1. Select the text block that begins with **Eight years in business**.

2. Open the **Text** menu.

3. Select **Fast Format**. The menu cascades.

4. Choose **Pick Up Attributes**.

5. Use the page number box to open the **Researching the Market** page. The page opens in the Freelance window.

6. Select the text block that begins with **Administered over 1,000 surveys**.

7. Open the **Text** menu again.

8. Select **Apply Attributes** from the Fast Format menu. The text block is reformatted, as shown in Figure 5.26.

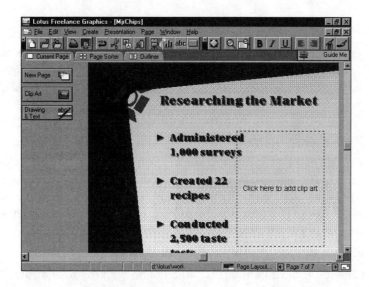

Figure 5.26 *The second text block reformatted.*

Click the **Undo** SmartIcon to change the text back to the way it looked before the steps above. Instead of opening the Text menu, you can quickly access Fast Format by using the shortcut menu. Click on the text block with the right mouse button. The Shortcut menu pops up. Select **Fast Format**, then choose **Pick Up Attributes** or **Apply Attributes,** depending upon what you want to do.

Indenting and Outdenting Text

Indenting text in books (including this one) and business documents signals the beginning of a new paragraph. Full-fledged paragraphs aren't really used in bullet style presentations because you're using phrases as bulleted text instead. But to drive home a bulleted point, you may want to add additional text that you can use as supporting facts. For instance, I've added more text to the Introducing Major Chips page after the first bullet. I've added two bulleted items: Super slow chip and Quickie chip. The Super Slow Chip and the Quickie Chip are Major Chips' computer chip products. Go ahead and add these two items to your bulleted list. Instead of leaving these two bulleted items as they are, we can reformat them so that they're indented. This way, the audience knows that these are supporting facts to the first point being made. Let me show you how to indent text lines.

Do It:

Do you remember when you clicked on the "Click here" prompt and a text block popped up with several buttons along the top of the box? No? Well, that's okay, because we'll open it together again and I can show you how to use them.

1. Double-click on the bulleted list on the Introducing Major Chips page. The text block appears.

   The first two buttons are the outdent (left arrow) and indent buttons (right arrow). The space between the two buttons indicates the text level. The next button, the one with the red arrow, decreases the point size of the text in the block. The button with the blue arrow increases the point size. The Tip button provides you with some keyboard shortcuts that you can use.

2. Position the cursor in front of **Super slow chip**.

3. Click the **Indent** button (that's the button with the right arrow). The text is indented, as shown in Figure 5.27. Notice that "Level 2" appears in the space between the two arrows now. Freelance provides you with a title and five additional text levels. Go ahead and keep clicking the **Indent** button to see how the different text levels appear, but make sure you come back to Level 2.

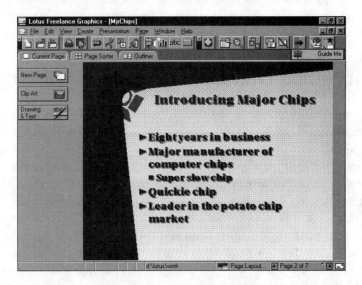

Figure 5.27 *Super slow chip indented.*

4. Next, position the cursor in front of **Quickie chip**.

5. Select the **Indent** button again to change the text level from Level 1 to Level 2.

6. Click **OK** when you're finished making changes.

These two paragraphs are now indented and are obviously tied in with the first bulleted list item.

Rotating a Text Block

Instead of curving your text into fantastical shapes and curves, you can do a simple text rotation. You may want to rotate text to create labels for charts or tables, or you may want to rotate clip art. Freelance lets you freely rotate text or rotate in 45 degree increments.

Do It:

Since we just finished working with the bulleted list on the Introducing Major Chips page, let's have some fun with it and rotate it. Here's how:

1. Click once on the bulleted list to select it.

2. Open the **Text** menu.

3. Select **Rotate**. The cursor changes shape to a curved double arrow with a plus sign.

4. Click on the upper-left corner handle of the text block and hold the left mouse button down. The text block is outlined by a dashed line.

NOTE

To rotate text blocks in 45 degree increments, press and hold down **Shift** while you drag the text block.

5. Drag the **cursor** down the page. The outline begins to rotate.

6. Release the **cursor**. The text is now rotated and looks similar to Figure 5.28.

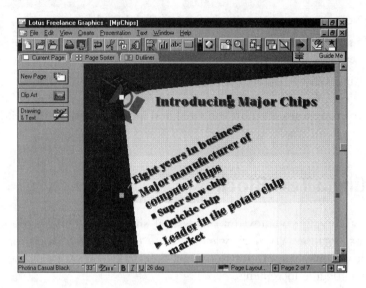

Figure 5.28 *Rotated text.*

You cannot rotate charts, organization charts, or tables, but everything else is fair game. Before we end this chapter, let's continue to have some fun and align text blocks.

Aligning Text Blocks

Unlike aligning text, aligning text blocks doesn't require you to use the Infobox. You can align the left sides or the right sides of two or more text blocks. You can align the top or bottom of text blocks and you can even center text blocks in a row, a column, along a point, or on the page. To show you how this works, I'm going to align the title of the Introducing Major Chips page and the bulleted list.

Do It:

Here's how to align text blocks:

1. Select **Introducing Major Chips**.
2. Press the **Shift** key and select the bulleted list. Now both text blocks are selected.

3. Open the **Text** menu.

4. Select **Align**. The Align Objects dialog box, as shown in Figure 5.29, pops up.

Figure 5.29 *The Align Objects dialog box.*

5. Choose the **Center in a column** radio button. Notice that the thumbnail changes to reflect the alignment selection.

6. Click **OK** to align the text blocks. The text blocks immediately realign.

This feature is helpful when you've resized several text blocks on a page and you want them to be realigned. I'm not saving these alignment changes, but this gives you a good idea of how alignment works.

From Here...

Well, are you a text connoisseur yet? If you've worked through this entire chapter, you must be! Not only do you know how to add pages and add text to them, but you can work with text colors, borders, indenting, styles, shadows, rotation, and alignment, among other things. And, what's even better is that the skills you learned here are applicable to Freelance charts, tables and objects.

What's next? So far we've been working in Current Page view which allows you to see one page at a time. That's fine if all you want to do is create each page individually—but what if you want to view all the text? You could move back and forth between pages or you could print all the pages out and flip through them.

Frankly, that's a waste of time, energy, and paper. A faster and easier way to view all the text is to use Outliner view. In Outliner view, all the text is displayed as an outline. That makes it easier to check the text for logic and sequencing. In the next chapter I'll show you how Outliner view works.

teach yourself...

Freelance Graphics 96

CHAPTER 6

Working in Outliner View

(Viewing text from a different perspective)

So far we've been working in Current Page view, which allows you to focus on individual pages within the presentation. You can create pages and enter text and graphics on each page, change page layouts, and move between pages. Current Page view is a great way to begin creating a presentation. At some point during the creation of your presentation, however, you'll probably need to take a step back and look at the overall presentation and focus on different aspects of it, specifically the text and page sequence.

Focusing on text can be difficult in Current Page view. Since you can only view one page at a time, you need to move back and forth between pages to check the text. It's hard to keep track of all the text and if your presentation consists of multiple pages, it gets pretty cumbersome to move between pages. To overcome this daunting organizational task, Freelance has another view called *Outliner*. Outliner view allows you to concentrate your energy on the text because it displays the text in an outline. The text is displayed as headings, bullets and indents. It even has a canary-yellow background with lines that remind you of old-style legal pads.

In Outliner view, you can do everything that you can in Current Page view and a little more. To help you in the creation process, Freelance allows you to add, edit and delete pages and text, and move text and pages within the presentation. You can even begin designing your presentation in Outliner view by entering text or importing outlines from Word Pro or ASCII text. You can collapse and expand all the text or just a page of text, which can help you check the text flow. We now have several pages in our presentation. Let's switch views and I'll show you how to work on the presentation in Outliner view.

Changing to Outliner View

Changing to Outliner view is a simple process that you can do at any point during the presentation. In fact, it's probably a good idea to change to Outliner view occasionally just to spot check the text.

Do It:

I've opened the Major Chips presentation and it's displayed in Current Page view. Here's how to change to Outliner view:

❖ With the presentation open, click on the **Outliner** tab. The Page View changes to look like Figure 6.1.

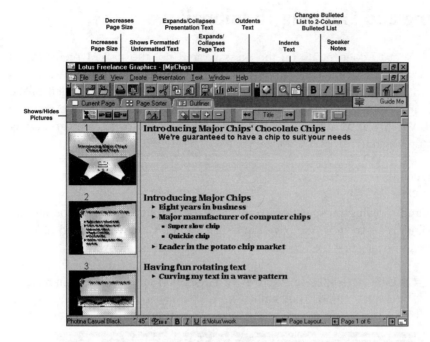

Figure 6.1 *Outliner View.*

 To the left of the text is a thumbnail of each presentation page. A number appears above each thumbnail. This is the page number—you'll notice that it changes to include a plus sign (+) when you collapse the text and move the page around.

N O T E

Most of the buttons and menus do the same thing in Outliner view as they do in Current Page view. Take a couple of minutes, however, to familiarize yourself with the Outliner buttons I've pointed out in Figure 6.1. In the following sections I'll show you how to use the cool stuff you find here.

Hiding and Showing Thumbnails

When I want to concentrate on the message and not the look, I prefer things "plain vanilla." That's where hiding and showing presentation page pictures comes in. The presentation pages are displayed as thumbnails to the left of the outline and Freelance allows you to hide the thumbnails when you're working on text. When you want to see how the text looks on the page, you can display the pictures again.

Do It:

Hiding and showing presentation pages involves using the same button switch. The default is set to show the page thumbnails, so I'll show you how to hide the presentation pages first then display the pages again. Here's how:

1. Click the **Show/Hide Pictures of Pages** button to hide the thumbnails in the left column. The Outliner View changes to look like Figure 6.2.

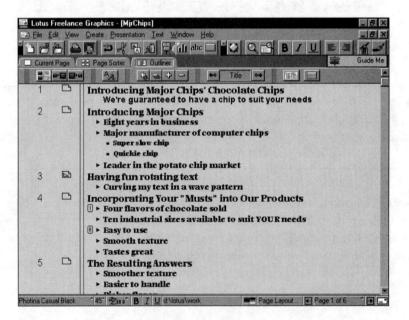

Figure 6.2 *Hiding pictures of pages.*

KEYBOARD

To hide the thumbnails, you can press **Alt-V**, then **G**. To show the presentation pages again, press **Alt-V**, then **G** again.

N O T E

When you hide the pages, small page icons appear in place of the thumbnails. Some of the page icons also display symbols. These symbols indicate that the page contains more than text, (clip art, tables, diagrams or charts). Plain icons indicate the page only has text. Icons with triangles signal that there are graphics on the page. Tiny bar charts on the icon indicate that there are charts. Icons with organization charts signal that an organization chart appears on the page.

To display the page thumbnails:

2. Click on the **Show/Hide Pictures of Pages** button. The thumbnails are once again visible.

If you change the text, you may want to see how these changes affect your page layout. Helpful features in viewing changes are the Increase Page Size and Decrease Page Size buttons. Let's move on and see how these buttons work.

Changing the Thumbnail Size

Not only can you hide thumbnails in Outliner view, but Freelance allows you to increase and decrease the thumbnail sizes too. You have three size choices: small, medium and large. It sounds just like your choice at a fast food restaurant, doesn't it? Unless you've changed the page size, it's set to medium when you open Outliner, so you can increase or decrease the thumbnails. After making changes to a page, it's helpful to enlarge the thumbnail and see how it affects your page layout. In this section, I'll show you how to enlarge the pages.

Do It:

To increase the thumbnail size from medium to large:

1. Select the **Increase Page Size** button to increase the size of the thumbnails, as shown in Figure 6.3.

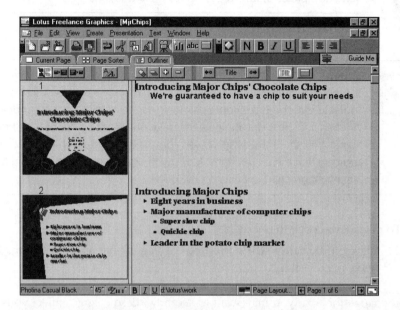

Figure 6.3 *Thumbnails increased in size.*

KEYBOARD

To increase the size of the thumbnails in the left column, press **Alt-V**, **Z**, then **L**. The presentation thumbnails pop up as shown in Figure 6.3.

2. To change the thumbnails back to medium, choose the **Decrease Page Size** button. The thumbnails immediately change.

When you increase the thumbnail size, notice that the text area decreases in size. This doesn't affect the amount of text you can add. If you increase the size of a thumbnail, you should know how to decrease it too.

You may not want your Outline view to be so plain vanilla as to hide the thumbnails entirely. Just as there are different types of vanilla, there are different levels of plain too. If you'd prefer to see the thumbnails but you don't want them to occupy too much space in the Freelance window, then you can change the size of the thumbnails to small.

Do It:

As you learned already, Freelance gives you one button to increase the size of the thumbnails and one to decrease them. You've already used the Decrease Presentation Page button. Now you're going to use that same button again to decrease the size of the pictures further. Here's how:

1. Click the **Decrease Page Size** button to decrease the size of the thumbnails.
2. To change the pictures back to medium, select the **Increase Page Size** button.

You can just make out the layout of the thumbnails when they're that small. Notice that when you reduce the size of the pages, the text area increases in size.

Viewing Text in Draft Mode

Do you remember in Chapter 2 that I told you Outliner is a partial WYSIWYG display? WYSIWYG stands for *what you see is what you get*. That means that when you look at a page in Current Page view, the page appears exactly as it will when you print it. Outliner view is a partial display because you're only seeing how the text looks, nothing else. Any tables, charts, clip art, or other graphics that you've added don't appear in Outliner. But the text in Outliner view is displayed in the fonts and attributes that you chose earlier. Viewing text in draft mode is helpful with those hard to read fonts, and if you print the outline in draft mode, it'll print quicker. If you'd prefer not to see the text as it appears, then Freelance allows you to change that too. Here's how:

Do It:

To temporarily strip the text in Outliner view of all its formatting:

1. While in Outliner View, select the **Formatted/Unformatted Text** toggle to view your text in draft mode. The text is stripped of any formatting, as shown in Figure 6.4.

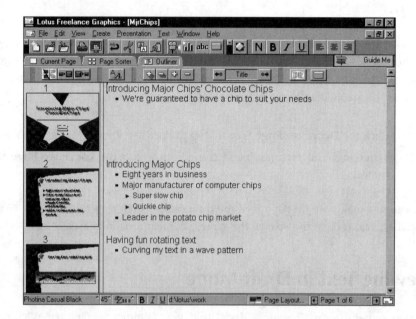

Figure 6.4 *The text in Draft Mode.*

2. Choose the **Formatted/Unformatted Text** toggle again to display your text formatted.

KEYBOARD

To change your text from draft mode back to formatted text, you can choose the View menu then select **Draft Mode** again. This deselects Draft Mode and changes your presentation text back to formatted text.

While all these buttons I just showed you are really cool and helpful features that allow you to concentrate on your text in an outline format, Outliner view allows you to do many more important things, such as add pages and text and move them around. Let's dig in and see how to do these things now.

Adding a Page

While looking at your presentation in Outliner, you may find gaps in the logic of your presentation or that you need to add another page. So now what do you do? You could add the page by going back to Current Page view and move between pages until you find the right place to add it. But you can do it much more quickly in Outliner mode.

Adding a page (or multiple pages) to your presentation is just as easy in Outliner View as it was in Current Page view. After looking through the presentation, let's add a page titled Agenda.

Do It:

Let's add the Agenda page after the page titled Introducing Major Chips. To do this:

1. Select the **Introducing Major Chips** page by clicking on the page thumbnail or anywhere in the text for that page. A rectangle appears around the picture and text, as shown in Figure 6.5.

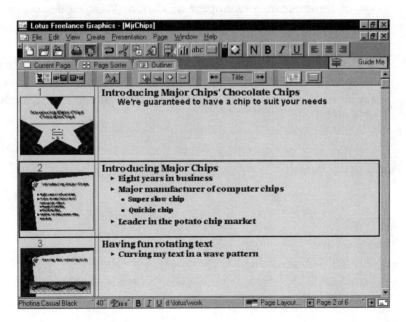

Figure 6.5 *A page selected in Outliner View.*

NOTE In Outliner view, page text is displayed as a long list or outline. To move between pages of text in Outline view, you can use the scroll bar to the right of the text to move up and down between pages.

Notice too, that when you highlight the page, the SmartIcons bar changes. Figure 6.6 shows you the new SmartIcon bar that pops up.

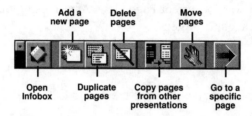

Figure 6.6 Page Outliner SmartIcon bar.

Most of these SmartIcons appear in Current View mode too, so you should be familiar with them. I'll show you how to use the SmartIcons specific to Outliner View as we continue throughout this chapter.

2.   Click on the **Add a new page** SmartIcon. A blank bulleted list thumbnail appears immediately after the highlighted Introducing Major Chips page and a blinking cursor is positioned at the first line of text, as shown in Figure 6.7.

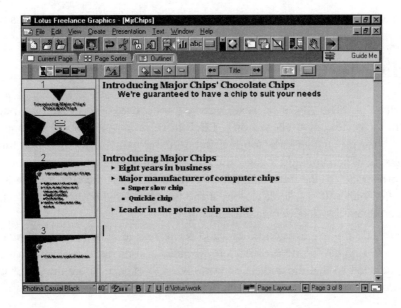

Figure 6.7 *A new page added.*

NOTE

Freelance automatically adds a new page using the bulleted list page layout. If you want to choose a different page layout, open the **Page Layout** box on the Status bar. The Switch Page Layout dialog box pops up. Select a different page layout and then click **OK**. The thumbnail changes to display the new page layout.

SHORTCUT

To create a new page in Outliner View, press **F7** to add a page.

Now that we've added a page and the cursor is blinking, let's add text to this page.

Adding Text to a Page

In Chapter 4, "The ABC's of Text," you learned how to add text to a page in Current Page view. You clicked on a **Click here** prompt and started typing. You can add text in Outliner view too but you don't have any "Click here" prompts or text blocks. When you add a page, the cursor is immediately positioned at the line that corresponds to the page title. When you press **Enter**, the cursor is positioned at the first bullet. If you look closely at the thumbnails when you enter text, you can see the text blocks opening and closing.

Let's title this page **Agenda** and add some text in a bulleted list format that reflects the structure of the presentation. Agendas or topic-to-be-discussed pages are often included so that the audience knows what to expect during the presentation. Let's add text to the new page now.

Do It:

With the cursor positioned at the beginning of the new page, here's what you do:

1. Type **Agenda**. Notice that when you type, the thumbnail to the left changes to display the information that you've entered.

2. Press **Enter** to start typing the bulleted list. Freelance immediately opens the next text block on the page, and the cursor is positioned at the first line of the new text block. In this case the second text block is a bulleted list, so my cursor is positioned to the right of a bullet, as shown in Figure 6.8.

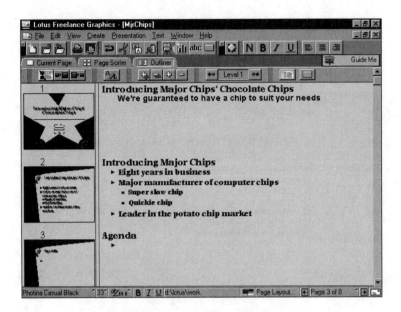

Figure 6.8 *Beginning a bulleted list.*

3. Type **Company Introduction** on the first bulleted line.

4. Press **Enter** again to begin a second line of text. The cursor is positioned to the right of the second bullet, just like it is when you enter text in Current Page view.

5. Type **New Product Introduction** on the second line.

6. Press **Enter** to start a new line of text.

7. Type **The Results**.

To complete this page, enter **Market Research**, **Our Products**, and **Product Availability** on three separate lines, as I've done in Figure 6.9.

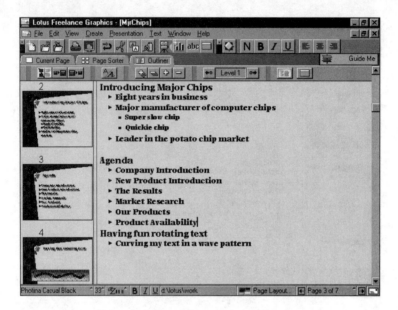

Figure 6.9 *The new page with text entered.*

Text is automatically formatted based upon the text properties associated with the text block. To change the text properties, you can open the Infobox by clicking on the **Infobox** SmartIcon. The Text properties page is displayed and you can change the format of the text. We've just entered several lines of text and the page thumbnail has changed to reflect this addition. Upon reviewing the text though, there are three items that really should be indented a text level. Let's do that now.

Indenting Text

Freelance provides you with an **Outdent** and **Indent** button, and the good news is that you don't have to open and close anything else to use them—they're right there in the Outliner window.

After looking at the text we entered in the Agenda bulleted list, let's indent *The Results, Market Research, Our Products,* and *Product Availability* one text level now. Let me show you how.

Do It:

To indent text:

1. Click and drag the cursor to select **The Results**, **Market Research**, **Our Products**, and **Product Availability** paragraphs as I've done in Figure 6.10. A rectangle appears around the text selected.

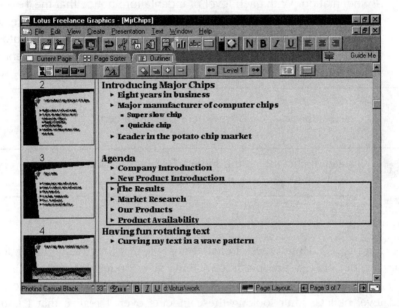

Figure 6.10 *Selected text.*

NOTE

To select an entire page of text, you can click on the page thumbnail. A rectangle appears around the picture and text, indicating that it has been selected. You can select a paragraph of text by clicking on the bullet. A rectangle appears around the selected text. To select an entire text block (which includes multiple paragraphs), click on the red margin line and drag the resulting rectangle so that all the text is included within the rectangle outline. To select several pages, press the **Shift** key and click on the page pictures. All the page pictures and corresponding text are surrounded by a rectangle.

2. Click on the **Indent Text** button (that's the right arrow in the Text Level box). All four lines of text are indented and a new bullet style appears before the text. Level 2 appears in the Text Level box.

Freelance has five levels of indentation from which you can choose. To indent the text another level, click on the **Indent Text** button again. Continue clicking the button until you find the right level of indentation. With each level of indentation, notice that the Text Level box changes to indicate which level of indentation you have selected. Every time you change the level of indentation, Freelance automatically reformats the text to the style associated with that indent level for your SmartMaster Look.

3. To deselect the text, click anywhere on the screen.

Instead of clicking on the **Indent Text** button, you can quickly change a text level by pressing the **Tab** key.

The reason that I indented these bulleted items is that they really fall under the overall category of New Product Information. New Product Information is a first level bullet; therefore, the topics that appear as supporting bullets should be second level bullets. After looking these indents over, I realize that I had you indent one line that shouldn't have been indented. We need to outdent Product Availability. Let's do that now.

Outdenting Text

What is outdenting? Well, if indenting is moving text to the right, then outdenting changes the text level to the left. For instance, a level three indent would change to a level two indent if you select the **Outdent** button once. The text is immediately reformatted to reflect the new text level. Let's outdent Product Availability once so that it's a level one indent again.

Do It:

To outdent text a level:

1. Select **Product Availability**.

2. Click on the **Outdent Text** button (that's the left arrow in the Text Level box). The line of text is outdented and Level 1 appears in the Text Level box, as shown in Figure 6.11.

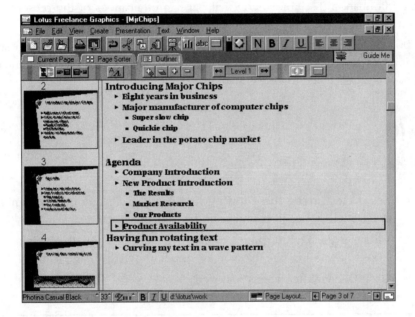

Figure 6.11 *Text outdented.*

3. Click anywhere outside the text block to deselect the paragraph.

To outdent text quickly, you can press **Shift-Tab**. The text is outdented a level.

SHORTCUT

The next level up from 1 Level 1 is a title. If you outdent a Level 1 bulleted item to a title, Freelance adds a page and the bulleted item becomes the page title. Let's move on and I'll show you how to remove pages and text from the presentation in Outliner view.

Deleting a Page

After reviewing presentation text in Outliner view, you may decide you've covered all the information that appears on that page in other areas of the presentation, so you don't need the page any longer. It's easy to remove a page.

Do you remember that page I used in the last chapter to show you some examples of how to curve text? Well, that page still exists in the presentation and now is a good time to delete it. Here's how:

Do It:

To delete a page in Outliner view:

1. Select the **Having fun rotating text** page by clicking on its thumbnail. A rectangle appears around both the thumbnail and text.

2. Click on the **Delete pages** SmartIcon. The Deleting Page dialog box pops up, warning you that you are about to delete a page with graphics.

3. Click **OK** and the page is removed.

KEYBOARD

You can also delete the page by pressing the **Delete** key.

Removing a page is easy. When you make major changes like adding or removing a page, it's a good idea to save the file by pressing **Ctrl-S**. We've inserted the Agenda page in the wrong place. The Agenda page should appear before the Introducing Major Chips page, not after it as it now appears. Let's move it.

Moving a Page

You'll probably move pages around while you're creating the presentation. That's okay, because Freelance allows you to move pages around to your heart's content. In this section, I'll show you how to move a page. We need to move the Agenda page so that it's in front of the Introducing Major Chips page.

Do It:

To move a page:

1. Click on the thumbnail of the **Agenda** page and hold down the left mouse button. The cursor turns into a small hand.

2. Drag the cursor upward until a thick black line appears (see Figure 6.12) above the **Introducing Major Chips** page. This indicates the page insertion point.

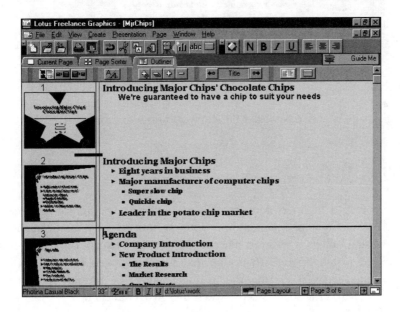

Figure 6.12 *The page insertion point.*

3. Release the left mouse button. The Agenda page appears above the Introducing Major Chips page now, as seen in Figure 6.13.

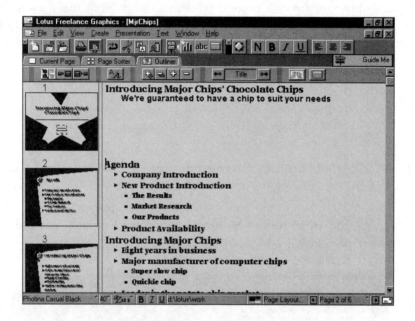

Figure 6.13 *The pages switched.*

Moving a page is very easy. Next I'll show you how to move text.

Moving Text

Lest we forget, a bulleted item is really considered a paragraph in Freelance. So when I say "moving a paragraph," you can translate that to mean moving a bullet. Moving bullets works just like moving a page—except on a smaller scale, of course. I just happened to notice that we transposed two bullets on the **Agenda** page. Do you see them? The bullet with "The Results" after it should appear after Market Research. Let's switch these two bullets now.

Do It:

To move a paragraph to another location within the presentation:

1. Select **The Results** bullet and hold down the left mouse button. The paragraph is selected and the cursor turns into a hand.

2. Drag the cursor down until a black line appears. This is the paragraph insertion point.

3. Release the left mouse button to place the paragraph. The Results bullet now appears after Market Research.

You can follow these same steps to even move text to a different page. Now that we've changed the bulleted items, the flow is more logical. Let's make one more change to this page.

Changing Bulleted Lists from One Column to Two

We're probably going to add more bullets to the Agenda page as we progress through the book. Let's change the bulleted list we just created into a 2-column bulleted list page now. Freelance gives you a shortcut so that changing a bulleted list page to a 2-column bulleted list page isn't a major effort.

Do It:

Here's how to switch from a bulleted list to a 2-column bulleted list page:

1. Select **Product Availability** on the Agenda page.

2. Click on the **2-Column bulleted list** button. A marker with two lines in it appears beside the bullet, as shown in Figure 6.14. This indicates that the line of text is the first line in the second column. If you look at the thumbnail, you can see that the page layout has changed to a 2-column format.

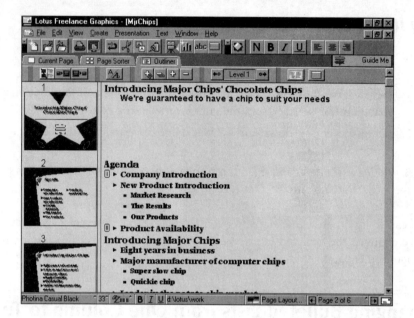

Figure 6.14 *A 2-column bulleted list.*

N O T E

If you decide that you don't want to create a 2-column bulleted list after all, click the **Undo last command or action** SmartIcon or press **Ctrl-Z**. The markers disappear and the page layout changes back to a bulleted list.

I like how this looks a lot better, especially since I'll be adding more text later.

Now is a good time for me to tell you that the Copy, Paste, Cut and Undo buttons work the same way in Outliner view that they do in Current Page view so I'm not going to show you how to use them here. You've already seen how they work in Chapter 4. Let's continue to focus on the features that make Outliner view unique.

Using the Outline Features

As the name implies, Outliner view is about viewing the presentation in outline format—complete with text levels and, if you want, stripped of any formatting. In Outliner mode, you can collapse your presentation text to view page titles, and to check for topics and logic, or you can collapse page text after reviewing the contents. Of course, you can also expand the text for the entire presentation or just the page.

Earlier in this chapter I told you that you can import an outline from Word Pro or import an ASCII file. I also told you that you could create your entire presentation in Outliner view. If you create an entire outline in another program and import it into Outliner view, you could have almost an entire presentation on your hands before you've even been working in Freelance for ten minutes. Not bad, huh? This gives you a huge head start. Also, if your co-workers don't have Freelance on their computers, how do you show them the presentation text? You could give up your computer for the day and go on a long coffee break, or you could print out an entire copy of the text in outline format.

In this section, I'll show you how to collapse and expand your presentation text and page text, as well as show you how to import and print out an outline.

Collapsing and Expanding Presentation Text

Collapsing and expanding the entire text is a great way of checking for page sequence, covered topics, and the flow of the presentation. You can quickly skim through collapsed text to see the grand view of the presentation without getting caught in the details. Unless you've selected the **Collapse** button already, the presentation text appears in its entirety. Let's collapse it now.

Do It:

With all the text visible, here's how to collapse the text:

1. Click the **Collapse text in the entire view** button (that's the one with the multiple dash (-) signs). Now you can only see the presentation page titles, as shown in Figure 6.15.

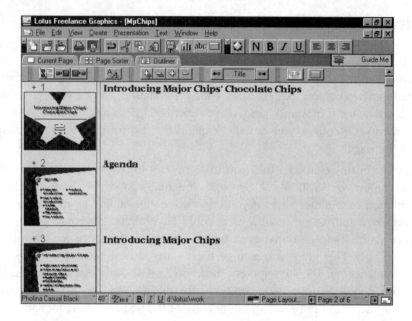

Figure 6.15 The presentation text collapsed.

 The page number appears above each thumbnail in Outliner View. When the presentation text is collapsed, a plus (+) sign appears before the page number of some of the pages. This indicates that more text appears on the page.

N O T E

We may want to expand the text again at some point. Here's how:

2. To show all the text in the presentation, click the **Expand text in the entire view** button (the button with the multiple plus (+) signs). All the text appears in Outliner View again.

All you can see are the page titles when the text is collapsed. That's certainly a helpful feature when determining the topics you've discussed and where in the presentation they appear. Collapsing and expanding page text is just as easy.

Collapsing and Expanding Page Text

Collapsing and expanding text for a particular page is particularly handy when your entire presentation text is collapsed. As you scroll down, you may wonder what topics are discussed on a page. Instead of expanding the entire presentation to check on one page, Freelance allows you to expand just that page. I'll show you how to collapse and expand page text right now.

Do It:

Let's collapse the Agenda page. Here's how:

1. Click the **Agenda** thumbnail.

2. Choose the **Collapse text in the page** button (that's the button with a single dash (-)). The page text is collapsed and now you can only see the page title.

3. To display the page text again, click on the **Expand text in the page** button, which is the button with a single plus (+) sign. The page text is displayed in Outliner View, as shown in Figure 6.16.

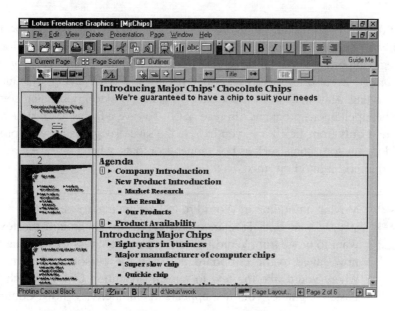

Figure 6.16 *The page text expanded.*

Instead of scrolling through pages and pages of text to locate a specific page, you can quickly find the page using the collapse and expand features. With the outline collapsed, scroll down until you locate the title of the page you want, then you can expand just that page or the entire presentation again. It's really that easy. Let me show you how to get a head start designing your presentation next.

Importing Outlines

You may have been working on an outline of your presentation long before you ever opened Freelance. Creating an outline and seriously thinking about your presentation before you actually design it are definitely pluses. But what if you could take the actual outline you've been working on in Word Pro, Microsoft Word or WordPerfect and import it into Freelance? That would be an A++! If you have a good outline established, it can be used as the basis for a solid foundation upon which the presentation can be built. Instead of opening Freelance and entering text as you think of it, why not use the outline? I'll show you how to import an outline now.

Do It:

If you've created an outline in Word Pro already, then you're set to import the text. If your outline is in another program, you need to save it in ASCII before you can begin importing it. ASCII stands for *American Standard Code for Information Interchange*. It's also known as *text-only*. It's just a way of saving your file with no formatting. Almost all word processing programs, desktop publishing software, and other applications programs can read ASCII. To save a file as ASCII or text-only, select **text-only** from the choices you have in the save dialog box for your program. You'll lose any formatting, such as bold, indents or fonts, when you save it as ASCII. Now, to import it into Freelance:

N O T E

Moving an outline in Word Pro to Freelance follows a different set of steps. Open both Freelance and Word Pro. Highlight the text you want to move from Word Pro into Freelance. Press **Ctrl-C**. The text is now saved to the clipboard. Position the cursor in Outliner view where you'd like the text to appear and press **Ctrl-V**, which is the Paste command. Your text appears in Outliner view now. Continue to copy and paste text from Word Pro to the Outliner view until your outline is complete.

---

1. With the Outliner view open, select the **Open an existing file** SmartIcon. The Open dialog box pops up, as shown in Figure 6.17.

Figure 6.17 *The Open dialog box.*

2. Choose **ASCII Text (TXT)** from the File of Type drop down list. ASCII Text (TXT) pops up in the File of Type window.

3. Click the **Look in** drop down list box arrow to locate your outline on the hard disk.

4. Select the document you want to import into Freelance.

5. Click **OK** to import the outline into Freelance. The outline appears in Outliner view.

NOTE When you import the file, Freelance creates a new page for any text that isn't indented. If all the text is indented to the same level, then the text is imported as level one paragraphs. You can change the text level of any paragraph by using the **Outdent** and **Indent** buttons.

Importing an outline or copying and pasting an outline is quite a jump start for a presentation. Either way, at some point during the design process you may want to print out the text and pass it around.

Printing Outliner Text

It's always a good idea to get feedback from your coworkers or fellow presenters when creating a presentation. But sharing presentation text may not be convenient. You may work on the tenth floor and be one of only three people with Freelance on your computer and the coworkers you really want to share the outline with are on the third floor and, of course, they're not the other two people with Freelance on their systems. You could print out each and every page of the presentation thus far, but all you really want them to read right now is the text. Instead of printing out every page, Freelance allows you to print just the text in outline form. Here's how.

Do It:

With the Outliner tab selected:

1. Click on the **Print** SmartIcon. The Print dialog box pops up, as shown in Figure 6.18.

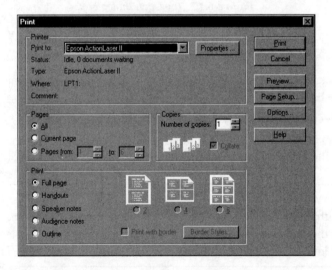

Figure 6.18 *The Print dialog box.*

2. Choose the printer you're connected to from the "Print to" drop down list box in the Printer section of the dialog box.

3. Select the pages you want to print from the Pages section of the dialog box.

   ❖ To print all the pages of your presentation, select the **All** radio button.

   ❖ Choose the **Current Page** radio button to print only the page that is selected.

   ❖ You can also print a page range by selecting the **Pages From** radio button and then using the increment buttons to select the page numbers you want to print.

4. Using the increment buttons, choose the number of copies you want to print out from the Copies section of the dialog box.

5. Next, choose **Outline** from the Print area within the dialog box.

6. Click on the **Print** button to print the outline. The printing status dialog box pops up telling you the outline is being printed. You can press the **Cancel** button to stop printing the outline if you decide you don't want to print it after all.

Freelance uses a default font to print out the outline which may or may not be the same font you're using in the presentation. In addition, underlined words or special attributes used when formatting your text may not print as you see them in Outliner view. That doesn't mean the text isn't formatted the way you want, it's just that some of the formatting is stripped out in Outliner view. You'll also notice that the thumbnails don't print out either.

From Here...

You can now enter, format, and manipulate presentation text and pages in Current Page and Outliner views. I think you deserve a pat on the back.

In the next several chapters I'm going to show you how to create charts, tables and objects, and how to add clip art and logos to the presentation. In Chapter 7, I'll show you how to create all kinds of charts that can help clarify numerical data for your audience. You'll learn how to create charts such as bar, pie, line, scatter, and radar.

CHAPTER 7

Working with Charts

(Pack your presentation with visual impact)

Charts are a major asset to any presentation for two reasons: they relieve the monotony of staring at bulleted lists, and they can present numeric data much more clearly than words alone. Yes, bullets help make the text look more interesting, but charts can really liven things up. Not only can an audience look at data presented in a clear and colorful manner, but they can read and interpret it for themselves. Much more importantly, charts can reinforce the ideas that you've already presented.

Freelance allows you to create over 10 different types of typical business charts for your presentation. Of course you can add legends, titles, and axes labels, and format your charts to use colors, borders, grids, 3-D, and a lot more. Freelance also lets you incorporate data from other programs such as Lotus 1-2-3, dBase, and Excel, as well as ASCII text. Determining which type of chart to use is often a matter of your personal preferences. But certain types of data comparisons lend themselves to a specific chart type. Here are the basic chart types available to you in Freelance:

❖ Bar Chart

❖ Stacked Bar Chart

❖ 100% Stacked Bar Chart

❖ Line

❖ Area

❖ Pie

❖ Hi/Low/Close/Open

❖ XY (Scatter)

❖ Radar

❖ Mixed

❖ Number Grid

To help you choose the type of chart that may work best for you, here are descriptions and examples of the more commonly used chart types.

❖ **Bar Charts.** Bar charts use bars to represent data, hence the name bar chart. The bars in a bar chart can be vertical or horizontal. They are usually used to compare two or more series of data. For example, Major Chips sold over 3 billion dollars worth of computer chips in 1995. How does this figure break down month to month? You can use a bar chart to show computer chip sales on a monthly basis for 1995. In Figure 7.1, I plotted Major Chips' 1995 computer chip sales data. The numbers running up the line to the far left (that's the Y-axis) represent the dollars earned from sales. Along the X-axis (that's the line running across the bottom of the chart) are the names of the months. Each bar represents the dollars earned for the specified month

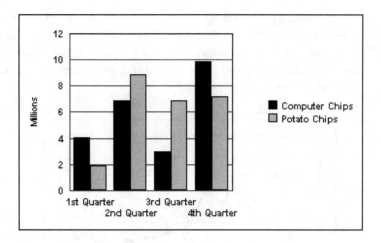

Figure 7.1 *A bar chart.*

❖ **Stacked Bar Charts.** You can also create *stacked* bar charts, which are variations of the standard bar charts. Continuing with the example I used earlier, Major Chips produces two types of computer chips: the Quickie Chip and the Super Slow Chip. I could use a stacked bar chart to show you how much of the monthly sales are attributable to the Quickie Chip vs. the Super Slow Chip. Each bar still represents the total sales dollars for a specific month but the bar consists of two colors or patterns now: one representing the dollar amount for Quickie Chip sales and the other color representing Super Slow Chip sales.

❖ **100% Stacked Bar Charts.** The third type of bar chart, 100% stacked, looks a lot like stacked bar charts. The difference is that the Y-axis in a 100% stacked bar chart is automatically formatted to reflect percentages. Therefore, each colored section of a bar represents a percentage of the total. If it helps, think of it as a pie chart in the shape of a bar.

❖ **Line Charts.** Line charts use lines to display changes in a series of data over a period of time. They're great for showing trends such as profits earned over a five-year period or production during the course of a year. For example, Major Chips documents the total number of pounds of potato chips that are produced on a daily basis. I've created a line chart, shown in Figure 7.2, which shows the daily poundage produced for the month of December. Each point on the line represents the pounds produced for the specified day of the month. On the 15th of December, for instance, 289 pounds of potato chips were produced. The overall trend of this chart indicates that production went down toward the end of the month. Of course, we could use a line chart to compare several items over a period of time.

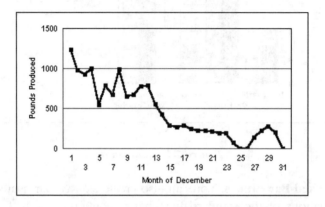

Figure 7.2 A line chart.

❖ **Pie Charts.** Pie charts show a series of data in relation to the whole. For instance, Major Chips' potato chips occupy a 39% share of the potato chip market. The other 61% of the market is divided between 3 other companies. In Figure 7.3, I've created a pie chart that shows where Major Chips fits into the entire potato chip market. Each pie piece represents a company and the size of the pie is determined by the percentage of the market the company occupies.

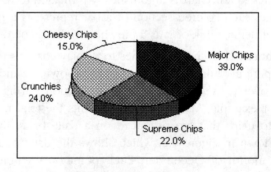

Figure 7.3 A pie chart.

Freelance allows you to create exploding pie pieces, multiple pie charts, and, just like other chart types, you can add 3-D effects.

❖ **High/Low/Close/Open Charts.** These charts are sometimes referred to as *stock market charts*. Hi/low/close/open charts are highly specialized charts that are used to monitor temperatures, stocks, and commodities. Figure 7.4 shows a typical high/low/close/open chart.

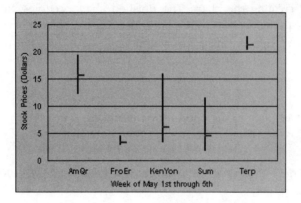

Figure 7.4 *A high/low/close/open chart.*

Now you have a good idea of how some of the charts are used and the different selections available to you. Different types of data lend themselves to different types of charts, as is the case with line and pie charts. There is no doubt that charts can help liven a presentation, present data much clearer than words, and help your audience remember the information better.

Freelance has several page layouts for charts from which you can choose. In the next section, I'll show you how to select the different page layouts.

Choosing a Chart Page Layout

You may use several charts throughout a presentation, so Freelance gives you several chart page layouts to help add variety. You can select from pages that contain one chart, two charts, four charts, and charts and bulleted lists. Each chart layout page contains "Click here" prompts to help you create the type of chart you want. Naturally, any chart page you select incorporates the same SmartMaster look that you have been using all along. We're working in Current Page view again, so click the **Current Page** tab to return if you're still in Outliner view.

Adding a 1 Chart Page

A 1 Chart page contains two "Click here" prompts: one to create a page title and the other for creating the chart. The finished chart occupies almost the entire page so you can really show information details on a chart this size. Here's how to add a 1 Chart page to your presentation.

Do It:

To add a 1 Chart page to the end of the presentation, first locate the last page in the Major Chips file. Then:

1. In Current Page view, click on the **New Page** button. The New Page dialog box pops up.

2. Select **1 Chart** in the Select a page layout list box.

N O T E   Don't forget that the thumbnail to the right of the Select a page layout list box displays the page layout of the selection and gives a brief explanation of how that page is usually used within a presentation. It's a helpful way to decide whether that really is the page that you want to use.

3. Click **OK** to add the 1 Chart page immediately after the current page in your presentation. The 1 Chart page pops up, as shown in Figure 7.5.

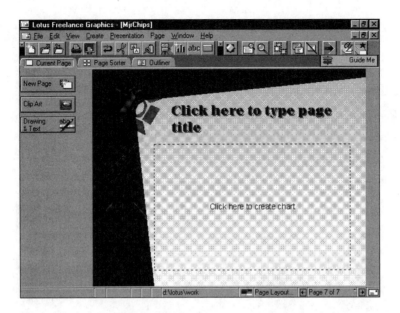

Figure 7.5 *The 1 Chart page.*

1 Chart pages look very similar to the other page layouts the you've worked with so far. The only difference is the kind of "Click here" prompts on the page. Let's keep this page for the presentation. We'll return to this page and add a chart later.

Adding a 2 Chart Page

2 Chart pages contain 2 charts that are positioned side by side on the page. This is a great way for you to compare the information in the two charts. Your chart sizes are reduced so that both charts can fit on the page. Let me show you how to add a 2 Chart page to your presentation.

Do It:

Here's how to add a 2 Chart page to your presentation:

1. Select the **New Page** button. The New Page dialog box opens.
2. Choose **2 Charts** in the Select a page layout list box.
3. Click **OK** to add a 2 Charts page to the presentation. A 2 Chart page pops up in the window, as shown in Figure 7.6.

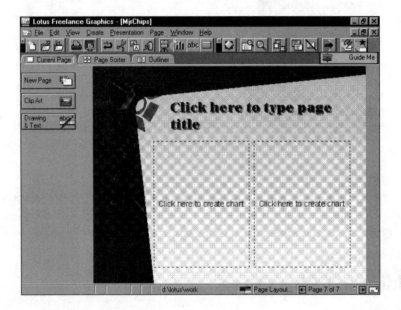

Figure 7.6 *A 2 Chart page.*

Each chart in a 2 Chart page is created individually, so you could have a line chart and a pie chart on the same page, or you can make both charts the same type. It's up to you. This principle holds true for 4 chart pages as well. In the next section, you'll learn how to add a 4 chart page to your presentation.

Adding a 4 Chart Page

Four charts on a presentation can get tight because all four charts have to fit into the same area that was available for 1 or 2 charts. These chart page layouts are good for comparison purposes as well, but keep in mind that reading charts that small can be difficult. 4 Chart page layouts are just as easy to add to a presentation as any other page layout.

Do It:

To add a 4 Chart page layout:

1. Click on the **New Page** button.
2. Select **4 Charts** from the Select a page layout list box.
3. Click **OK** to add a 4 Charts page to your presentation. A 4 Chart page appears in Current View.

If you plan on using a 4 Chart page, you may want to limit the style of charts for easy comparison and clarity. You can, however, create any type of chart you want in each chart area, because you create each chart individually.

Adding a Bullets & Chart Page

If you worked through Chapter 4, you've already added a Bullets & Chart page. If that's the case, then skip ahead to the next section. If you didn't add a Bullets & Chart page, I'll show you how to add a Bullets & Chart page layout now. Bullets & Chart pages look like 2 Chart pages except that the "Click here" prompt to the left allows you to add a bulleted list to the page. The "Click here" prompt to the right lets you create a chart. This is a great page to show data in a chart format and be able to point out specific items on the chart at the same time. So, let's add a Bullets & Chart page.

Do It:

To add a Bullets and Chart page:

1. Open the New Page dialog box by selecting the **New Page** button.
2. Choose **Bullets & Chart** from the Select a page layout list box.
3. Click **OK** to add a Bullets & Chart page to the presentation. The Bullets & Chart page opens, as shown in Figure 7.7.

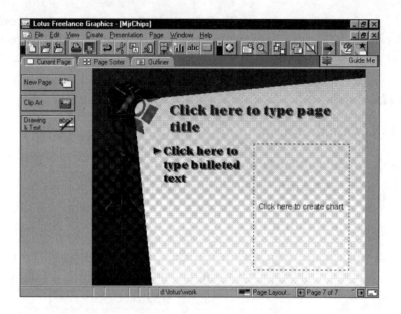

Figure 7.7 *A Bullets & Chart page.*

I'm going to show you how to add a chart to an already existing page later in this chapter. Right now, let's create a chart on the 1 Chart page that we just added.

Creating a Chart

Creating a chart is a little more complicated than adding text to a presentation. We have lots of choices and decisions to make regarding the look of the chart. The first decision is to determine what chart type to use. Before we do, we need to have some data. Now, the purpose of this page is to show how well Major Chips is doing financially in both the computer chip and potato chip markets. In creating this chart, we need to show eight years' worth of sales dollars for two different products. If your 1 Chart page isn't in the Freelance window, display that page now.

Do It:

The best type of chart for the data is probably a stacked bar chart. Here's how to select a chart type:

1. Click on the **Click here to create chart** prompt. The Create Chart dialog box pops up, as shown in Figure 7.8.

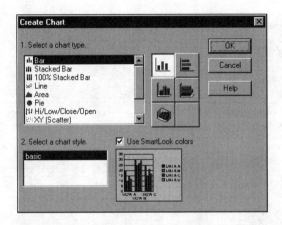

Figure 7.8 *The Create Chart dialog box.*

2. Select **Stacked Bar** from the Select a chart type list box.

3. Next, choose the **vertical with-depth** (that's the second selection down in the first row from the left) in the chart type icon.

    ❖ The top row of icons control the orientation, vertical and horizontal, of the bars in the chart. The second row of icons allows you to choose with-depth. With-depth adds a dimensional look to the chart. Select the icon in the third row to display the bar chart in three dimensions (3-D).

    ❖ **Basic** is the default style listed in the Select a chart style list box. If you find yourself making a lot of charts and constantly changing the chart attributes, you may decide to create a chart style for future use. If that's the case, the next step is to choose a chart style from the Select a chart style list box. In Chapter 5, *Text Properties*, you learned how to create a text style. Follow the same steps to create a style for a chart.

    ❖ Freelance automatically uses the same color scheme associated with your SmartLook color when creating a chart. If you'd prefer to use a red/gray/blue/yellow color scheme then deselect the **Use SmartLook Colors** check box.

4. Click **OK** after you've made your selections. The Edit Data dialog box pops up, as shown in Figure 7.9.

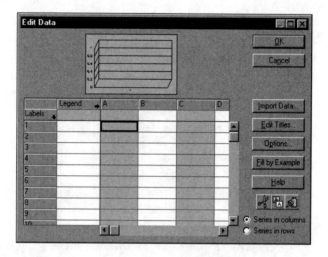

Figure 7.9 *The Edit Data dialog box.*

NOTE

You may decide later that the chart you're selecting now doesn't really work with the data and point you're trying to make. You can change the chart by clicking anywhere in the chart area. The chart handles appear and a Chart SmartIcon bar appears. Select the **Set chart type** SmartIcon. The Chart Properties dialog box pops up. Select a different chart type and choose a chart effect. As soon as you make the selection, the chart changes to the new chart type. When you're satisfied with the selection, close the Chart Properties dialog box. To quickly change to a Bar, Line or Area chart, select the SmartIcon that corresponds to that chart type.

The Edit Data dialog box allows you to enter your numeric values. However, as the name implies, this is also where you'll make numeric changes to your information as needed. Keep the dialog box open because we're going to create a legend for the chart next.

Creating a Chart Legend

You can enter and edit numeric data using the Edit Data dialog box. You can also create legends and X-axis labels for the chart using this dialog box. The main area of the dialog box consists of cells that are organized very much like a spreadsheet with rows and columns. You can also edit the numeric information using this dialog box, but we'll discuss that later.

You've probably looked at road maps before. Did you ever notice the little corner of the map where the map company tells you what all the lines and colors mean? That area of the map is called the *legend*. Charts usually have legends too. Without them it can be impossible to figure out what you're actually looking at on the chart. Since we're using a stacked bar chart, we're adding two sets of data. Each set of data in the stacked bar appears in a different color. To differentiate between each data series, we need to identify what each colored portion of the bar represents. That's where the legend comes in.

Do It:

You can create a legend when you first begin entering data or you can create it later. Either way, you need to be in the Edit Data dialog box. Here's how:

1. Select the **A** cell in the Label row as I've done in Figure 7.10 to enter the Legend information.

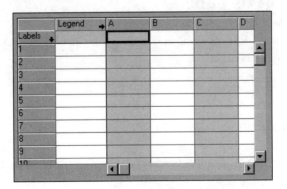

Figure 7.10 *A cell highlighted.*

2. Type **Computer Chips** in the cell.

3. Press the **Tab** key to move to the next cell to the immediate right. The first cell in the **B** column is selected now.

You can move between cells in the Edit Data dialog box by pressing the arrows on your keyboard too.

N O T E

4. Type **Potato Chips** in the B cell. You've entered all the information you need to create a clear legend for your audience.

Once the chart has been placed on the page, you can hide the legend or show it by selecting the **Show chart legend** SmartIcon.

N O T E

As you enter information, notice that the thumbnail sketch of the chart changes. In the above steps, you're creating the legend for the chart; as you enter this information it appears to the right of the chart. This legend location is the default but you can move it to another area on the page. I'll show you how later. Next, let's create the X-axis labels.

Creating X-Axis Labels

To enter X-axis label information, you need to be in the Edit Data dialog box. Let's enter X-axis labels now.

Do It:

Here's how to design the X-axis labels:

1. Select the Row 1, Legend Column cell as I've done in Figure 7.11.

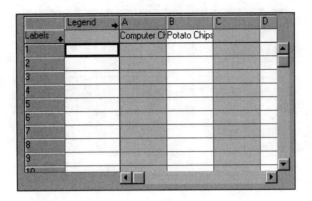

Figure 7.11 *Row 1, Legend Column cell selected.*

2. Type **1988** in the cell.

3. Press the **Down Arrow** to move to Row 2, Legend Column.

N O T E

If you look at the thumbnail, notice that 1988 now appears below the X-axis of the chart. As you continue to add the years, you'll see them appear in the thumbnail. If you'd prefer not to see a preview of the chart, select the **Options** button and click on the **Show Chart Preview** check box to remove the check. Select **OK**. Your preview chart selection is now turned off.

---

4. Enter **1989** in the cell.

5. Press the **down arrow** again to move to Row 3, Legend Column.

6. Type **1990** in the Row 3, Legend Column cell.

7. Again, select the **down arrow** to move to Row 4, Legend Column.

8. Type **1991** in the cell.

9. Continue to add **1992**, **1993**, **1994** and **1995** by following the above steps until your Legend column looks like Figure 7.12.

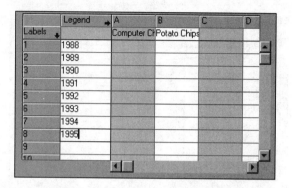

Labels	Legend	A	B	C	D
		Computer C	Potato Chips		
1	1988				
2	1989				
3	1990				
4	1991				
5	1992				
6	1993				
7	1994				
8	1995				
9					
10					

Figure 7.12 *1988 to 1995 X-axis labels.*

SHORTCUT

Instead of manually entering values that are sequential, you can enter **1988** in the Row 2, Legend Column and then use the Fill by Example feature. Click on 1988 and drag to select the cells from Row 2 down to Row 8. Click on the **Fill by Example** button. A value appears in each cell from 1988 to 1995 now. Fill by example works for numbers, dates, months—any value that follows a sequence. This is a much quicker way of creating a long list of numbers.

We have our legend and X-axis information entered. All we need now is the data.

Entering Data for a Chart

The locations (or addresses) of cells in spreadsheet programs are usually referred to by a row number and then a column letter, for example cell 5A is located in Row 5, Column A, and cell 26Z is located in Row 26, Column Z. We'll be using the same addressing procedures, so when I write "cell 2B", I'm going to assume that you understand which cell I'm referring to. Let's enter this data into the Edit Data dialog box now.

Do It:

Let's enter the computer chip sales numbers first in Column A, then we'll enter the potato chips sales data in Column B. Here's how:

1. Select cell **1A**. We're entering the sales figure for 1988 in this cell.
2. Type **578,000** in the cell.
3. Press the **down arrow** to select cell 2A.

Again, notice that the thumbnail changes to show the information that you've entered. In this case, we now have a very large blue bar in the thumbnail.

N O T E

---

4. Enter **983,000** in the cell.
5. Press the **down arrow** again to select cell 3A. A second bar appears in the thumbnail now.

Instead of typing data over again, you can import it into the Edit Dialog box. Freelance allows you to import data from Lotus 1-2-3, dBase, Excel or ASCII. To do this, select the **Import Data** button. The Open dialog box pops up. Locate the file that you want to import. Click **OK** to import the data.

N O T E

---

6. Enter **1,567,000**.
7. Press the **down arrow** again.
8. Enter **1,752,000** into cell 4A.
9. Select the **down arrow**. You now have cell 5A selected. That corresponds to the year 1992.
10. Type **2,548,000** in the cell.
11. Press the **down arrow** to select the 6A cell.

12. Following the steps above, continue to enter the data. Enter **3,740,000** in Row 6, **5,235,000** in Row 7 and **5,958,000** in Row 8. The entered data appears as shown in Figure 7.13.

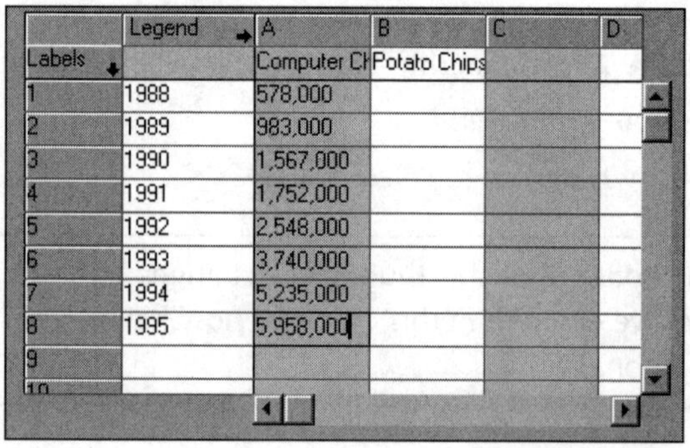

Labels	Legend →	A	B	C	D
		Computer Ch	Potato Chips		
1	1988	578,000			
2	1989	983,000			
3	1990	1,567,000			
4	1991	1,752,000			
5	1992	2,548,000			
6	1993	3,740,000			
7	1994	5,235,000			
8	1995	5,958,000			
9					
10					

Figure 7.13 Computer chip sales for 1988-1995.

Half the data is now entered. Following the steps I described above, enter **387,000** in Row 1, Column B; **542,000** in Row 2, Column B; **710,000** in Row 3, Column B; **1,050,000** in Row 4, Column B; **1,178,000** in Row 5, Column B; **2,890,000** in Row 6, Column B; **3,752,000** in Row 7, Column B; and **4,250,000** in Row 8, Column B. Next, let's create some titles for the chart.

Creating Chart Titles

Charts usually have titles for the X- and Y-axes. This helps a person reading the chart understand what the X and Y-axis information means. Charts often have an overall title too. Let's name the chart and axes now.

Do It:

We've added the information into the Edit Data dialog box, now it's time to give the chart some titles. Here's how:

1. With the Edit Data dialog box open, click on the **Edit Titles** command button. The Edit Titles dialog box pops up.

2. Type **Major Chips' Sales History** in the top line of the Chart Title text box.

   ❖ Optionally, you can add a brief note to the chart to clarify or add any additional information.

3. Select the **Axis Titles: X** line and type **Fiscal Year**.

4. Select the **Axis Titles: Y** line and type **Dollars Earned**. The Edit Titles dialog box should now look like Figure 7.14.

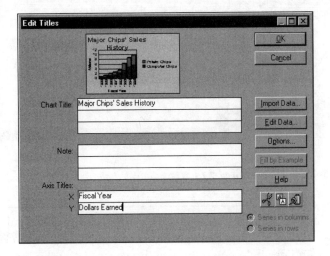

Figure 7.14 *The Edit Title dialog box with data.*

If you want to return to the data, click the **Edit Data** button in the Edit Titles dialog box. Don't do that now, though; it's time to view the completed chart on the page.

5. Click **OK** to see the chart on the presentation page. The page pops up as shown in Figure 7.15.

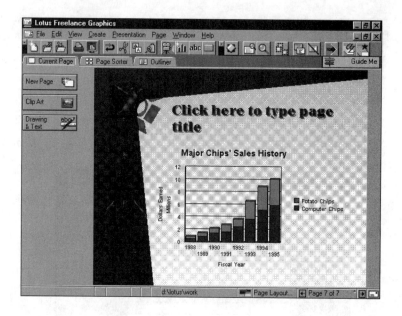

Figure 7.15 *The completed chart.*

Many chart types automatically display the horizontal grid lines, which are the lines that appear in the completed chart in Figure 7.15. These lines help guide the eye; however, select the **Turn horizontal grid on/off** SmartIcon if you prefer not to display the grid lines.

NOTE

Now that you know how to create a chart, let's add a chart to the Bullets & Chart page that we added in Chapter 4. I'll take you through the design process quickly now that you know how to do it yourself.

Adding a Chart to a Bullets & Chart Page

Major Chips surveyed 1,000 professionals in the industrial baking industry to determine how the chocolate used in their products could be improved. Smoother texture was the number one answer with a resounding 47.6%; easier to handle came in second with 32%; 17% said they would like a richer flavor, and only 3.4% said they would like to see prices reduced. For the Bullets &

Chart page we added earlier, we've already added text to the bullets section (we did that in Chapter 4, *The ABC's of Text*) to reflect this numeric information. Let's visually reinforce these answers by creating a pie chart that displays the results. Follow along with me while I quickly add a pie chart to the page.

Do It:

With the Bullets & Chart page in the Freelance window, here's how to create a pie chart using the data I gave you:

1. Click the **Click here to create chart** prompt. The Edit Data dialog box pops up.

2. Select **Pie** from the Select a type list box window.

3. Choose the **width-depth** icon for the single pie.

4. Press **OK**. The Edit Data dialog box pops up.

5. Select cell **1A**.

6. Moving down Column A, enter **47.6**; **32**; **17**; and **3.4**, as shown in Figure 7.16.

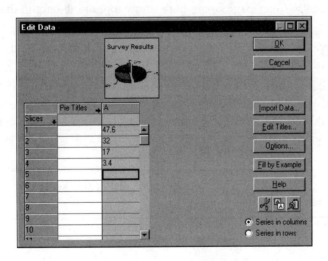

Figure 7.16 *Column A with data.*

7. Select the **Row 1, Pie Titles** Column cell.

8. Moving down the Pie Titles Column, type **Smoother**; **Easier**; **Richer**; and **Cheaper**.

9. Select the **Edit Titles** button. The Edit Titles dialog box pops up.

10. Type **Survey Results** in the first line of the Chart Title window.

11. Click **OK**. The pie chart appears on the page.

The numbers and text are almost unreadable. Using the Text properties page in the Infobox (which you learned about in Chapter 5), I've enlarged the text.

Editing Data in a Chart

Freelance allows you to open the Edit Data dialog box and make changes whenever you want. I've noticed that two numbers need to be changed in the chart on the Bullets & Chart page I just finished entering. Tag along with me and I'll show you how to correct this typo.

Do It:

With the Bullets & Chart page open, here's how to edit the data in the chart:

1. Select the **Survey Results** chart by clicking anywhere in the chart area on the page.

2. Click the **Show/edit chart data** SmartIcon to open the Edit Data dialog box. The Edit Data dialog box pops up. Instead of 47.6, the first number should read 47.4. The last number, instead of reading 3.4, should be 3.6. We need to change these numbers now.

KEYBOARD

To open the Edit Data dialog box using the keyboard, press **Alt-R**, then **E**.

---

3. Double-click on **47.6** to select the cell text. A blinking cursor appears in the cell.

4. Using the **backspace** key, delete the number **6**.

5. Type **4** instead.

6. Next, double-click on **3.4**. The cell is selected and the cursor is positioned in the cell.

7. Delete the number **4** from the cell.

8. Enter the number **6**.

9. Click **OK** to return to the chart and see your changes.

Changing data is really quite simple and you can continue to make changes as often as you like. The Edit Data dialog box allows you to make changes to your numeric data and chart titles. But what if you don't like the font or point size? You prefer to have a border around the entire chart? You want to position the legend in another location? You can do all those things and more.

Changing Chart Properties

The chart properties dialog box works the same as the text properties dialog box that I showed you in Chapter 5. You learned how to change fonts, point size and colors, and add borders and shadows. You can do all that with the chart properties dialog box too, and you can also change other properties as well. You can change the locations of the chart legend, the titles and the labels. The chart properties dialog box also allows you to create exploding pie slices, hide slices, re-sort the pie slices, and include the pie totals in the chart title. To show you how the chart properties page works, I'll show you how to explode all the pieces of a pie.

N O T E You can explode a single pie piece as well but you don't need to use the Chart Properties dialog box. Instead, click on the pie slice you want to explode. Drag the pie piece away from the remaining pieces until you've positioned it the way you want it.

Do It:

Let's explode the pieces of the pie chart we created in the previous sections. This is great for highlighting specific data that you want to point out to the audience. Let's do it now:

1. Select the pie chart so that the handles appear around the chart area.

2. Click the **Open Infobox** SmartIcon (that's the one with the yellow box tilted on its corner). The Chart Properties dialog box pops up.

3. Open the **Properties for:** drop down list box.

4. Select **Plot**. The Plot properties page appears, as shown in Figure 7.17.

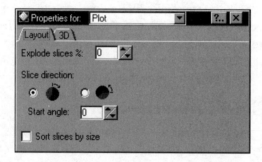

Figure 7.17 The Plot properties page.

5. Click the increment **up arrow** in the Explode slices % text box until **20** appears in the window.

6. Click the **Close** button to close the properties dialog box and see the changes you've just entered.

Just like the Text Properties dialog box, the Chart Properties dialog box is a powerful tool that can help you change the formatting of your chart.

Another chart type that we haven't discussed yet is the organization chart. In the next section, I'll show you how to create an organization chart for the presentation.

Understanding Organization Charts

Organization charts are different from any of the charts I've shown you thus far. For one thing, organization charts don't use numbers as data, they use text. In addition, organization charts graphically show how people or departments relate to one another within a company or organization. You can have several levels within the chart to accommodate the president or CEO, managers and support staff.

Adding an Organization Chart Page Layout

The easiest way to create an organization chart is to add an organization chart page layout. Page layouts for organization charts include a "Click here" prompt to add a title to the page and a "Click here" prompt to create the chart. Let's add the page now.

Do It:

Go to the last page in the presentation so that we can add this page to the end of the file. Here's how to add an organization page layout to the presentation:

1. Click the **New Page** button. The New Page dialog box pops up.
2. Select **Organization Chart** from the Select a page layout list box.
3. Click **OK**. The organizational page layout page pops up.
4. Title the organization chart page **The Driving Force Behind the New Division**.

Creating an Organization Chart

Creating an organization chart involves clicking on "Click here" prompts and making selections from dialog boxes. You have to give some information too. Let's do it now.

Do It:

Choosing a style for the organization chart is really a matter of personal preference. With the organization chart page open:

1. Click on the **Click here to create organization chart** prompt to begin. The Organization Chart Gallery, shown in Figure 7.18, pops up.

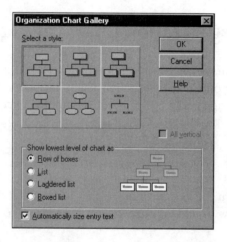

Figure 7.18 *The Organization Chart Gallery.*

2. Choose an organization chart style from the **Select a style** icons. I've chosen the middle icon in the top row.

3. Next, select the **List** radio button from the Show lowest level of chart as section of the dialog box to show the lowest level as a list of people.

   ❖ Freelance automatically resizes the text to fit into the chart blocks, unless you turn the default off. You can still resize the text if you want. If you'd prefer to resize text entirely by yourself, click on the **Automatically size entry text** check box to remove the check from the box.

4. Click **OK**. The Organization Chart Entry List dialog box pops up, as shown in Figure 7.19.

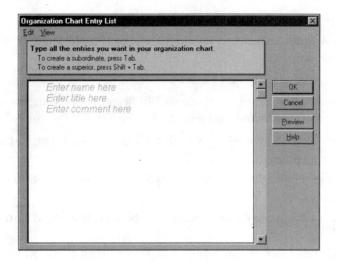

Figure 7.19 *The Organization Chart Entry List dialog box.*

It's time to enter the data for the organization chart.

Entering Data for an Organization Chart

Major Chips is forming a new division that only handles the chocolate products. The President of the Division is Eric Beatty, who has four vice presidents: Julie Duffy, Barb Weadock, Ralph Esposito, and Tom Cassidy. Each vice president has at least two subordinates. Let's begin entering data now.

Do It:

Let's enter the name of the company owners and work our way down the ladder. Here's how to enter data:

1. With the Organization Chart Entry List dialog box open, type **Bob Refos/Ellen Nacey** in the first line with the "Enter name here" prompt.

2. Press **Enter** to move the cursor down to the next line. The "Enter title here" prompt appears on this line.

3. Type **CEO & President** on the second line.

4. Press **Enter** to move to the third line which contains the "Enter comment here" prompt.

5. Enter **Major Chips** on the third line.

6. Press **Enter** again. An indented bullet appears with the three entry prompts. This is the next level in the organization hierarchy.

7. Type **Eric Beatty** where the "Enter name here" prompt appears. Press enter again.

8. At the "Enter title here" prompt, type **President**. Press **Enter** to move to the third line.

9. Enter **Chocolate Chip Division** on the third line. Press **Enter** again.

Another bulleted set of prompts pops up. These prompts are on the same level as the one where we entered Eric Beatty's information. The next entry, however, is really a subordinate of Eric's so this set of prompts should be indented again to indicate that the next entry is a subordinate of the previous entry.

Creating Subordinates

Organization charts are designed to show who works for whom, therefore, subordinates need to be clearly labeled as such. Eric Beatty is the president of the Chocolate Chip division but the next entries are all subordinates who work for him. Let's translate this into a visual representation in the chart.

Do It:

We need to create two different levels of subordinates for this chart. Here's how:

1. With the cursor positioned at the "Enter name here" prompt, press the **Tab** key. The prompt automatically indents one level as seen in Figure 7.20.

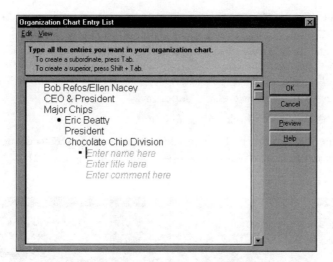

Figure 7.20 *Entry prompts indented one level.*

NOTE

If you make a mistake or someone gets a promotion, you can change the entry to a superior. To create a superior, press **Shift-Tab**. The entry prompts are immediately outdented a level.

2. Type **Julie Duffy** on the first prompt line. Press **Enter**.

3. Type **Vice President** on the second line. Press **Enter** again.

4. Enter **Marketing** on the third prompt line. Press **Enter** to begin a new entry series.

The next entries are Julie's subordinates so now we need to indent yet again.

5. With the cursor positioned at the "Enter name here" prompt, press the **Tab** key. The prompts are indented another level.

6. Enter **Louise Simons** at the "Enter name here" prompt. Press **Enter** to create another entry section.

7. Enter **George Thomas**. Press **Enter**.

The next entry is Barb Weadock, another vice president, so we need to outdent a level.

8. Press **Shift-Tab** to create a superior.

9. Type **Barb Weadock** on the first line.

10. When you're finished typing all the entries, click **OK** to create the organization chart. The chart pops up, as shown in Figure 7.21.

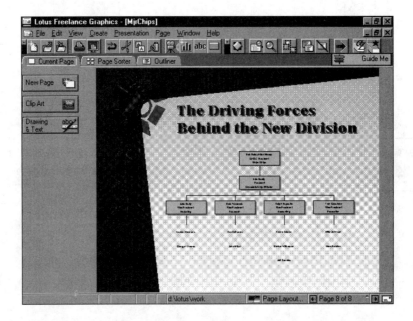

Figure 7.21 *The organization chart.*

To view an organization chart before you place it on the page, click the **Preview** button. The chart appears and you can click **OK** to place the chart or **Change** to return to the Organization Chart Entry List dialog box. You can also click the **Preview** button and hold down the left mouse button. The chart appears and when you release the left mouse button, the data pops back up.

The chart looks pretty good, however, it turns out that Tom's last name is spelled wrong. Let's do some editing.

Editing an Organization Chart

To edit the data in the organization chart, you need to reopen the Organization Chart Entry List. When the dialog box opens, you can change entries to subordinates or superiors and you can add additional positions. After reviewing the chart, I've noticed that the name Simmons is misspelled. I also noticed that we didn't include Larry Mittler's name. Let's open the dialog box and make these corrections.

Do It:

With the chart on the screen, here's how to open the Organization Chart Entry List and edit the data:

1. Click the **Organization Chart** to select it.
2. Click the **Edit organization chart data** SmartIcon. The Organization Chart Entry List pops up.
3. Scroll down the list box to locate **Louise Simmons**.
4. Position the cursor in front of the m in Cassidy and type the letter **m**
5. Click **OK** to see the chart. Simons is now spelled as Simmons in the organization chart.

Good, that was really easy. Now let's add Larry Mittler's name and position.

Adding a Staff Position to an Organization Chart

Freelance allows you to add one staff position per organization chart. You're further limited by the fact that this staff position can only report to the top person in the chart. The staff position appears on the chart a little differently than what we've entered before: it juts out to the side, just below the superior position. Let's add a staff position to the chart now.

Do It:

Larry Mittler's official title is Executive Administrative Assistant. Here's how to add Larry's name and title to the organization chart:

1. Select the organization chart in the window.

2. Choose the **Edit organization chart data** SmartIcon. The Organization Chart Entry List pops up. You can't add a staff position by typing it in the list box.

3. Next, open the **Edit** menu.

4. Select **Staff** from the menu. The Organization Chart Staff, shown in Figure 7.22, pops up.

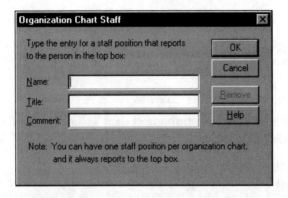

Figure 7.22 *The Organization Chart Staff.*

5. Enter **Larry Mittler** in the Name text box.

6. Type **Executive Administrative Assistant** in the Title text box.

   ❖ You can also add a comment such as the division Larry works in, his floor number or his telephone number.

7. Click **OK** when you've finished entering the data. The Organization Chart Entry List box appears in the window again.

8. Click **OK** again to return to the organization chart on the page. The organization chart now looks similar to Figure 7.23.

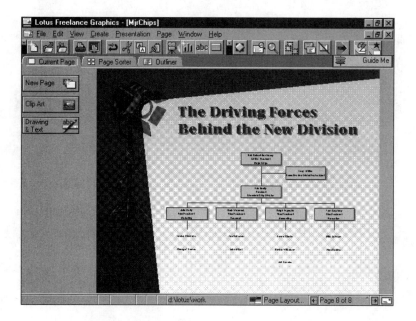

Figure 7.23 *The organization chart with a staff position.*

From Here...

Charts help alleviate boredom in a presentation, but more importantly, they help translate information from text to a visual representation that will probably help your audience remember the meaning longer.

Another way to show numeric data is to create a table. Tables don't have quite the same visual impact as charts, but they are useful in displaying text and/or numbers. In the next chapter, I'll show you how to add a table page layout, create a table, edit it and change table properties.

Title page, SmartMaster look: mmpastel

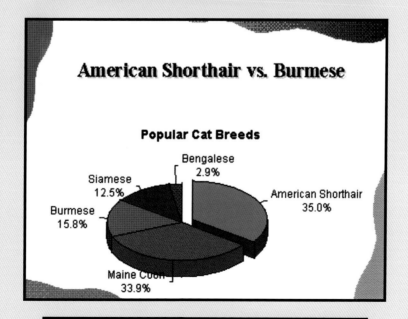

Pie chart, SmartMaster look: festive

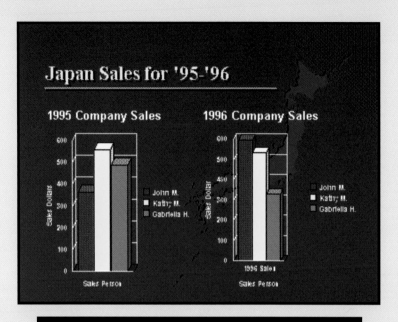

Two bar charts, SmartMaster look: japan

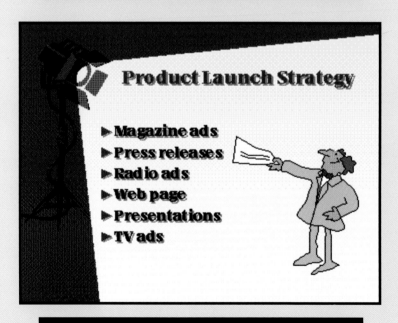

Bulleted list, SmartMaster look: spotlite

Flow Shapes diagram, SmartMaster look: bluegray

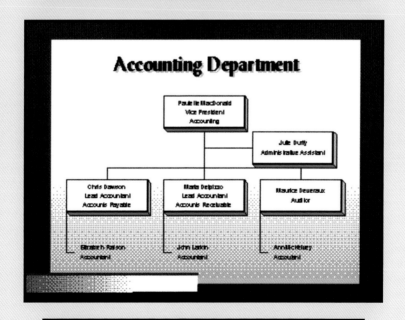

Organization chart, SmartMaster look: bluegray

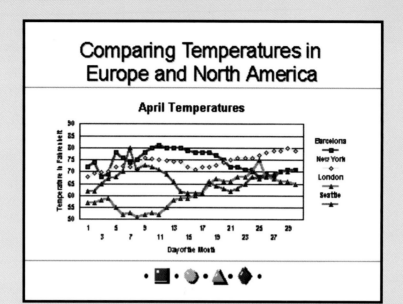

Line chart, SmartMaster look: buttons

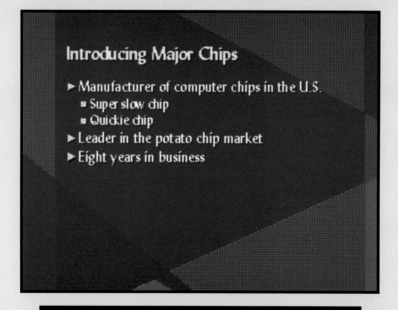

Bulleted list, SmartMaster look: mmblue

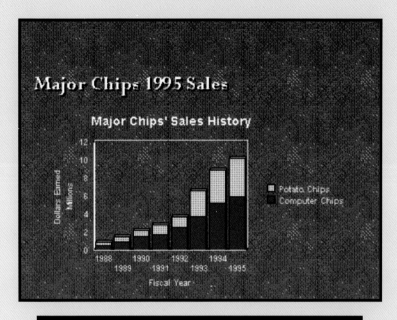

Stacked bar chart, SmartMaster look: txblue

Table, SmartMaster look: 3line

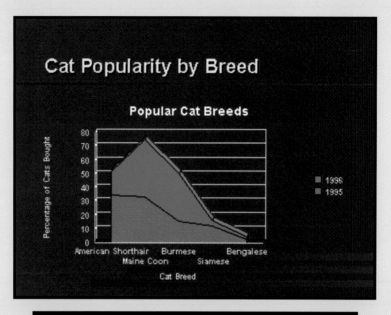

Area chart, SmartMaster look: gradline

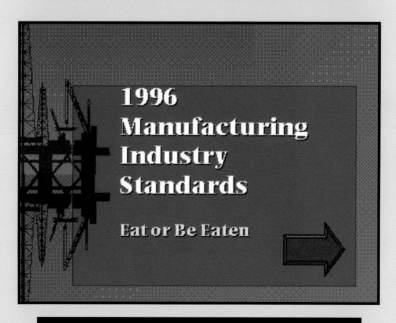

Title page, SmartMaster look: oilrig

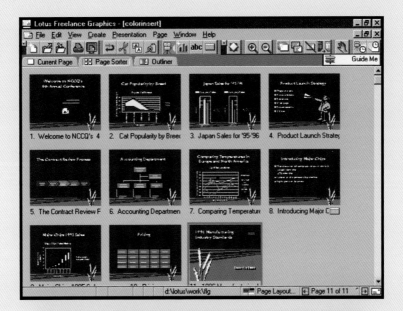

Page Sorter view, SmartMaster look: farm

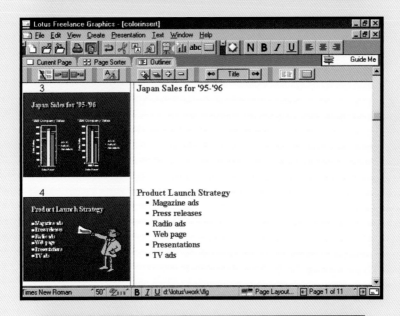

Outliner view, SmartMaster look: gradate3

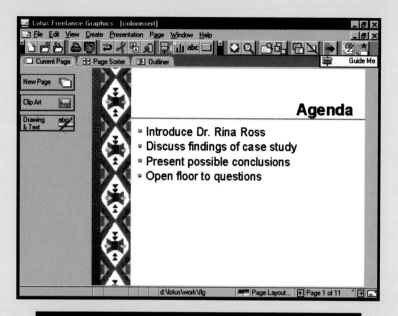

Bulleted list: SmartMaster look: southwst

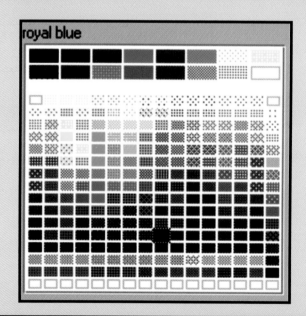

Color palette: Royal blue

CHAPTER 8

Working with Tables

(Displaying data in boxes)

Tables are used to display numbers and text in a column and row format. Creating a table involves selecting a table style and the number of rows and columns you want to include. Once you've created a basic table, you can add or delete columns and rows, move columns and rows around, create borders, shadows, reformat the text, select background colors, and most of the other properties we discussed in Chapter 5, *Text Properties*, and Chapter 7, *Charts*.

Major Chips is introducing a new line of products, namely their brand of Milk, Dark, Bittersweet, and White chocolate. Naturally, potential customers will want to know how the product will be sold, for example in ounces or pounds, and the cost per unit. Chocolates will be sold in 10, 25, and 50 pound quantities and, depending upon the size and type of chocolate, the price ranges from $10.95 to $64.95. Let's create a table displaying the cost of each chocolate based upon the quantity sold.

How did we begin creating a chart or a bulleted list? By adding a page layout, of course. Tables are no exception. There is a table page layout listed in the standard page layouts that Freelance provides. Let's select it now and start working on our table.

Adding a Table Page Layout

Adding a table page layout begins with the New Page dialog box. Freelance provides you with only one style of table page layout; therefore, you don't have to agonize over whether to have one table, two tables or four tables on a page like you did with charts. The page contains two "Click here" prompts, one to title the page and the other to create the table.

Do It:

With the Major Chips presentation open to the last page, here's how to add a table page layout:

1.   Open the New Page dialog box by clicking the **New Page** button.

2.   Select **Table** from the Select a page layout list box.

3.   Click **OK** to add the page. The Table page layout appears, as shown in Figure 8.1.

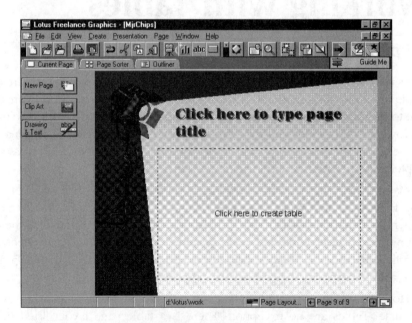

Figure 8.1 *The Table page layout.*

4. Title the page **Pricing** by opening the text block.

Creating a Basic Table

Freelance allows you to create tables with up to 30 columns and 50 rows. Naturally, the table is resized to squeeze all that information on the page. And if you really create a table that size, it'll be difficult to read and look unattractive. Some people like to add all kinds of data to a table that isn't really necessary—don't fall into that trap! Be selective with the data you add. But if you really have that much data to include, you may want to break the table down into smaller comparisons over several pages instead. By now you have probably gotten the hang of adding your own data to a page, so let's dive right in.

Do It:

With the Table page layout in the Freelance window:

1. Click on the **Click here to create table** prompt. The Table Gallery dialog box, shown in Figure 8.2, opens.

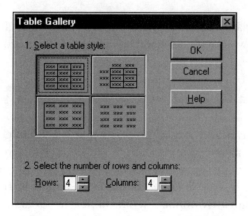

Figure 8.2 *The Table Gallery dialog box.*

2. Choose a table style from the Select a table style section of the dialog box. I'm choosing the table style to the left in the top row. The table is entirely boxed in and lines appear between the columns and rows.

N O T E

If the table has more than 2 columns and 4 rows, it's a good idea to include lines between cells in the table. Lines assist readers in reading the chart accurately because they guide the eye across rows and down columns easily. In addition, if there are any other objects such as logos or clip art on the page, it's a good idea to have a border around the entire table to visually separate the two objects.

3.   Use the increment buttons to select **3** rows in the Select the number of rows and columns section of the dialog box.

4.   Next, select **4** columns.

5.   Click **OK**. The table pops up on the page.

N O T E

You can really create a table on any type of page—it doesn't have to be a table page layout. If you want to add a table to a different layout page, choose **Table** from the Create menu. The Table Gallery dialog box pops up. Follow the steps outlined in this chapter to continue creating a table.

This looks pretty blasé right now but as we continue through the chapter, we'll jazz it up. Right now, though, let's add some data to the chart.

Adding Data to a Table

In Freelance, you can add text or numbers into a cell table or you can add a combination of numbers and text to a cell, such as dollar signs and periods. You may have worked with spreadsheet applications such as Lotus 1-2-3 or Excel before and, in that case, you know that individual cells in spreadsheets can be assigned mathematical formulas. While tables in Freelance look similar to spreadsheets, you cannot assign formulas to individual cells. You are, therefore, adding discrete pieces of data into each cell which do not depend upon the values in other cells.

Each cell is able to contain a certain number of characters per line. This number depends upon the width of the cell. If you enter more characters than the first line can contain, the cell automatically increases in height and a second line of text is created.

Do It:

Follow along with me and I'll show you how to enter data into the first row of the table. Afterwards, use these steps to guide yourself in entering data for the second and third rows too.

1. Select the table by double-clicking on it. A thick blue line appears around the table edges.
2. Position the cursor in the Row 1, Column 1 cell.
3. Type **$10.95** in the first cell. Use the **Tab** key to move to the next cell.
4. Type **$10.95** in the second cell.
5. Enter **$15.95** in the third cell moving across the table.
6. Next, enter **$19.95** in the fourth cell.
7. Click in the Row 2, Column 1 cell. Your table should look like Figure 8.3 now.

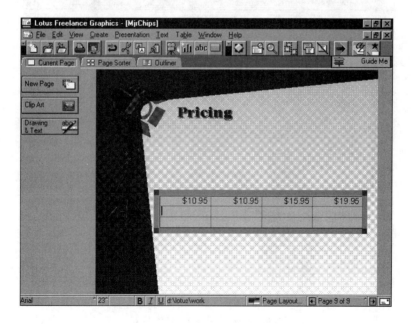

Figure 8.3 *The first table row.*

N O T E

Using the **Tab** and **Shift-Tab** keys to move between cells or the direction arrows to move between characters is an easy way of getting around a table. There are some fancy ways of moving around a table too. Press the **Home** key once to return to the beginning of the first line in a cell. Press **Home** twice to return to the beginning of the first cell in the row. To move to the end of the line in the current cell, press the **End** key once. Press the **End** key twice to move to the end of the last cell in the row. To go to the beginning of the first cell in the table, press **Ctrl-Home**. To move to the end of the last cell in the table, press the **Ctrl-End** keys. When you have a very large table, these can help you quickly move through the table. You can also click in a cell to move to it.

Good, you've filled in the first row of the table. Following the steps above, enter **$25.95**, **$22.95**, **$32.95**, and **$39.95** across the second row. Next, enter **$45.95**, **$45.95**, **$55.95**, and **$64.95** in the third row. Your table should look like Figure 8.4. I had you make a typo so that I can show you how to edit data in the table.

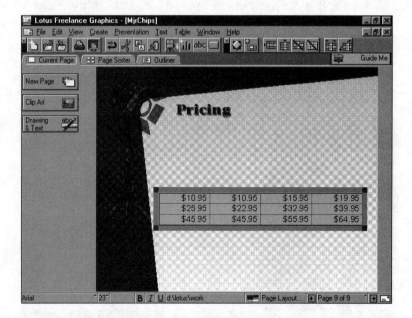

Figure 8.4 *The table with data.*

Editing Data in a Table

Editing table data is really quite simple. You can correct typos and remove entire rows or columns of text if you decide that you don't want the information displayed in the table after all. When we added text in the previous section, I had you incorrectly type a price. Let's correct it now.

Do It:

To correct a typo:

1. Click in the $22.95 cell.

2. Use the **Backspace** key to delete the second 2 in $22.95.

 To delete an entire word, click and drag over the entire word to select it, then press the **Delete** key. You can also delete the text in an entire row or column by clicking and dragging across a row or column and pressing the **Delete** key.

3. Type **5**. $25.95 should now appear in the cell.

In the next section we'll add a row and create column titles.

Inserting a Row

After creating a table, you may find that you haven't added enough rows to the table or you may decide that you want to add more information than you initially intended. To fit all this data, you can insert a single row or multiple rows to a table. Just remember that while 50 is the maximum number of rows you can have in a table, 8 rows is really the maximum number of rows that your audience is able to read. If you have to create a table with more than 8 rows, try to break the table down into sections on different pages. Also, when you add a row, it assumes the properties of the table so you don't have to reformat it.

Do It:

To add a single row to a table:

1. Click in Row 1, Column 1 to select the chart.

2. Click the **Insert a Row** SmartIcon (that's the one with a right-pointing arrow pointing at a selected row). A blank row appears immediately after Row 1.

N O T E

To add several rows to a table, you can select the table, then open the Table menu. Choose **Insert**, then **Row/Column**. The Insert Column/Row dialog box pops up. Choose **Row** and use the increment buttons to increase the number of rows that you want to insert. Choose the radio button to insert the new row before or after the currently selected row. Click **OK** to add the rows to the table.

Now that you know how to enter data, type **Bittersweet**, **Milk**, **Dark**, and **White** in the cells of the new row. Now, let's move that new row to the top of the table.

Moving a Row

The row that we just added to the table is obviously in the wrong place. It should be the first row in the table, not the second. Let's move the row now.

Do It:

To move a row:

1. Select the second row (that's the row that we just inserted) by clicking and dragging across the row.

2. Click the **Move Row or Column** SmartIcon. The Move Column/Row dialog box, shown in Figure 8.5, pops up.

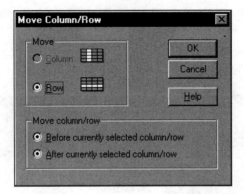

Figure 8.5 *The Move Column/Row dialog box.*

3. Click on the **Row** radio button.
4. Choose **Before currently selected column/row**.
5. Click **OK**. Row 2 becomes Row 1 now.

Now we have column headings. To further clarify the information in the chart, we need to add another column to the table and enter some text.

Inserting a Column

While working on the table, you may need to add a column. In our Major Chips table, we need to add a column and insert text to indicate the pounds.

Do It:

We need to add one column to the table. To add a single column to a table:

You can add multiple columns (up to 30) by choosing **Insert** from the Table menu, then choosing **Row/Column**. Don't forget that you need to consider the audience. They probably won't be able to read the data if you have 30 columns.

N O T E

1. Select Column 1 by clicking in the first cell and dragging the pointer down to the last cell.

2. Click on the **Insert a Column** SmartIcon. A blank column appears, as shown in Figure 8.6, after Column 1.

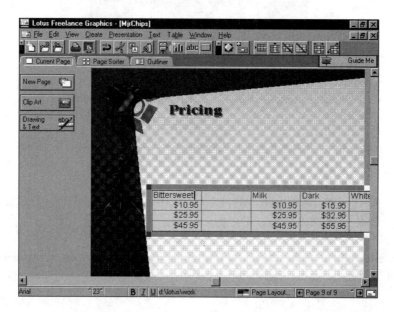

Figure 8.6 *A column inserted.*

As you can see in Figure 8.6, part of the table is hanging off the page right now. Using your knowledge about clicking and dragging (Chapter 2), move the table so that all the cells appear on the page.

Moving a Column

The column that we just added to the table needs to be moved. Follow along with me and I'll show you how to move a column.

Do It:

To move a column:

1. Click in the second column.

2. Select the **Move Row or Column** SmartIcon. The Move row/column dialog box appears.

3. Click on the **Column** radio button.

4. Choose **Before currently selected column/row**.

5. Click **OK**. Column 2 is now Column 1.

After you've moved the column, type **Quantity**, **10 Pounds**, **25 Pounds**, and **50 Pounds** in the column you just added starting in Row 1, Column 1. It's really starting to look like a table now.

Creating a Border

Borders are used to make items stand out. You can surround an entire table with a border, place a border on the top or bottom, or add a border to the left or right sides of the table. Freelance allows you to change the line styles of the border and even fill the interior of a border.

Do It:

Let's place a border around the entire perimeter of the table. To add a border:

1. Select the table by clicking on it.

2. Click on the **Infobox** SmartIcon.

NOTE

Make sure that Table appears in the Properties for: window. If it doesn't, open the Properties for: list box and select **Table**. The Infobox changes to reflect the Table properties.

3. Select the **Borders & Colors** tab (that's the tab with the colorful lines).

4. Choose a border. I'm choosing the first button from the left in the second row. It's the border selection with the line around the image. A border appears around the table. You may not see the border at first because of the line width selected by default.

5. Open the **Width:** drop-down list box.

6. Select a thick line near the bottom of the box.

7. Close the Infobox. The border around your table should look similar to Figure 8.7 now.

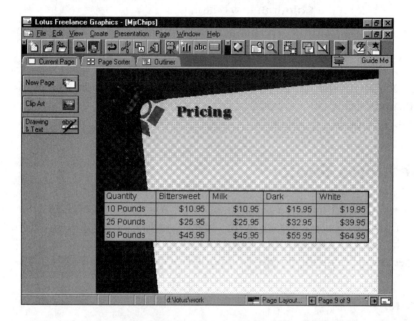

Figure 8.7 A border around the table.

Optionally, you can change the style, width and color of the border by opening the drop-down list boxes in the Lines and Colors tab. Simply click on the drop-down list arrow and make a selection. The drop-down list closes and the changes are made.

N O T E

In the next section, I'll show you how to change the color of the cells in the first row.

Coloring the Interior of Cells

When you create a table, the cells are assigned a color based upon the SmartMaster Look you selected when you began creating the presentation. But you're not stuck with the default colors. You can change the background color of a single cell or a row of cells to make them more noticeable.

Do It:

Since the first row of the table contains titles, let's change the background color of the first row so that it's aztec blue instead. To change the color of multiple cells:

1. Select Row 1.
2. Open the Infobox. *Selected cell(s)* should appear in the Properties for text box.
3. Select the **Borders & Colors** tab.
4. Choose **Aztec Blue** from the Pattern Color drop down list box.
5. Close the Infobox.

The background color of the row, is now aztec blue. The background color appears as a shade of gray if you don't have a color monitor.

Aligning Text in a Row or Column

When you enter data, text is automatically left justified and numbers are right justified. To give the table a uniform look and make it easier to read, you can change the alignment of text or numbers. You can even center justify the entire table. Let's center our text now.

Do It:

To change the alignment of data in the table:

1. Select the cells in the table.
2. Open the Infobox.
3. Select the **Alignment** tab from the Infobox.
4. Choose the **Centered** buttons in the horizontal and vertical rows. The data in all the cells is centered vertically and horizontally in each cell, as shown in Figure 8.8.

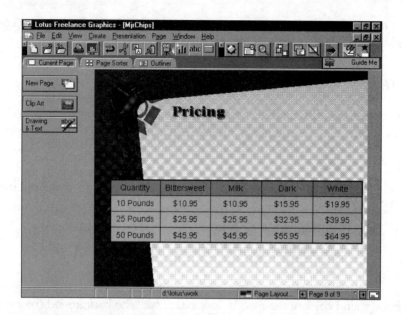

Figure 8.8 *The text centered in each cell.*

Let's continue changing the properties of the table by changing the height of a row.

Changing the Height of a Row

There are several reasons why you may want to change the height of a row: to fit data into cells or to create a visual separation between rows. You can even reduce the size of a row and fill it with a different color for an artistic look, signaling a change in the type of information. Next, let's increase the height of the row.

Do It:

To change the height of a row:

1. Select Row 1.

2. Click on the **Change Size of Selected Row or Column** SmartIcon.

3. Choose the **Columns & Rows** tab (that's the one with the colored row and column). The Columns & Rows properties page appears, as shown in Figure 8.9.

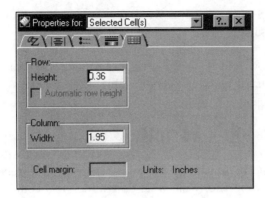

Figure 8.9 *The Columns & Rows properties page.*

4.   Enter **103** in the row height text box.

5.   Close the Infobox. The height of Row 1 increases.

To quickly change the height of a row, you can double-click the table to select it. Then, position the pointer above a line in the row that you want to change. The pointer turns into a double-ended arrow. Click and drag the cursor up or down to decrease or increase the row height. This technique also works for columns.

Changing the Width of a Column

You may need wider columns to fit data on one line or you may find that one column needs to be wider than the others. Either way, you don't have to have uniformly spaced columns if that doesn't suit your purposes.

Do It:

To change the width of a single column follow the steps below, except that you only need to select the column you want to change. To change the width of all the table columns:

1.   Select the entire table by double-clicking on it.

2.   Click on the **Change Size of Selected Row or Column** SmartIcon. The Infobox pops up with the Columns and Rows tab selected.

3. Type **1.75** in the Column Width text box. The width of each column is reduced slightly.

Let's see, you know how to create a table, add and edit data, change the table properties. But what if you don't like the table style?

Changing a Table Layout

After reviewing the presentation, you and your team may decide that the table layout just isn't appropriate. Well, what do you do? You could begin by deleting the entire table but that means you'd have to add the data in all over again and that's really too much work. Freelance allows you to change the table layout at any time during the design process.

Do It:

Let's change the table from its current layout to one where the data is boxed in but the titles aren't. Here's how to change a table layout:

1. Select the table.
2. Choose **Table** from the Properties for: list box in the Infobox.
3. Select the **Table Layout** tab (that's the odd looking one with a grid pattern). The Table Layout properties page opens, as seen in Figure 8.10.

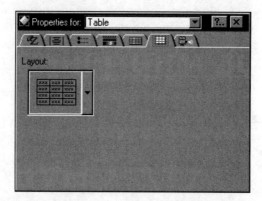

Figure 8.10 *The Table Layout properties page.*

4. Choose a layout from the drop-down list. I've chosen the layout to the right in the top row.

5. Close the Infobox. The layout changes.

If you don't like the way that looks, click the **Undo** SmartIcon to reformat the table back to the way it was.

Deleting a Column or Row

In Freelance, if you want to delete the text in a row or column, all you need to do is select the row or column. Then choose **Clear** from the Edit menu. The column is still there but the text is gone. Removing a row or column is just as easy; however, you need to follow a different set of steps. Creating a table, just like a chart or text, is a matter of creating and editing data and its properties. You may decide that you don't want to display data that appears in a column or that you added too many rows.

Do It:

We're not really going to remove this row permanently. We need the data, so after you follow the steps outlined below use the **Undo** command to reinsert the column.

1. Select Column 1.

2. Click on the **Delete Rows or Columns** SmartIcon. The Delete Column/ Row dialog box pops up, as shown in Figure 8.11.

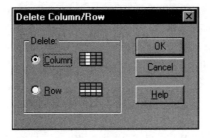

Figure 8.11 *Delete Column/Row dialog box.*

3.   Choose the **Column** radio button.

4.   Click **OK** to delete the column. The column is immediately deleted.

Remember to **Undo** the delete!

Deleting a Table

Your boss just came in and told you that the table you designed needs to be completely changed. While all tables are changeable, you may have made so many properties changes that starting from scratch is the easier thing to do.

Do It:

To delete a table:

1.   Select the table.

2.   Click on the **Delete Entire Table** SmartIcon. The table is immediately deleted.

The "Click here to create table" prompt reappears on the page again. You can now begin the whole design process over by clicking on the **"Click here"** prompt. Don't forget to use the **Undo** command to undo the delete command. We really do want to keep this chart.

Resizing a Table

After creating a table, you may find that the table looks too small in comparison to the overall page. Or maybe it's just the opposite—it occupies too much space on the page. In Freelance, you can resize a table so that it fits perfectly. Resizing is just a matter of clicking and dragging the handles.

Do It:

The table that we created in this chapter is a little too large for the page. Let's resize the table now. Here's how:

1. Click on the table. Handles appear around the edges of the table.

2. Select and drag a handle to resize the table. When you resize the table to your preference, release the left mouse button.

The table is off center. Let's move it so that it's completely on the yellow portion of the SmartMaster background.

Moving a Table

After you've finished working on the table, you may have to move it so that the page looks pretty. Every page of your presentation should appear balanced—that's one reason why you chose a SmartMaster Look. But during the process of designing a table, you may find that the items on the page have become unbalanced. To reestablish the equilibrium, you can move the table.

Do It:

Let's move the table to the right. Here's how:

1. Select the table.

2. Click on the table with the left mouse key and drag the table to the right. The pointer turns into a hand.

Good, now our table page is done. This is also a good time to tell you that you can follow the same steps that I described in Chapter 5, "Text Properties," to change text properties, such as bold, italics, increase the point size or change the font in a table.

From Here...

In this chapter, you learned how to add a table layout page, create a basic table, add and delete columns and rows, add and edit data, resize a table, and move a table in the page. Have your creative juices started flowing yet?

In the next chapter we'll start working with the Drawing and Text menu. If you've ever worked with a drawing program such as Illustrator, Freehand, or Photoshop, you'll be familiar with some of the tools that you'll encounter in the next chapter. If you haven't used these programs before, no sweat. You'll be a whiz when you've finished the chapter. Maybe drawing isn't of interest to you? Well, there's still something for you in Chapter 9—I'll show you how to create and add text to flowcharts.

CHAPTER 9

The Art of Objects

(Working and playing with the drawing tools)

In this chapter, you'll learn how to use Freelance's drawing tools to create your own objects and artwork. You don't need years of artistic experience to create a little cartoon, a funny drawing, a basic logo, or redesign the office layout. Drawing lines, squares, circles, arcs and curves, as well as making them look pretty, are some of the things you'll learn to do in this chapter.

During the tutorials, you'll be working with open and closed objects. What's the difference between the two? *Closed objects* are objects whose beginning and ending points are the same. A circle, a square and a triangle, for example, are all closed objects. *Open objects* have different starting and ending points. A line, a curve and an arc are all good examples of open objects. You'll learn how to draw both kinds of objects and how to convert open objects into closed objects. I'll also show you how to fill objects with colors and patterns and, of course, group them into more complicated objects. You'll be able to draw and edit objects by the time you finish this chapter.

Before we dive in, let me give you some composition tips. The first tip is to balance the objects on the page. Try to spread the objects on the page so that it doesn't look cluttered and the audience can see what they're looking at. Another good idea is to size the drawing in relation to the other items on the page. Don't make one object huge and the rest really small; try to size them so that the eye isn't drawn to one part of the page over and over again (unless that's your intention). The most important elements of the object should be larger or more colorful than the rest of the drawing. For example, make the name slightly larger and in a different color from the background when making a logo. And lastly, try to use a common background, color, or shape to tie together elements within the drawing.

Where do we start? By adding a page layout of course.

Adding a Basic Page Layout

Okay, you've learned how to add almost all the standard page layouts to your presentation that Freelance provides you. The next page layout that we're going to work with is called the Basic Layout page. This page is a little unusual because Freelance provides you with only a "Click here to create title" prompt. There are no other prompts on the page.

Do It:

To add a Basic Layout page to the presentation:

1. Click on **New Page**.
2. Choose **Basic Layout** from the Select a page layout list.
3. Click **OK** to add the page to the presentation. The Basic Layout page appears in the Freelance window, as shown in Figure 9.1.

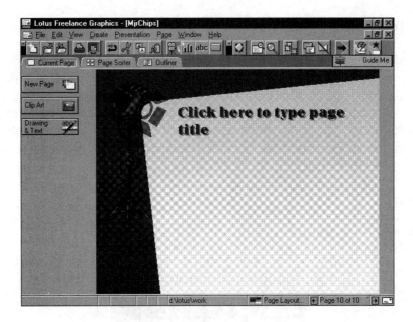

Figure 9.1 *The Basic Layout page.*

You can design a Basic page layout to suit your own needs. You can use it to create a drawing or clip art, or you can add your own text blocks and charts (see Chapter 15, "Customizing SmartMasters"). Let's get started.

Understanding the Drawing and Text Palette

Freelance has ready-made diagrams available, but you can also create your own diagrams or even artwork. In Freelance, you can draw rectangles, circles, ellipses, lines, polygons, arcs, curves, and a bunch more. While the Tools palette isn't as sophisticated as a dedicated drawing program, it is pretty handy. In addition, you can add objects that contain text blocks. Once you add the object to the diagram or artwork you can add your own text.

When drawing, it's a good idea to have the drawing grid and rulers displayed. These tools help make your work a little easier.

Displaying the Drawing Grid

Instead of eyeballing where an object should be placed on the page or visually trying to align objects with one another, you can use the drawing grid. The drawing grid is a series of dots that appear at regular intervals on the page. These dots help align and place objects on the page. And, to make drawing even easier, you can choose to have the **Snap to grid** feature active. While you can see the grid displayed on the screen, it doesn't appear on the page when the page is printed out. Let's display the drawing grid now.

Do It:

To display the drawing grid:

1. Choose **Set Units & Grid** from the View menu. The Set Units & Grid dialog box pops up, as shown in Figure 9.2.

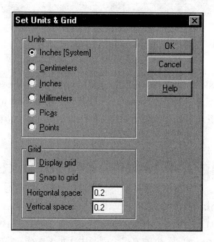

Figure 9.2 *The Set Units & Grid dialog box.*

2. Click on the **Points** radio button in the Units section of the dialog box.

    I prefer to use points but you can choose any unit of measurement you prefer from the items displayed in the Units section. By selecting the units now, you're also setting up the rulers.

3. In the Grid section of the dialog box, click in the **Display grid** and the **Snap to grid** check boxes.

4.   Click **OK**. The presentation page is displayed with the grid.

Next, let's display the rulers.

Displaying the Rulers

Rulers are the quickest and easiest way to measure an object. In Freelance, the rulers show the exact location of a selected object on the page as well as the object's measurements. The vertical ruler (the one to the left of the page) shows where the top and bottom edges of the object appear. The horizontal ruler (the one that runs across the top of the page) displays the location of the right and left edges of the selected object. Before we begin drawing, let's display the rulers.

Do It:

To display the rulers:

❖   Choose **Show Ruler** from the View menu. The rulers are displayed in the Freelance window now, as shown in Figure 9.3.

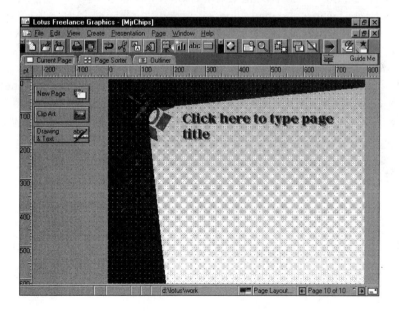

Figure 9.3 *The rulers displayed.*

While looking at the rulers, move the pointer to different locations on the presentation page. Notice the set of lines that move every time you move the pointer? These lines indicate where the pointer is currently located on the page. The rulers use the same units of measurement that were chosen when you opened the Set Units & Grid dialog box earlier, so if you want to change them, you need to open the Set Units and Grid dialog box again.

You may find yourself creating a lot more artwork in Freelance than you expected. If that's the case, you may want to customize the SmartIcon Bar so that you aren't constantly having to open the menu to toggle back and forth between displaying and hiding rulers, showing and hiding the grid, and snapping the grid on and off.

For the next several sections, I'm going to show you how to use the Tools palette to create a mouse. But before we begin drawing the mouse, we need to open the palette.

Opening the Drawing & Text Palette

The Tools section of the palette contains the tools necessary for drawing arcs, arrows, circles, ellipses, curves, lines, polygons, polylines, rectangles, squares, and freehand drawing. The next portion of the palette is the Shapes with text section. This section contains common shapes used in diagrams and clip art with text blocks that you can add your own text to. Another section of the Tools palette is called Connectors. This is where you can choose different lines and arrows to connect the objects together. There is also a special section in the palette that you can use to create flowcharts. Here's how to open the palette.

Do It:

To open the Drawing & Tools palette you need to click on one item.

❖ With the presentation page open, click on the **Drawing & Text** button to the left of the page image. The Tools palette, shown in Figure 9.4, opens.

Figure 9.4 *The palette.*

To move the palette, just click on the bar at the top and drag it anywhere in the Freelance window.

Okay, the grid is on the page, the rulers are displayed above and to the left of the page, and the palette is open. What are we waiting for? Let's start drawing.

Drawing Circles and Ellipses

What's the difference between an ellipse and a circle? Well, the simple answer is that circles are perfectly round while ellipses look like squashed or elongated circles. In this section, we need to make several circles and ellipses. Let's do it now.

Do It:

With the Drawing & Text palette open, let's draw a circle first. Here's how:

1. Click on the **Circle** icon in the Tools palette. The pointer turns into a crosshair pointer.

2. Hold down the **Shift** key as you drag the pointer.

3. Release the left mouse button and a circle appears on the page.

You have one perfectly round circle. We'll use this circle as the mouse's head. Now, make a smaller circle following the steps above. We'll use the second circle as a mouse eye. Since mice have two eyes, later I'll show you how to duplicate the one small circle so that we have two. Next we need to make the mouse's body and legs by drawing ellipses. Here's how:

1. Click on the **Circle** icon in the Tools palette again.

2. Press the left mouse button down and drag the pointer.

3. Release the mouse button and an ellipse, such as the one shown in Figure 9.5, appears on the page.

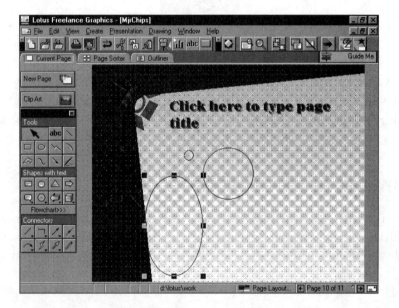

Figure 9.5 *An ellipse.*

When you use the circle tool with the **Shift** key held down, you get a circle. When you use it by itself, you draw an ellipse.

N O T E

Draw one more ellipse, but make this one smaller than the one we just created. We'll use the second ellipse and a duplicate as the mouse's haunches. The page is getting crowded now. Let's move the objects we've created and start organizing them.

Moving Objects

In previous chapters, you learned how to move text, tables and charts on the page. Moving objects works the same way. Let's move the objects so that it starts to really look like a mouse now.

Do It:

Let's move the objects we've created.

1. Select the ellipse. Handles appear around the object.

2. Click on the object and hold the left mouse button down. The pointer turns into a hand.

3. Drag the object so that it's immediately underneath the circle.

4. Next, click on the small ellipse to select it.

5. Drag the ellipse so that it overlaps the large ellipse, as shown in Figure 9.6.

Figure 9.6 *The ellipses overlapping.*

6. Click and drag the small circle so that it's positioned in the large circle, as shown in Figure 9.7.

Figure 9.7 *A circle within a circle.*

Our mouse is looking a little lopsided. Let's replicate the small circle and the ellipse.

Replicating an Object

Let's replicate the small circle and then the ellipse so we can give our mouse a little balance.

Do It:

To replicate an object:

1. Select the small circle.
2. Choose **Replicate** from the Edit menu. Two small circles now appear within the large circle, as shown in Figure 9.8.

Figure 9.8 *The circle replicated.*

KEYBOARD

You can select the object and then press **Ctrl-F3** to replicate it.

Now that you know how to replicate objects, replicate the small ellipse.

Aligning Objects

Aligning objects is a matter of lining up their edges or centering them along an imaginary line. Let's align our circles along their top edges, so that they're even.

Do It:

To align an object:

1. Select a circle.

2. While pressing the **Shift** key, click on the second circle.

Normally, when you select one object and then click on another, you deselect the first object. By pressing the **Shift** key and then clicking on two objects, you're telling Freelance that you want both objects selected at the same time. Following the same steps, you can select two text blocks, two objects, an object and a text block—in short, any combination.

3. Choose **Align** from the Drawing menu. The Align Objects dialog box pops up, as shown in Figure 9.9.

Figure 9.9 *The Align Objects dialog box.*

4. Choose the **Align tops** radio button.

5. Click **OK** to align the objects.

6. Position the small circles within the large circle, so that they look like round eyes. After doing that, replicate the ellipse and position them alongside the larger ellipse. You now have a skeleton of a mouse.

Adding Colors and Patterns

Colors and patterns add texture and interest to objects. For our mouse, let's fill the eyes with a pattern and color.

Do It:

To apply a pattern to an object:

1.   Select the small circles (they're the mouse's eyes).

2.   Click on the **Open Infobox** SmartIcon. The Lines & Colors properties page appears with Selected Circles/Ellipses in the Properties for: text box.

3.   Open the Border Color list box and select **50% gray**.

4.   Open the Interior Pattern drop-down list and select the second pattern in from the left in the last row.

5.   Select **Black** from the Pattern color drop-down list.

6.   Choose **50% gray** from the Background list. The mouse's eyes should now look similar to Figure 9.10.

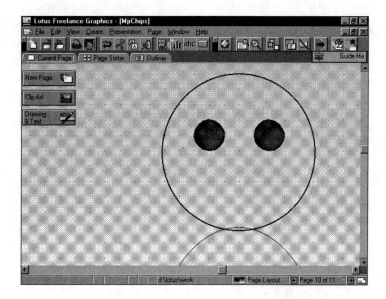

Figure 9.10 *Objects with patterns and colors.*

Following the steps we just went through, change the head, body and leg colors so that the object borders are 50% gray and filled with a solid pattern in 25% gray. We need to add ears to our mouse.

Drawing Arcs

An *arc* is a straight line with a curve in it. The beginning point of an arc is different from its end point, unlike a circle or ellipse where the beginning point *is* the end point. When you draw an arc, you need to specify the beginning and end points first, then specify how much of a curve you want. To show you what I mean, let's draw an arc now and use it as a mouse ear. By the way, if the page title is getting in the way, move it aside for now.

Do It:

To draw an arc:

1. Click on the **Arc** icon in the Tools palette. The pointer changes shape.

2. Click on the top edge of the mouse head, slightly off center.

3. Move the pointer to the side of the mouse's head and click again. A very light, dashed line appears.

4. Next, click off of the mouse's head anywhere between the two points. An arc appears similar to the one in Figure 9.11.

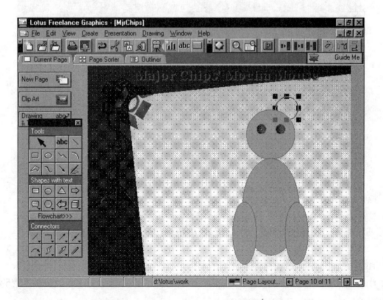

Figure 9.11 *An arc for a mouse ear.*

Flipping Objects

In Freelance, flipping an object means that the object is mirrored. Flipping our mouse from top to bottom, for example, gives us an entirely upside down object with the head on the bottom and the feet up in the air. You can also flip an object from side to side. Flipping objects is a very helpful feature for the very reason that we're doing it. Instead of drawing another arc to match the one we've already drawn, we can replicate the original arc and then flip it. We're left with two matching arcs that can fit on either side of the head. Let's do it now.

Do It:

First, you need to replicate the original arc by following the steps outlined earlier. Now, to flip the object:

1. Select the replicated arc.
2. Click on the **Flip left to right** SmartIcon.
3. Drag the flipped arc so that it appears on the other side of the head. Your mouse should look similar to Figure 9.12 now.

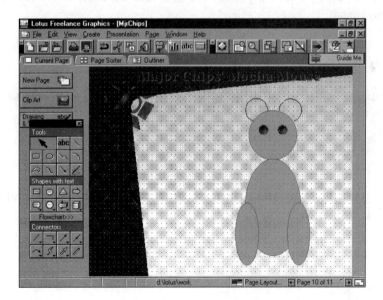

Figure 9.12 *The mouse.*

N O T E Freelance also provides you with a SmartIcon that allows you to flip an object from top to bottom. It appears in the SmartIcon bar beside the Flip left to right SmartIcon.

If you have trouble getting the mouse ears to abut the head, open the Set Units and Grids dialog box and click on the **Snap to grid** check box. This turns the Snap to feature off and you'll probably find it easier to move the objects.

Converting to Polygons

There are some situations where you may want to fill the space created between the sides of an arc just like you can fill in a circle or a square. The space within a circle or square is entirely enclosed, so Freelance doesn't have a problem with adding a pattern or color to this area. The space within an arc, however, is open, so Freelance can't fill the space—or can it? Well, Freelance can't fill an arc with a color or pattern the way it is, but if you convert the arc to a polygon, then Freelance can fill it. The mouse's ears should be filled in with a color and perhaps a pattern too, but first we need to convert the arcs into polygons.

Do It:

Converting to polygons also works for curves and lines too. Here's how to convert our arcs to polygons:

1. Select the right arc.
2. Choose **Convert** from the Drawing menu.
3. Select **To Polygons**. A line appears between the beginning and ending points, as shown in Figure 9.13.

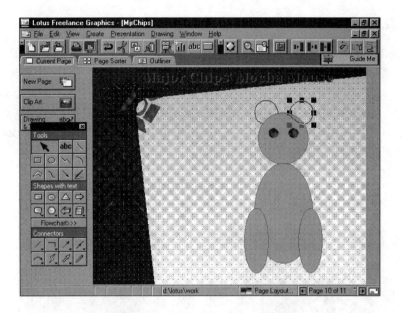

Figure 9.13 *An arc converted to a polygon.*

You can also revert to lines by selecting **To Lines** in the Convert menu. The line created when we converted to polygons doesn't affect the integrity of the arc; now we can fill the space with a color and pattern. Go ahead and convert the other arc into a polygon and then fill both the ears with a graduated fill in 50% gray using the Borders & Lines properties page in the Infobox.

Assigning Object Priority

Our ears look pretty good, but notice that we can still see the line that connects the arc's beginning and ending points. You may run into this problem often when you're creating objects. To get around this, Freelance allows you to assign a priority to each object. Using this feature, you can bring objects into the foreground or send them into the background. Let's send our mouse's ears into the background.

Do It:

To send an object into the background or bring it forward:

1. Select the ears.

2. Choose **Priority** from the Drawing menu.

3. Choose **Send to Back**. The ears move behind the head, and appear as shown in Figure 9.14.

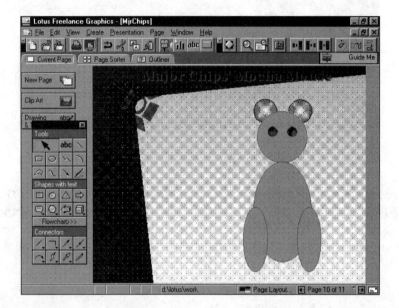

Figure 9.14 *The ears moved to the back.*

While you're assigning priorities to objects, send the left mouse leg to the back too. Next, let's give this mouse a nose.

Drawing Polygons

Polygons are closed objects that have three or more sides. Freelance gives you a special tool to create rectangles and squares because they're often used, but there is another tool that you can use to create polygons. Let's use this tool to create the mouse's nose in the shape of an upside down triangle.

Do It:

To create a triangle:

1. Click on the five-sided polygon in the Tools palette. Move the pointer onto the page but don't place it on top of the mouse yet.

2. Click on the page and then move the pointer to the right about half an inch.

3. Click the pointer again. A dashed line appears between the two points.

4. Move the pointer down about half an inch and click again. Another line appears between the point you just created and the point you created in Step 3. This line is the second side of the triangle.

5. Click on the first point you made in Step 2 to complete the third side of the triangle. Your triangle should look similar to Figure 9.15.

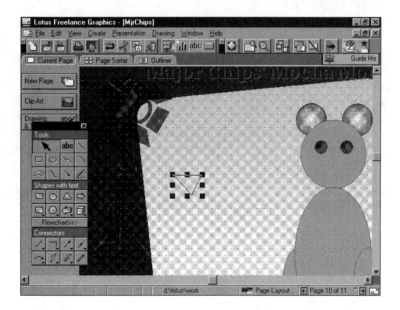

Figure 9.15 *A triangle.*

Fill the triangle with a graduated pattern and color it pink coral. Now, this triangle is a little too large to pass for a mouse nose so let's make it smaller.

Changing the Size of an Object

You've already learned how to resize an object by grabbing and dragging the handles. Resizing this way works okay but you're not reducing the object in proportion. To change the size of an object proportionally, Freelance provides you with three SmartIcons that reduce or increase an object or make two objects the same size. Let's reduce the size of the triangle now using the Make Selected Object Smaller SmartIcon.

Do It:

To change the size of an object:

1. Select the triangle.
2. Click on the **Make Selected Object Smaller** SmartIcon. The triangle is reduced in size slightly. Continue clicking on the icon until the triangle gets really small.

   ❖ You can click on the **Make Selected Object Larger** SmartIcon to gradually increase the size of an object. If you want to make two objects the same size, highlight both objects and then click on the **Make Selected Objects the Same Size** SmartIcon. For example, we could use this SmartIcon to make the mouse ears the same size.

   When you've reduced the triangle, drag it onto the mouse's face and place it off center, as I've done in Figure 9.16.

Figure 9.16 *The mouse has a nose.*

Grouping Objects

Now that we have several objects on the page, it's probably a good idea to group the objects; otherwise, we may accidentally select objects that we don't want. *Grouping objects* means that all the objects are combined to make one large object. This makes handling numerous objects easier and quicker. If you didn't group the objects, for example, and decided to move them, you'd have to select each object in the drawing. Here's how to group objects.

Do It:

To group objects:

1. Select the eyes, ears, nose, and head of the mouse.
2. Click on the **Group Objects** SmartIcon. The multiple handles disappear and are replaced by eight handles that appear around the entire mouse head.

Freelance now recognizes the mouse head as one object instead of multiple objects. If you decide to ungroup the objects later, simply click on the object, open the Group menu and choose **Ungroup**. Go ahead and group the body and legs with the head. Now the mouse is one entire object. Let's add a mouth to the face.

Zooming In

Pages in Current Page view aren't displayed in full size; therefore, enlarging an entire page can be a big help when trying to get the details right. To work on a small section of the page, it helps to really zoom in to see what you're doing. We want to give our mouse a mouth. Let's zoom in.

Do It:

To zoom in on an object:

1. Click on the **Drag to Zoom in on an Area** SmartIcon.
2. Next, click on the mouse's face. The object is enlarged slightly.

To zoom in further, continue clicking the SmartIcon and then the mouse's face. Now let's get started drawing the mouth.

Drawing Curves

Curves are similar to arcs: they have different beginning and ending points. They can look like arcs, or they can be straight lines with little kinks in them. We're using the curve tool to create the mouse's mouth.

Do It:

We're still zoomed into the mouse, so here's how to create a curve:

1. Select the button that looks like a straight line with curved edges from the Tools palette.

2. Click on the mouse's face, just below the nose.

3. Move the pointer over about half an inch and then down about a quarter inch and click again.

4. Next, move the pointer over half an inch and up a quarter of an inch, and click the mouse button.

5. Click the mouse button again, after moving the pointer so that it's positioned half an inch over and down a quarter of an inch.

6. Finally, move the pointer about half an inch over and up a quarter of an inch. You can't see anything yet, but you really do have the makings for an excellent curved line.

7. Click on the pointer tool in the Tools palette. A curved line, similar to the one in Figure 9.17, appears on the mouse drawing.

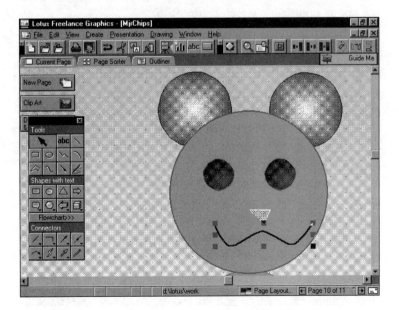

Figure 9.17 *A curved line.*

The curve I created looks uneven and needs to be adjusted. A good way to make adjustments to an item such as the curves we created is to use Points Mode. Follow along with me and I'll explain Points Mode and how to work in it.

Adjusting Objects in Points Mode

Objects are comprised of lots of tiny points that you normally can't see. When we created the curve, we created a point each time we clicked. Since we clicked five times, we have five points to work with. Using these five points, we can make changes to the curve but adjusting just those five points probably won't change the curves as we'd like. To make fine adjustments to an object, you can add, delete or move points by using Points Mode. You can change the shape of any object, except connectors, text shapes, and grouped objects.

Do It:

Here's how to use Points Mode:

1. Select the curve.

2. Choose **Points Mode** from the Edit menu. The curve changes to display the points on the curve (see Figure 9.18).

Figure 9.18 *The curve in Points Mode.*

These are the points that we created when we clicked during the Drawing Curves steps earlier. Notice that the pointer changes also to include a little circle. This indicates that you're in Points Mode. The points are clear squares right now, but when you select a point, it's filled.

3. Click and drag the right end point to shorten the line.

4. Shorten the left side of the curves by clicking and dragging the left end point.

5. Click and drag the center point upward toward the nose.

6. Choose **Points Mode** from the Edit menu again to turn exit Points Mode.

Creating curves using the curve tool, creates curves that are known as *Bézier curves.* Bézier curves are irregular curves because the shape is not perfect. A good example of a Bézier curve is a roller coaster. One side of the curve is a gradual slope but the other side of the curve is steep, indicating a Bézier curve. Freelance gives you these little handles, called *control points,* on the curve points so that you can adjust the angle of the curves. If you haven't noticed any control points, select one of the points on the curve and take a closer look. If you click and drag on a control point on the Bézier curve handles, you can adjust the slope of the curve. Go ahead and try it.

I've adjusted the curves as much as I can using the points that were already there. Let's add a point to adjust a different section of the curve.

Adding Points

Points Mode allows you to refine the shape of a curve, a line, or an object. But if you're using only the points that are on the object, you may have difficulty adjusting specific areas because there aren't any points to grab and drag. For example, I'd like to adjust the space between the second and third points, and between the third and fourth points on the curve, but it's difficult because there aren't any points in that section of the curve. In that case, Freelance allows you to add additional points to the object so that you can readjust the shape more easily.

Do It:

Here's how to add a point to an object:

1. Select **Points Mode** from the Edit menu.

2. Choose **Add Point** from the Edit Points cascade menu located under the Edit menu. Instead of a circle on the pointer, there is now an "x."

N O T E

You may find, when you're in Points Mode, that you need to remove a point because the resulting object isn't what you wanted, or you can't adjust the shape as you'd like. To remove a point you need to be in Points Mode. Open the Edit Points menu and choose **Delete Point**. In addition, you may find that you want to splice two portions of the object together that weren't originally joined. In that case, use the **Break at Points** selection in the Edit Points menu.

---

3. Click on the curve between the second and third points from the left. A new point appears on the curve now.

You can click and drag this point just like you can any other point, and this new point has control points that can help you adjust the slope of the curve. Go ahead and experiment with the points and adjust your curves at the same time. Next, we'll zoom back out and then add some whiskers.

Zooming Out

Zooming in is a helpful feature when you need to concentrate on small areas within the window. But it's a good idea to zoom back out sometimes so that you can see the overall picture.

Do It:

We've been zoomed in on our mouse's face long enough. Let's zoom back out to see how the entire picture looks. Here's how:

❖   Click on the **Show Whole Page** SmartIcon to view the entire page.

N O T E

You can also gradually zoom back out by opening the View menu and selecting **Zoom Out**.

Now we can see the entire mouse again. Let's add some whiskers.

Drawing Lines

You'll probably want to use lines when you're drawing objects with straight edges. Freelance isn't known for its drawing tools; however, they're certainly sufficient for drawing a building or a seating plan for the office. Let's draw something simple with the line tool now.

Do It:

To draw a straight line:

1. Click on the **line** icon in the Tools palette.
2. Click next to the mouse's nose on the right side and drag the pointer.
3. Release the left mouse button and a line appears.

Lines are probably one of the simplest objects to draw. Draw two more lines on the right side of the nose, and then draw three lines on the left side of the nose. Your mouse should appear similar to Figure 9.19.

Figure 9.19 *The mouse with whiskers.*

I admit it—I cheated a little bit. When you weren't looking, I drew the teeth using the polygon tool and then I drew a line down the center of the polygon. I also changed the priority of the polygon so that it was "sent back one." As you add new objects, you should continue grouping them too.

Drawing Squares and Rectangles

Squares and rectangles are one of the most basic drawing tools that you can use to create more complex objects. But squares and rectangles are also great for creating borders around text or other objects. Don't forget that you can use video and bitmap images in your Freelance file and an attractive, professional way to present these images is with a border around them.

Do It:

To draw a rectangle:

1. Click on the **rectangle** icon.
2. Click on the page and drag the pointer. A dashed rectangle appears so that you can see the dimensions of the object.
3. Release the left mouse button and the rectangle appears in solid lines.

To draw a square, hold down the **Shift** key while you drag the pointer in Step 2. And of course you can change the thickness, color and style of the lines for any object by selecting the Lines & Colors properties page in the Infobox. I've cheated a little more and completed the mouse using all the tools that I've shown you in this chapter. We have a cute cartoon. Let's add a shape with text and make it look like he's saying something.

Understanding Shapes with Text

Within the Drawing & Tools palette is a palette called *Shapes with Text*. This palette contains commonly used shapes such as circles, ellipses, rectangles, squares, triangles, cylinders, crosses, polygons, and arrows. You can use these shapes to create all kinds of drawings including office seating plans, floor plans, and more complicated objects. True, you could have drawn all these objects using the Tools palette, but what makes the objects in the Shapes with Text palette special is that they're already drawn and they have an area where you can add your own text. I'm going to show you how to work with this palette in detail in the next chapter, but, to complete our mouse, let's add a shape with text.

Adding a Shape with Text

You know those bubble shapes that cartoonists use in their drawings to indicate that the character is thinking or saying something? They're often referred to as *word balloons*, and Freelance has a variety that you can use. You can add word balloons to your own drawings, or you can add them to bitmap images and clip art. Since our mouse is done—or near completion—let's add a word balloon now.

Do It:

To add a word balloon to a page:

1. Open the **Drawing & Text** palette.
2. Click on the first button in the second line of the Shapes with Text section. A palette pops up with a variety of word balloons from which you can choose.
3. Click on the last word balloon in the top row. The pointer turns into a crosshair.
4. Click on the page and drag the pointer. A dotted rectangle appears indicating the dimensions of the object.
5. Release the left mouse button when the object is the size you want. A word balloon appears on the page, as shown in Figure 9.20.

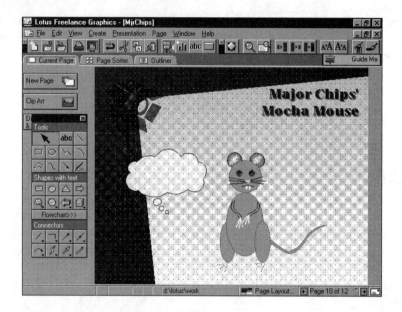

Figure 9.20 *A word balloon.*

6. Position the word balloon above the mouse's head by clicking and dragging.

Very good. Let's add some text to the word balloon and then we can call it quits.

Adding Text to a Shape

There is a difference between adding text to a shape and adding text to a Shape with Text. When you add text to a Shape with Text, the text becomes a part of the shape so when you move the shape the text moves too. When you add text to an object, you have to group the text and object before they can move together. In this section, we'll add text to a Shape with Text but I'll also tell you how you can add text to any object.

Do It:

Let's add text to the word balloon we just added to the page. Here's how:

1. Double-click on the word **balloon**. A text block, seen in Figure 9.21, appears.

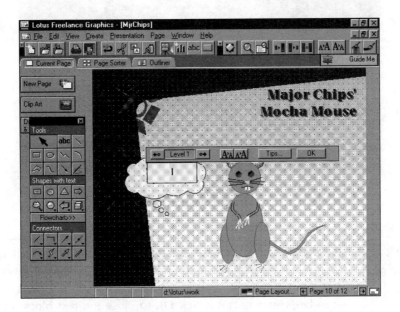

Figure 9.21 *A word balloon text box.*

2. Type **Mmmm, chocolate. My favorite food, after cheese of course!**

3. Click **OK** to close the text block. Just like all the other text blocks you've worked with, click anywhere outside the word balloon to deselect the text. Your word balloon looks similar to Figure 9.22 now.

Figure 9.22 *One terrific mouse, if I do say so myself.*

NOTE To add text to an object, draw the object first. When you're ready to add text, click on the **ABC** button in the Tools palette. Position the cursor on top of the object and click again. A text block pops up and you can begin typing text. Click **OK** to close the text block and the text appears on the object.

I turned the Display grid feature off so that you can see the final product better. Not bad, huh? Be sure to save Mocha Mouse because we'll use him in the next chapter.

There are a couple of tools in the Palette that I skipped over. But let me tell you a little about them now:

❖ **Arrows**. You can draw arrows to connect two objects together using the Arrow tool in the Tool Palette. Don't confuse them with Connectors though (we'll discuss Connectors in the next chapter).

❖ **Freehand**. The button with the pencil on it in the Tools Palette is the Freehand tool. This tool allows the mouse to function like an electronic pencil or pen. You can draw angles, squares, text, lines or curves. To temporarily stop drawing using the Freehand tool, press the **Backspace** key and position the crosshair at a new location. Creating an object using this tool can be difficult because it's not easy to control the movements of the pointer while drawing.

❖ **Polylines**. The polylines tools appears as a jagged line. This tool allows you to draw lines with angles. This is particularly useful when drawing an object that has straight and curved edges. Unlike the Polygon tool, Polylines creates open objects. If you want to fill an object created as a Polyline, then you need to convert to polygons first.

From Here...

You've learned how to work with the Tools palette to create your own drawings in this chapter. There are plenty of features on the Drawing & Text palette that we haven't discussed. In the next chapter, "Using Clip Art and Diagrams," I'll show you how to use many of the features that we skipped here.

I also have some good news: you don't need to create your own drawings and clip art. Freelance provides you with clip art images and diagrams that can be incorporated into the presentation. I'll show you how to access all these images and show you how you can create your own diagrams too. Let's move on.

CHAPTER 10

Using Clip Art and Diagrams

(Breaking up text is easy to do)

After finishing Chapter 9, you should have a good drawing that you can use repeatedly in this presentation or in any other presentation you design. But before you do that, you need to save it into the clip art library where it can be readily stored and accessed. Clip art is a fun way of adding humor and restating your message. It's a good idea to include some sort of art every couple of pages to keep the presentation interesting. Besides the clip art you create or import, Freelance comes with numerous pieces of clip art. There are cartoons, people, continents, symbols, computers, animals, arrows, buttons, tools and much more for you to use. In addition to clip art, Freelance also provides you with ready-made charts and diagrams. You can select from flow and Gantt charts; graphs; hub, triangle and network diagrams; and timelines, just to name a few. And, of course, you can create your own charts or diagrams and save them in the diagram library too.

In this chapter, I'll show you how to select and add clip art to a page, and add your own clip art to the library. I'll also show you how to choose a diagram and add your own text to it, edit colors, patterns or borders, and create your own diagrams which you can save and use later. Do you remember the Bullets & Clip Art page layout that we added to the presentation and titled *Researching the Market* in Chapter 4? We're finally going to add clip art to that page now. But before we add the clip art, you need to open the Researching the Market page or add another Bullets & Clip Art page layout to the presentation, whichever you prefer. In the next section I'll review how to add a Bullets and Clip Art page.

The Bullets & Clip Art page layout is divided almost in half so that you can add text to one side of the page and clip art to the other half. If you created the Major Chips presentation pages along with me throughout the book, then all you need to do is use the Page Number box on the Status bar to open the page titled Researching the Market. If you didn't, just add another Bullets & Clip Art page to the presentation. Either way, it's easy to add the page.

Whether you just added a page or went back to the Researching the Market page, I'm assuming that you have a Bullets & Clip Art page in the Freelance window. Let's add clip art to it now.

Adding Clip Art

Clicking on a **Click here to add clip art** prompt opens a dialog box that puts all the available clip art at your fingertips. You can peruse the clip art or go directly to a specific piece. After making your selection, the clip art is added and automatically sized to fit the page. The point of using clip art is to reinforce your message, so choose clip art with that idea in mind. The Researching the Market page discusses how Major Chips listened to customers and conducted research in the industry, so let's add some clip art to this page that ties in with the research theme.

Do It:

To add clip art to a Bullets & Clip Art page:

1. Click on the **Click here to add clip art** prompt. The Add Clip Art or Diagram to the Page dialog box, shown in Figure 10.1, appears.

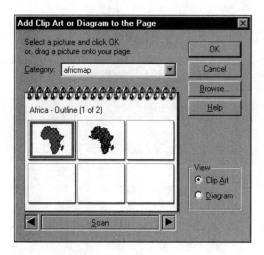

Figure 10.1 *The Add Clip Art or Diagram to the Page dialog box.*

N O T E

You can add clip art to any page in the presentation, too. Instead of following Step 1 above, click on the **Clip Art** button to the left of the presentation page in Current Page view. The Add Clip Art or Diagram to the Page dialog box shown in Figure 10.1 appears in the window. To select clip art, continue following the steps below.

❖ Normally, when you click on the **Click here to add clip art** prompt, the **Clip Art** radio button is selected in the View area of the dialog box. If you're not using a prompt to add Clip Art to the page, you may have to select this radio button to view Freelance's clip art selections.

2. Open the **Category** drop-down list to go directly to a clip art topic.

N O T E

You can view all the clip art in sequence by clicking the **Scan** button beneath the displayed pictures. After clicking the **Scan** button, it turns into the Stop Scan button. When you see clip art that you want to look at more closely, press the **Stop Scan** button and use the left and right arrows to move between pages.

3. Select **Cartoons**. The drop-down list box closes and a page of cartoon figures appears, as shown in Figure 10.2.

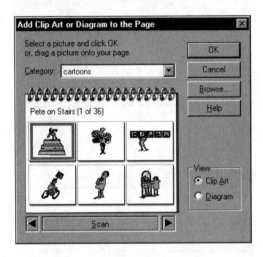

Figure 10.2 *Cartoon clip art.*

❖ "Pete on Stairs (1 of 36)" appears just above the first picture. Each picture has its own title. To see the title, click on the picture.

4. Click the right arrow four times until "Coworker 2 (19 of 36)" appears.

5. Click on **Pete Getting Comments (23 of 36)** (the middle picture in the bottom row).

6. Click **OK** to place the clip art on the page. Pete Getting Comments appears on the page, as shown in Figure 10.3.

Figure 10.3 *Pete Getting Comments on the page.*

The picture is automatically sized so that it doesn't interfere with the bulleted list. If you're adding clip art to a page layout that doesn't have a "Click here to add clip art" prompt, such as a bulleted list page, then you'll probably need to resize the clip art. To do this, select the clip art and drag a handle (they're located in the corners). Do you remember the Mocha Mouse that we created in the last chapter? Let's turn it into clip art now.

Adding to the Clip Art Library

You may find that you're using your company's logo a lot, or you've created a drawing that you want to use in future presentations. Instead of importing or recreating the piece of art every time, you can add it to the library. You can add logos, clip art, bitmaps, and text to the library. The *library* is Freelance's term for the area where the clip art or diagrams are stored within the program. There are two libraries: one for clip art and the other for diagrams—but you can add logos, bitmaps, and text to either library. When you add an image to the clip art library, you can access it just like I outlined in the previous section. I'll show you how to view the diagram library later. Let's add the mouse that we created in the previous chapter to the clip art library now.

Do It:

To add a drawing to the clip art library:

1. Select the mouse on the page titled *Major Chips' Mocha Mouse*. If you didn't save the mouse, then use a piece of text or some other graphic that you'd like to store in the library.

WARNING

Before adding the mouse to the clip art library, make sure all the pieces of the mouse are grouped together to form one object. If the entire mouse isn't grouped, then Freelance will save ungrouped objects as individual pieces of clip art.

2. Choose **Add to Library** from the Create menu.
3. Select **Clip art Library** from the cascading menu. The Add to Clip Art Library dialog box, shown in Figure 10.4, opens. Notice that the "flg" file folder is open in the Look in: text box. This is where Freelance stores clip art by default.

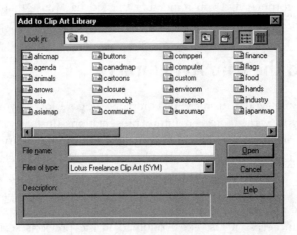

Figure 10.4 *The Add to Clip Art Library dialog box.*

4. Click on **custom**. Custom appears in the File name: text box now. This is where you'd probably save clip art that you created; however you can add clip art to any of the files listed in the window.

5. Click **Open** to add the mouse to the custom file. The Add to Clip Art Library dialog box closes and you're returned to the presentation page.

Click on the **Clip Art** button and choose **custom** from the Category drop-down list. The mouse appears on the page, as shown in Figure 10.5. Now we can use it any time we want.

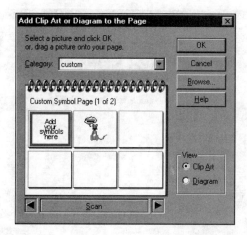

Figure 10.5 *The mouse in the custom category.*

Adding Text to Clip Art

You can add text to any object and this includes clip art. You may want to add a short joke to the clip art. Remember that *Researching the Market* page with Pete Getting Comments on it? Go back to it and we'll add text at the bottom of the picture.

Do It:

To add text to clip art:

1. Click on the **ABC** button in the Tools palette.

2. Click and drag on the page below the clip art. A text block appears when you release the left mouse button.

3. Type **Pete juggling too much information**.

4. Click **OK** to close the text block.

The text appears on the page but it needs to be formatted. Using the text properties page, change the font to **Arial** and make the point size smaller. Also, change the attributes to **Bold**. Your clip art should look similar to Figure 10.6.

Figure 10.6 *Clip art with text.*

Understanding Diagrams

Diagrams usually contain different shapes with text labels, and connectors to show the relationships between the shapes. Diagrams, like charts and tables, visually clarify your verbal message. Use diagrams to show processes. For example, a diagram works well to explain how a production line works, or what steps need to be taken in order to complete a project. Diagrams are also useful in explaining structures, such as a company's organization, or how the different departments within a company interact. Freelance has ready-made diagrams that you can incorporate into the presentation. You can choose from flowcharts, Gantt charts, timelines, hub charts, sections, and much more. In fact, you can probably find most typical business diagrams within the diagram library. And if you can't use any of the diagrams that you find, you can create your own using the Drawing & Text palette. Let's begin by adding a Diagram page layout to the presentation.

Adding a Diagram Page Layout

The next page layout that we're going to work with is called the Diagram page layout. As is the case with almost all the other page layouts, the Diagram page layout has two "Click here" prompts: one to add a title to the page and the other to create a diagram. Go ahead and add a Diagram page layout now.

This page isn't much different from any of the other pages that we've added to the presentation thus far. The "Click here" prompts work the same as they have all along so let's start by adding a Freelance diagram to the presentation.

Adding a Diagram

The purpose of the diagram that we add next is to show the audience how Major Chips handles orders. A flowchart would help display the information more clearly than words alone. Let's add one now.

Do It:

To add a Freelance diagram to the page:

1. Click on the **Click here to create diagram** prompt. The Add Diagram dialog box, shown in Figure 10.7, opens.

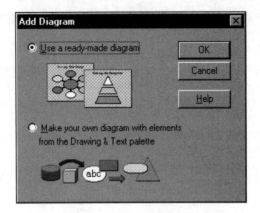

Figure 10.7 The Add Diagram dialog box.

2. Select the **Use a ready-made diagram** radio button, if it's not already selected.

3. Click **OK** to continue. The Add Clip Art or Diagram to the Page dialog box pops up. This is the same dialog box that you used when you added clip art earlier. The diagram radio button in the View area of the dialog box is now selected by default.

4. Select **Flow** from the Category drop-down list. Flowcharts appear in the window.

5. Click on **Process (3 of 26)**. That's the last flowchart in the top row.

6. Click **OK** to place the chart on the page, as shown in Figure 10.8.

SHORTCUT

A quicker way to move the diagram from the Add Clip Art or Diagram to the Page dialog box to the presentation page is to click on the icon and drag it onto the page. The results are the same: the flowchart appears on the page.

The flowchart is a little too large for the page. Let's decrease its size a bit.

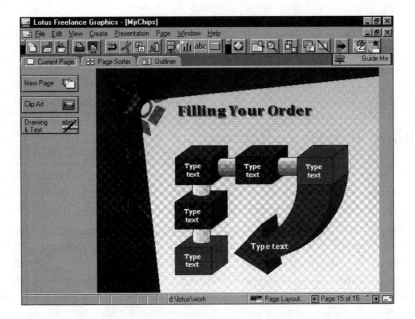

Figure 10.8 *The process diagram on the page.*

Changing the Size of a Diagram

A diagram or clip art can be increased or decreased in size so that it fits on the page and the audience can see the information being displayed. The diagram we added looks too large. Let's reduce it now.

Do It:

To change the size of a diagram:

1. Select the diagram. The handles appear around the diagram.

2. Position the pointer on top of a handle. The pointer turns into a double-ended arrow.

3. Click on the handle and drag it. Move the handle away from the center of the diagram to make it larger; move it closer to the diagram to make it smaller.

Now let's add text to the ready-made diagram.

Adding Text to a Diagram

Usually when you add a Freelance diagram to the page or create your own, you also want to add text to it. When a customer sends an order to Major Chips, it's routed to the Order Department. The Order Department determines what the customer is ordering and then forwards the product numbers and quantities to the Processing Plant. The Processing Plant adds the number of pounds needed to fill that order to the running total for the day. At the end of the day, the product numbers and quantities are sent to the Plant floor where the products are made. The completed products are shipped back to the Order Department, and the employees box and mail the orders back to the customer. Major Chips has the process so refined that it usually takes about three days for the order to be received and filled. Let's add this information to the flowchart we added to the page.

Do It:

With the diagram page in the window, here's how to add text:

1. Click on the diagram to select it.
2. Click on the **Type Text** prompt on the bottom block. A blinking insertion point appears on the block in a contrasting color.
3. Type **The Customer**.
4. Next, click on the **Type Text** prompt for the block immediately above the one we just added text to.
5. Type **Order Department**.
6. Click on the next block's **Type Text** prompt.
7. Type **Processing Plant** on the block.
8. Click on the **Text Type** prompt for the next block.
9. Type **Order Department**.

10. Finally, click on the **Text Type** prompt for the arrow. We're skipping the last block because we don't need it. I'll show you how to remove it later.

11. Type **Order Filled and Mailed**.

As you enter text into the Type Text prompts, it is automatically formatted to fit. You can reformat the text using the properties pages in the Infobox. Click anywhere off of the diagram to deselect it. The diagram now looks similar to Figure 10.9. Let's remove the unnecessary block now.

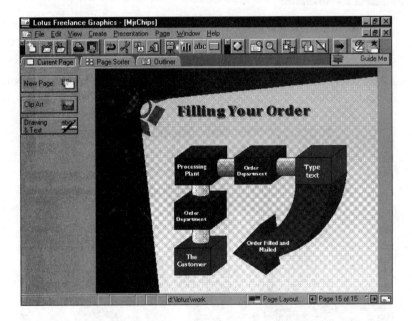

Figure 10.9 *The diagram with text added.*

Editing a Freelance Diagram

In Freelance, you can change and edit diagrams or clip art. You may want to change colors in a piece of clip art or alter the patterns in a chart. Sometimes a Freelance diagram will fit the bill perfectly, but there may be times that you'll have to edit it. The diagram that we selected and added text to has one extra block in it that we need to remove. Diagrams (and clip art) are comprised of multiple objects that are grouped together, just like our Mocha Mouse. When you select the diagram, you're selecting a grouped object. To edit a diagram, we need to ungroup it.

Do It:

To ungroup a diagram or clip art and edit it:

1. Select the diagram.
2. Choose **Ungroup** from the Group menu. The Ungroup dialog box pops up telling you that an object in a "Click here" block can't be ungrouped and that the page layout has to change from a Diagram to a Basic.
3. Click **OK** to continue. The diagram is ungrouped and appears as shown in Figure 10.10.

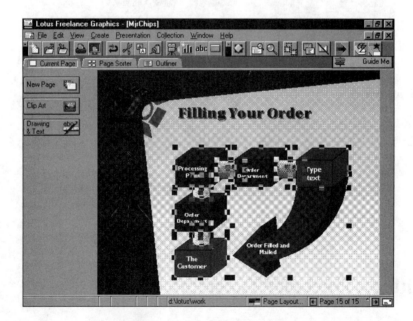

Figure 10.10 *The diagram ungrouped.*

4. Click anywhere on the page off the diagram to deselect all the objects.
5. Select the block and connector as I have in Figure 10.11.

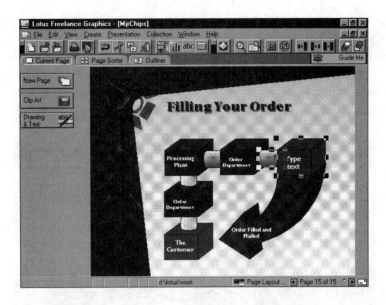

Figure 10.11 *The block and connector selected.*

6. Press the **Delete** key to remove the selected object. The diagram looks similar to Figure 10.12 now.

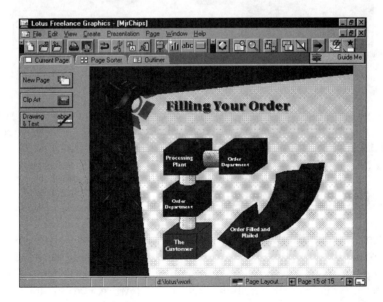

Figure 10.12 *The objects deleted.*

This looks silly now. We need to rearrange the blocks and then group them again. Use your knowledge of moving, sizing, aligning, and rotating objects to redesign the diagram, as I've done in Figure 10.13. You can also change the colors and patterns of an object when they're ungrouped by opening the Infobox and displaying the properties pages. Remember to group all the objects again when you've finished.

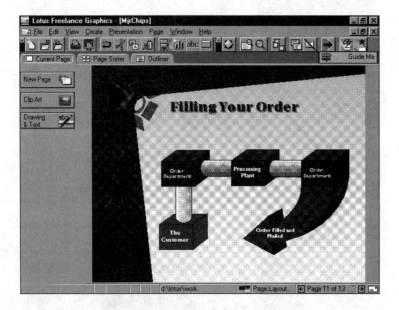

Figure 10.13 *The diagram rearranged.*

In some cases, it's easier to simply draw a diagram from scratch. And if you plan on using it often, it makes sense to save it in the diagram library. Follow along with me and I'll show you how to create your own diagrams.

Creating a Diagram from Scratch

While Freelance's diagrams come in handy, they may not always suit your needs. When that happens, Freelance provides you with the tools to make your own diagrams. Freelance provides you with numerous shapes that can be used to create any diagram. In addition, Freelance allows you to create flowcharts using common flowchart shapes. Let's draw a simple flowchart illustrating Major Chips' research. Researchers conducted over 1,000 surveys, incorporated this data into the development of the recipes, and then tested them. The recipes that passed the most taste tests made it to production.

Do It:

Let's begin creating our flowchart by adding another Diagram page layout. With the Diagram page layout in the window, here's how to create a flowchart of your own.

1. Click on the **Click here to create diagram** prompt. The Add Diagram dialog box pops up.

2. Select the **Make your own diagram with elements from the Drawing & Text palette** radio button.

3. Click **OK** to continue. The Drawing & Text palette appears in the Freelance window, as shown in Figure 10.14.

Figure 10.14 *The Drawing & Text palette appears.*

4. Click on **Flowchart>>>** to display the Flowchart palette, seen in Figure 10.15.

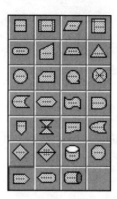

Figure 10.15 *The Flowchart palette.*

5. Click on the **Square** icon and drag the pointer to the page. The pointer turns into a hand.

6. Release the mouse button. The square appears on the page.

Continue clicking and dragging the icons on to the page as I've done in Figure 10.16. I've also aligned the objects using the Align feature that I showed you in Chapters 4 and 9.

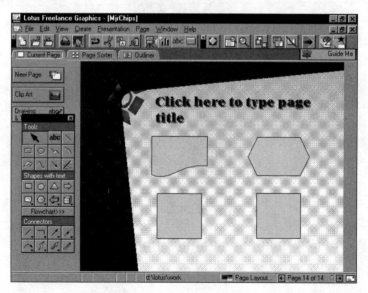

Figure 10.16 *Flowchart objects on the page.*

Adding Text to a Shape

Adding text to a shape is just as easy as adding text using a prompt. Also, the text automatically becomes a part of the shape when you add it. Move the shape, and the text moves too. Follow along with me and I'll show you how to add text to the flowchart.

Do It:

To add text to a shape:

1. Double-click on the first square in the bottom row. A text block appears.

2. Type **Conduct 1,000 surveys with consumers** in the text block.

3. Click **OK**. The text appears on the shape, formatted and centered (see Figure 10.17).

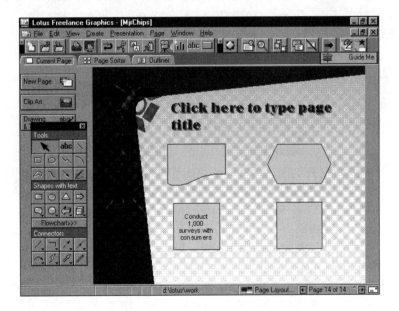

Figure 10.17 *Text on the shape.*

4. Next, double-click on the shape that looks like a torn page to open the text block.

5. Type **Design recipes based on consumer responses**.

6. Click **OK** to close the text block.

7. Double-click on the hexagon.

8. Type **Does recipe taste good?**

9. Select **OK** to close the text block.

10. Type **Send to manufacturing department** in the second square.

The diagram, as it is, doesn't mean anything. It's just a bunch of shapes with text on a page. To give it meaning, we need to add connectors.

Adding Connectors to a Diagram

Diagrams usually have connectors that indicate how the different shapes relate to one another. This relationship helps the audience understand how the diagram works, where to begin looking, and in which direction their attention should flow. Freelance allows you to add connectors to every object in the window. You can also connect text blocks, objects, tables, diagrams, charts, and clip art to each other.

Do It:

With the Drawing & Text palette open, here's how to add connectors between shapes:

1. Click on the **arrow** icon located in the first row, third column of the Connectors palette. A small palette containing various arrow styles appears.

2. Select the single arrow with no end points. It's the first arrow style in the top row.

3. Click and drag the crosshair pointer from the top of the square to the bottom of the shape that looks like a torn page. An arrow appears between the two shapes.

    Before you deselect the connector, notice the X at both ends. These indicate that it is connecting two handles. You can click and drag the ends of connectors to change the length. Notice that the end of the arrow doesn't touch the edge of the oddly shaped object. You'll probably encounter this often because the connectors connect object handles, not the object's edges. If you select the object that looks like a torn page, you can see that there is a space between the object lines and its handles.

4. Choose the single arrow with no end point style again from the Connectors palette.

5. Click and drag the pointer from the shape that looks like a torn page to the hexagon. An arrow appears between the two of these objects.

6. Click on the rounded arrow in the Connectors palette. A palette of rounded arrows appears.

7. Select the first rounded arrow in the first row (it's the one with the one arrow and no end points).

8. Click the pointer on the bottom edge of the hexagon and drag over to the object that looks like a torn page. A curved connector appears between these two shapes now.

9. Finally, select the single arrow with no end points again from the Connectors palette.

10. Drag the pointer from the bottom edge of the hexagon to the top edge of the square. Your diagram should appear similar to Figure 10.18.

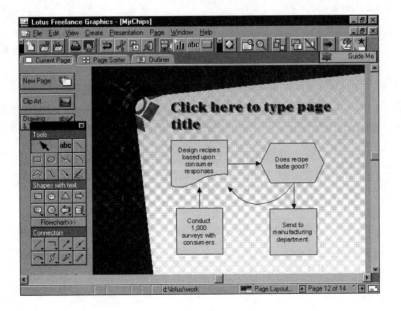

Figure 10.18 *A finished diagram.*

Using the technique I showed you earlier on how to add text to clip art, place a "Yes" beside the straight arrow pointing from the hexagon to the arrow; and place a "No" beside the curved arrow. All the objects are now connected to each other and, at a glance, the audience can tell how these shapes are related. If your connectors are coming out crooked and slanted, you probably need to align the objects. When you align the objects, their handles are aligned too. That means that when you draw a connector between two aligned handles, the connector should be straight.

Changing Connector Properties

You can also change the properties of connectors, which are a form of lines. Freelance lets you make the arrows thicker, and change the line styles and colors. Let's make the connectors in our diagram thicker.

Do It:

To change connectors:

1. Select all the connectors by holding down the **Shift** key while you click on each of them.
2. Choose the **Lines & Borders** tab in the Infobox.
3. Open the **Width** drop-down list.
4. Select a thicker line width from the list.
5. Close the Infobox. Your connectors should appear similar to Figure 10.19 now.

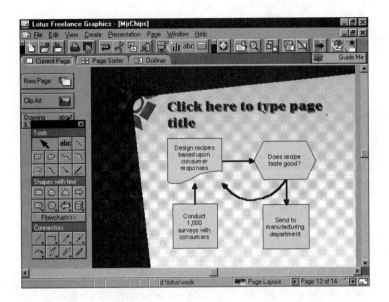

Figure 10.19 *The connectors are now more prominent.*

Group the items together, and in the next section we'll add the diagram to the diagram library.

Adding to the Diagram Library

You may find that the diagram you created for one presentation is going to be featured in all the company's presentations. Instead of importing or re-creating the diagram, you can add it to the library. Let's add the diagram we just created to the library now.

Do It:

To add a diagram to the library:

1. Select the grouped diagram.
2. Choose **Add to Library** from the Create menu.

3. Select **Diagram Library** from the cascading menu. The Add to Diagram Library dialog box, shown in Figure 10.20, opens.

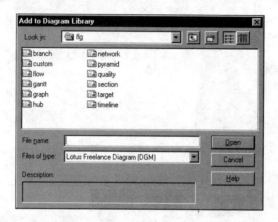

Figure 10.20 *The Add to Diagram Library dialog box.*

4. Enter **custom** in the File name: text box.

5. Click **Open** to add the diagram to the custom file. The Add to Diagram Library dialog box closes and you're returned to the presentation page.

Now you can use the diagram as often as you like.

From Here...

Together, we've added pages and text, created charts, tables, diagrams, objects and changed their properties. You've really learned a lot.

In the next chapter, we're going to switch gears a little and talk about color and palettes. We'll discuss color: what the human eye can see versus what you get on a monitor, primary colors; and a bit about cultural significance too. I'll show you how to change a color palette, edit your current palette and change to a black-and-white palette.

CHAPTER 11

Working with Color

(There's more to this than meets the eye)

Color—it's all around us. Our eyes are bathed in blues, reds, greens, whites, yellows, blacks and every conceivable color in between. Imagine the world in shades of white, gray and black—it would be a pretty drab looking place. Color adds interest to the world around us. But, what exactly is it? Why is the sky blue, my sweater red, and my car color described as "champagne"?

To explain color, we need to get a little technical here. First, the sun bombards the Earth with energy in the form of radiation, which is composed of waves. These waves have different frequencies (or lengths) of travel. Based upon wave frequencies, scientists have been able to identify the types of energy emitted by the sun. We know them as gamma rays, x-rays, microwaves, infrared, radio waves, and ultraviolet light. The last type of wave, and most importantly, the only one we can see with the naked eye, is light. Light is a very small portion of the waves emitted by the sun. This still doesn't explain why we see colors though.

Light is composed of several different wavelengths that we refer to as red, orange, yellow, green, blue, indigo and violet, commonly known as *Roy G. Biv*. When light hits an object, some of the wavelengths are absorbed by the object and some are reflected back. The waves that are reflected back compose the color that we see. My sweater is red, for example, because when light hits it, the sweater absorbs the orange, yellow, green, blue, indigo, and violet wavelengths. Red is the only wavelength that is reflected. Color is fluid, by nature. For example, there isn't a clearcut separation between the colors green and blue. In a true representation, the two colors would blend into one another—that's how you get such colors as turquoise and teal.

If you do a lot of design and layout work or if you'll be creating and modifying SmartMaster looks, then this chapter is for you. I'll show you how to work with color libraries and color palettes, create custom colors, and modify the colors that already exist. But before we start changing and creating colors, there are a few important concepts that you'll need to understand.

Understanding the Psychology of Color

Don't underestimate the power of color. Color has a definite impact on our moods. When designing your presentation, use a bright or unusual color to grab the audience's attention to an item. Don't use clashing colors or colors that blend. It hurts to look at green text on a hot pink background or black text on a gray background. Avoid using more than three main colors. That takes the focus away from the message. Avoid using the colors red and green together, such as red text on a green background, because some people are color blind and cannot differentiate between the two.

Color represents different things in different cultures. For example, brides in Western cultures usually wear white; the color white represents purity in this instance. But in many Asian countries, the bride wears red. This color represents fertility and celebration. Color also influences our moods. Yellows, oranges and reds (known as cool colors) tend to illicit feelings of excitement, intensity, passion, and cheerfulness. These colors are used in presentations to indicate warnings or competition. Blues and violets (known as warm colors) tend to make us feel secure, relaxed, and serene. These colors are good in presentations to indicate trust, balance and order. Green indicates growth and stimulation. Purple is often used for fantasy, magic, and mysticism. Gray, of course, is neutral; and brown signals security. Before you even begin changing colors in your presentation, know your audience! You don't want to accidentally insult foreign investors or use a color that makes your audience uncomfortable. Now that we know a little about how color affects us psychologically, let's discuss how it's reproduced.

Understanding Color Reproduction

Light can be categorized into additive and subtractive colors. Red, green and blue are called *additive colors* because when they are combined, they create white light. Yellow, cyan and magenta are called *subtractive colors* because an absence of light—known as black—is created when they are combined. To complicate things further, two additive colors make one subtractive color, and two subtractive colors make one additive color. For example, combining red and blue (two additives) makes magenta (a subtractive).

We can see millions of colors. Unfortunately, computer monitors, film, video and print can only reproduce smaller color ranges, or gamuts, than what we can see. And to add to this, film, monitors and print have slightly different gamuts. That means that when you create a color on the monitor, it may not look the same if you print it out or create film. You're using Freelance to create presentations on a computer. Computers, overheads and TV screens use additive colors. Photography and printing reproduce color using subtractive colors. What's the difference in the end as long as you're seeing color? Well, it's important to realize that the colors you create using print media aren't going to look exactly the same when they appear on film. So when you create a presentation on the computer with the intention of presenting it as a slide, be aware that the colors may not translate exactly as you planned.

Let's move on and learn about Freelance's color palettes and libraries, how to create your own colors, and how to convert CMYK (the subtractive colors) into RGB (the additive colors).

Opening Color Palettes

A *color library* consists of 256 colors. Freelance's SmartMaster designers took 64 colors from the color library and created a color palette for each SmartMaster look. Every SmartMaster look has a unique color palette that was designed specifically for it. This guarantees that the colors in each SmartMaster look good together. 48 of these colors are used throughout the presentation and the other 16 are alternative colors that you can add. The color palette establishes the look and tone of a presentation. Let's open the color palette for our SmartMaster look right now.

Do It:

With our Major Chips presentation open, here's how to access the SmartMaster look's color palette:

1. Open the Presentation menu, and choose **Edit Backdrop**. The Freelance window changes, as shown in Figure 11.1.

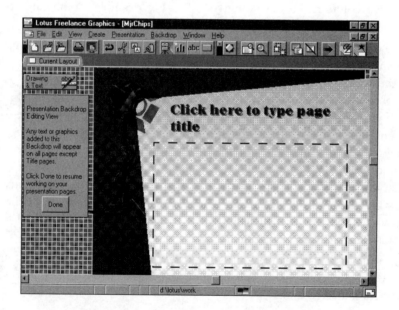

Figure 11.1 *The Presentation Backdrop Editing view.*

2. Next, select **Edit Palette** from the Presentation menu. The Edit Palette dialog box, in Figure 11.2, appears.

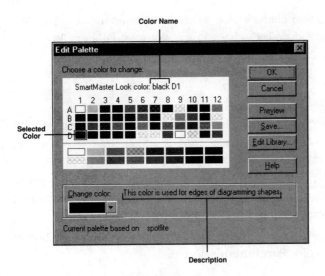

Figure 11.2 *The Edit Palette dialog box.*

The colors are laid out in a grid pattern. The colors in the columns labeled 1 through 12 and rows labeled A through D are the spotlite palette. The colors in the two rows below the palette are colors that match. Freelance designers recommend that you use one of these colors when making changes. Go ahead and click on the different colors in the color palette. The color you click appears in the Change color drop-down list and a description of where this color is used within the presentation appears.

The color that appears in Column 8, Row B is used as the background color in organization chart boxes, tables, and cell backgrounds. For example, in the table that we created on the Pricing page, this color is used in the cell background. It also appears in the organization chart we created. Let's change this background color globally so that everywhere in the presentation that this color appears will now be a new color.

Changing a Palette Color

The easiest way to make a color change throughout the presentation is to replace the color in the color palette. You can change the color of any detail in the presentation. The yellow color that appears in the background of the tables, cells and organization charts looks very light in comparison to the other yellows used in the presentation. Let's change the color to a darker yellow.

Do It:

With the Edit Palette dialog box still open, here's how to change a color throughout the presentation:

1. Click on the **Row B, Column 8** color in the color grid; that's the color we want to change. The Change color box and description changes to reflect your selection.

2. Open the Change color drop-down list box. The color library pops up with the color **Parchment** selected.

N O T E

You can move through the color library by clicking on a color and dragging the pointer. The names of the colors appear at the top of the library.

3. Double-click the color **light yellow** that appears immediately below the color Parchment. The color library closes and light yellow appears in the Change color box.

4. Click **OK** in the Edit Palette dialog box.

WARNING

Changing the color palette and then clicking on the **Save** button permanently changes the color palette for that SmartMaster look.

5. Click **Done** to exit the Presentation Backdrop Editing View. You're returned to the presentation.

You've just changed the color globally for this presentation. That's all there is to it, but what if you don't like the entire palette? Freelance allows you to change that too.

Switching Palettes

You could go into the color palette and change each color in the color grid, but there's an easier way. In addition to the color palettes assigned to each SmartMaster look, Freelance provides you with alternate color palettes. These alternate color palettes are unassigned so you can assign them to any SmartMaster you want. By changing the palette of a SmartMaster look, you can use the SmartMaster that you like so much, but you can also use a color scheme that you like better than the one assigned to it. Let's change the color palette of our presentation now.

Do It:

To change a color palette:

1. Select **Edit Backdrop** from the Presentation menu.
2. Choose **Switch Palette** from the Presentation menu. The Switch Palette dialog box, shown in Figure 11.3, appears.

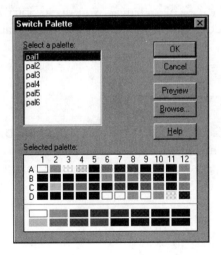

Figure 11.3 *The Switch Palette dialog box.*

The palette names that appear in the Select a palette list are the alternate palettes that are currently unassigned to any SmartMaster look.

3. Select **pal6** to choose that color palette.

N O T E

You can quickly view your changes by clicking on **Preview** and holding down the left mouse button. The SmartMaster appears with the color palette changes incorporated. Release the mouse button to return to the Switch Palette dialog box.

4. Click **OK** to choose the color palette.

5. Click **Done** to exit the Presentation Backdrop Editing View.

I definitely don't like this color palette. Let's get rid of it and restore the old color palette.

Restoring the Color Palette

Restoring the SmartMaster's original color palette is a handy technique to use when you realize that the color changes you made don't look so good. To do this, all you need to do is choose the SmartMaster look again. Let's do it now.

Do It:

To restore the color palette:

1. Open the Presentation menu and select **Choose a Different SmartMaster Look**. The Choose a Look for Your Presentation dialog box, shown in Figure 11.4, pops up. The SmartMaster you selected last appears in the dialog box.

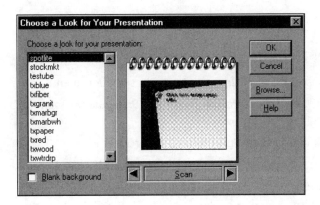

Figure 11.4 *The Choose a Look for Your Presentation dialog box.*

2. Select **spotlite** from the "Choose a look for your presentation" list box.

3. Click **OK** to change the SmartMaster look and restore the color palette. You're returned to the Freelance window.

The color palette is now restored. When you apply a SmartMaster look to the presentation, Freelance automatically uses the color palette associated with the new look. Changing colors in a palette is easy. You may decide that you don't like the extra palettes available to you. Or, after making changes to a palette, you may decide that you want to use this palette in other presentations too. In either case, you may want to create a new palette that you can make available to any other presentation.

Creating a Palette

Let's create our own palette that we'll use in a later chapter when we customize our own SmartMaster.

Do It:

To create a new palette:

1. Choose **Edit Backdrop** from the Presentation menu.

2. Next, select **Edit Palette** from the Presentation menu. The Edit Palette dialog box pops up.

3. Click on the color in Column 2, Row A.

4. Open the Change color drop-down list and select **Lemon**.

5. Click on the color in Column 3, Row A.

6. Select **Cherry Red** from the Change color drop-down list.

   Continue following these steps to change the colors in the color grid to the colors listed below.

Column 4, Row A	Raspberry
Column 12, Row A	15% Gray
Column 1, Row B	Cranberry
Column 8, Row B	Lemon
Column 9, Row B	Gold
Column 10, Row B	Gold
Column 12, Row B	Lemon

7. When you've completed changing colors, click the **Save** button. The Save As dialog box opens.

8. Type **Custom** in the File Name text box.

9. Select **Palette [PAL]** from the Save as type list box.

   ❖ The default location to save a color palette is in the flg folder already open. If you'd prefer to save the color palette in another location, locate the folder in the Save in list box.

10. Click **Save** to save the palette we just created. We're returned to the Edit Palette dialog box.

11. Click **OK** to exit the Edit Palette dialog box.

12. Click **Done** to return to the presentation window.

The palette that we just created has been incorporated into the presentation. Restore the original palette to the presentation by following the Restoring the Color Palette steps listed earlier. Let's discuss the color library next.

Opening the Color Library

Freelance stores a color library of 256 colors for every SmartMaster. Of the 256 colors in each library, approximately 64 are used to make a color palette. Each SmartMaster has its own color palette. The library has an area set aside where you can create and store up to 16 of your own colors. You can access these colors throughout the presentation. When you modify the RGB values of any color, remember that you're only changing the color within the SmartMaster look you are currently working in. I'll show you how to permanently change a color later. Let's access the color library for our presentation now.

Do It:

This color library contains all the colors available in the spotlite SmartMaster look that we're using for our presentation.

1. Select **Edit Backdrop** from the Presentation menu.

2. Open the Presentation menu again, and choose **Edit Palette**.

3. Click on **Edit Library**. The SmartMaster color library appears in the Edit Library dialog box, shown in Figure 11.5.

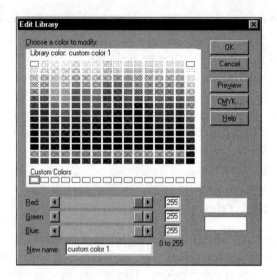

Figure 11.5 *The Edit Library dialog box.*

If you're a VGA user (your computer screen is 640 pixels wide, 480 lines high and 16 colors deep, which is usually the default), you may want to know which colors in the library are dithered and which aren't so that you know how they'll look when printed. *Dithering* is a technique of filling in the spaces between pixels to create a smooth finish and minimizing the differences between pixel colors. A gray scale, for example, where the colors smoothly transform from white to black without any obvious changes in color is an example of dithering. The colors in Freelance without dither are Red, Yellow, Olive, Neon green, Dark green, Turquoise, Aztec blue, Blue, Midnight, Hot pink, Plum red, Scarlet, White, 25% Gray, 50% Gray and Black.

If you want, you can modify any color within the library. In the next section, we'll alter the color scarlet.

Modifying a Color in the Library

Freelance strongly recommends that you don't modify the colors in a color library, but understands that you may have to in order to adjust a color for viewing or printing purposes. You'd probably want to adjust the colors in a color library if your printer isn't printing them the way you'd like them to or the color appears slightly too intense when creating a slide show. If you want to modify a color extensively, you're probably better off creating an entirely new color.

The color scarlet is used throughout the spotlite SmartMaster look. It's a dark color that will probably get darker when printed out. Let's lighten the color a little.

Do It:

Here's how to modify a color:

1. Select **scarlet** from the color library. Notice that color names appear at the top of the color grid. When you select the color, the Red values change at the bottom of the dialog box. The Green and Blue values will change too, depending upon the colors you select.

All colors that appear on your computer monitor are created using Red, Green and Blue. For example, when you select the color Azure, it's made up of 82 parts red, 145 parts green, and 239 parts blue.

N O T E

2. Click on the **Red left arrow** twice. The color in the box to the right changes.

3. Click **OK** to incorporate this change in the color library. The Edit Palette reappears.

If you are viewing the color in Black and White, you cannot modify the color library.

N O T E

The changes we made are hardly noticeable but rest assured, scarlet is now slightly lighter in appearance throughout the presentation. The color isn't permanently changed in the library either so if you create another presentation using the spotlite SmartMaster, scarlet will be the color that it was before we modified it. I'll show you later how to permanently change a color in a SmartMaster so that the SmartMaster always uses the new color.

Creating a Color

You may find that the color you need to include in a company logo doesn't exist on the color palette. Freelance allows you to create your own colors and save them in the color library for future use. Let me show you how to create a custom color now.

Do It:

We still have the Edit Palette in the Freelance window. To create a custom color:

1. Click on the **Edit Library** button.
2. Select the **Red** text box and type **53**.
3. Enter **0** in the text box for the color Green.
4. Select the **Blue** text box and type **48**. The settings in the Edit Library dialog box should appear. The resulting color appears in the box to the right.

To be able to use this color in any presentation that you create, you need to save it.

Saving a Custom Color

After going to the trouble of creating a custom color, naturally you want to save it so that you can use it whenever you want, in any presentation that you create.

Do It:

Our Edit Library dialog box is still in the window. To save the custom color we just created:

1. Type **Logo** in the New name text box.
2. Click **OK** to save the color and exit the Edit Library dialog box.
3. Click **OK** in the Edit Palette dialog box.
4. Click **Done** in the Edit Backdrop Presentation View message box. The Major Chips presentation appears in the window.

Display the Text properties page in the Infobox and then open the Text color drop-down list. At the very bottom, in the left corner, is the color we just added to the color library. But what if you have a specific color in mind but only know how to create it using Cyan, Magenta, Yellow and Black (subtractive colors)? If that's the case, Freelance can help translate the color from CMYK into RGB.

Changing Colors from CMYK to RGB

People who work with printers and designers often are probably more familiar with colors that are created using Cyan, Magenta, Yellow and Black. If you know how to create the color using the CMYK formula, you can easily convert it into RGB. Let's convert the CMYK formula into RGB.

Do It:

To convert from CMYK to RGB:

1. From the Presentation menu, select **Edit Backdrop**.
2. Select **Edit Palette** from the Presentation menu.
3. Click on **Edit Library** to open the dialog box.
4. Click on the second custom colors block. (The first one has the logo color that we just saved in it.)
5. Click the **CMYK** button. The CMYK to RGB dialog box pops up, as shown in Figure 11.6.

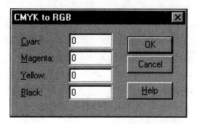

Figure 11.6 *The CMYK to RGB dialog box.*

6. Enter **100** in the Cyan text box; **75** in the Magenta text box; and **25** in the Yellow text box.

7. Click **OK** to convert the color from CMYK to RGB. You're returned to the Edit Library dialog box. The Red, Green and Blue settings have changed to reflect the color conversion. The resulting color appears in the Custom Colors section of the dialog box.

8. Enter **Invite** in the New name text box at the bottom of the Edit Library dialog box.

9. Click **OK** to exit the dialog box.

10. Click **OK** to exit the Edit Palette dialog box.

11. Click **Done** to return to the presentation.

You can access the color Invite by opening any color palette in the Infobox.

From Here...

You now know how to modify colors, create new colors, edit the color palette and library, restore colors and convert from subtractive to additive colors. You have the color basics with which to change the colors for the current SmartMaster or build your own. Next, we're going to give our presentation a final review using Page Sorter view. You'll learn how to switch from Current Page view to Page Sorter view, how to move pages around, and add speaker notes and audience notes.

CHAPTER 12

Polishing Up
Your Presentation

(You're almost ready to show off this masterpiece)

While creating this presentation, we've worked mostly in Current Page view. This allowed us to concentrate on designing one page at a time and to add our own graphics, tables, charts and text. I also showed you how to work in Outliner view. Outliner view allows you to concentrate on the text, and nothing else. Text is displayed in an outline format and you can add pages and text, move text around, and import text. I also mentioned that there is a third view, called Page Sorter. Page Sorter view allows you to concentrate on the overall presentation. The pages are displayed as thumbnails. You can move pages around, delete pages, import pages from other presentations, title pages and even add pages in Page Sorter view. This view mode allows you to work with the pages but not the text. It's a great way to polish up your work and get it ready for presentation.

In addition to working with Page Sorter view, you'll also learn how to create speaker notes and rehearse the presentation. You can add important facts, tips, and jokes to speaker notes, and refer to them throughout the presentation. Let's open Page Sorter view now.

Changing to Page Sorter View

Changing to Page Sorter view is a simple process that you can do at any point during the presentation. You may even find it helpful to view the presentation in Page Sorter periodically while you create it. Getting a different perspective is always helpful.

Do It:

With the Major Chips presentation open, here's how to change to Page Sorter view:

❖ Click on the **Page Sorter** tab. The Freelance window changes, as shown in Figure 12.1.

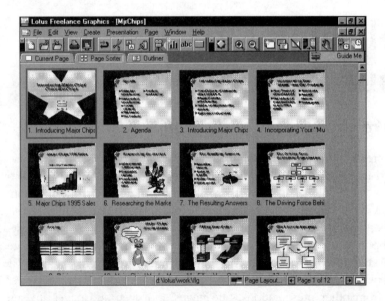

Figure 12.1 *The Page Sorter View mode.*

The presentation pages appear in the window. You can use the scroll bar to the right to move up and down in the window or you can decrease the size of the thumbnails so that you can see all the pages.

Decreasing the Thumbnail Size

You may want to decrease the size of the thumbnails if you have more pages in your presentation than can fit in the window. This is a helpful feature when you want to rearrange pages and see them in order.

Do It:

To decrease the size of the thumbnails in the window:

1. Click the **Zoom out** SmartIcon, it's the one with the magnifying glass and the minus (-) sign on it. The thumbnails decrease in size, as shown in Figure 12.2.

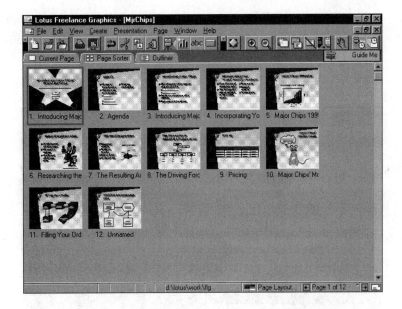

Figure 12.2 *The thumbnails decreased.*

Let's continue decreasing the size so that you see how small they can actually get.

2. Click on the **Zoom out** SmartIcon twice more. The thumbnails are reduced in size.

You can just make out the layout of the thumbnails when they're that small. Naturally, if you decrease the size of the thumbnails, eventually you may want to increase their size again.

Increasing the Thumbnail Size

In Page Sorter view, you can also increase the thumbnail size. While a decreased size can help in organizing page order, increasing the size can help you see the information contained on each page and the page layout. Let's increase the size now.

Do It:

To increase the thumbnail size:

1. Click on the **Zoom in** SmartIcon to increase the size of the thumbnails.

2. Continue clicking the **Zoom in** SmartIcon until your thumbnails look similar in size to Figure 12.3. This is the largest the thumbnails can get in Page Sorter.

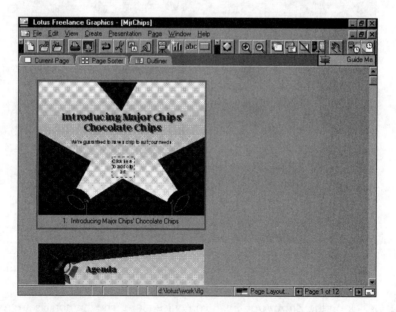

Figure 12.3 *The thumbnails at maximum size.*

3. Select **Zoom to full page** from the View menu to restore the size of the thumbnails.

That's all there is to decreasing and increasing the thumbnail sizes. While looking at the thumbnails, I've noticed that we should add a page at the end of the presentation.

Adding a Page

While looking at your presentation in Page Sorter view, you may decide that you need to add pages to continue the flow of the presentation. Page Sorter view allows you to add pages. You can't add text in Page Sorter view but adding a page to the presentation now allows you to save a place for it. When you add a page, it is automatically inserted after the currently selected page. Let's add a page to the end of the presentation now.

Do It:

To add a page in Page Sorter view:

1. Select the **Unnamed** page with the flowchart on it by clicking on the page thumbnail. A rectangle appears around the picture.

2. Click on the **Add a new page** SmartIcon. The New Page dialog box, shown in Figure 12.4, pops up.

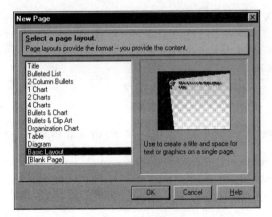

Figure 12.4 *The New Page dialog box.*

3. Select **Bulleted List** from the Select a page layout list box.

4. Click **OK**. A thumbnail of a bulleted list page appears in the Freelance window, as seen in Figure 12.5.

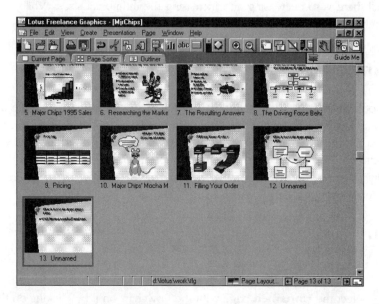

Figure 12.5 *The bulleted list page added.*

Since we've added the page, let's add text to it now.

Adding Text to a Page

Freelance doesn't allow you to work with text in Page Sorter view, so you have to return to Current Page or Outliner view.

Do It:

With the new page selected, here's how to enter text from Page Sorter view:

1. Double-click on the page. Freelance automatically returns you to Current Page view.

2. Title this page **Taking the Next Step**.

   Now is a good time to change the properties of this page before you add any more text. Position the insertion point at the first bullet. Open the Infobox and change the size of the text to **20**, and select **None** from the Bullets attributes style drop-down list. The bullets disappear and the text size is reduced. Continue adding text now.

3. Type **Product Launch: February 1996** and press **Enter** to start a new line.

4. Type **To place an order or request more information contact:** and then press **Enter**.

5. Using the text level arrows, select **Level 4**. This indents the text.

6. Type the following text in the text box:

   Catherine Castagna or
   Lauren Wolf
   Phone: (222) 555-1313
   Fax: (222) 555-1212
   E-mail: chocolate@majorchips.com
   999 Main St.
   Mytown, MM 99955-8833

Your page should look similar to mine in Figure 12.6.

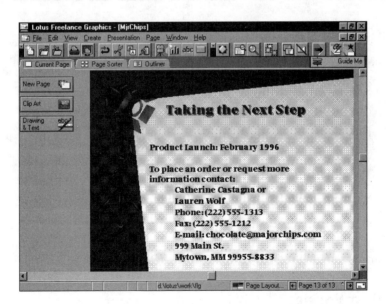

Figure 12.6 *The added page with text.*

7. Click the **Page Sorter** tab to return to Page Sorter view.

Hmmm, here's a good reason for using Page Sorter view—I just noticed that the flowchart page doesn't have a name. Let's take care of that now.

Naming a Page

Naming each page is Freelance's way of helping you identify each page within the presentation. Each page's name appears in the Go To Page dialog box, the List Pages dialog box, the Page Sorter view, and Outliner view. If you forget to add a title while creating the presentation, Freelance automatically names the page *Unnamed*. You have to open the page to title it. Looking through the presentation, it looks like we didn't add a title to the flowchart page and, therefore, *Unnamed* appears beneath the thumbnail. Let's name it now.

NOTE Page titles and page names are different. A page title appears at the top of each presentation page and helps your audience identify the topics that are addressed on that page. A page name helps you identify each page in the presentation. A page name is usually based upon a page title.

Do It:

To name a page:

1.   Select the flowchart page.
2.   Click on the right mouse button. The shortcut menu pops up.
3.   Choose **Page Properties** from the shortcut menu. The Infobox opens with the Page properties displayed.
4.   Type **Refining Our Recipes** in the Page Name text box.
5.   Close the **Infobox**. Our unnamed flowchart now has a name beneath it.

Remember, this doesn't add a title to the presentation page itself, it just names it. To add a title you need to open the page in Current Page or Outliner mode. Let's start rearranging the pages in the presentation.

Moving Pages

You'll probably need to move pages in the presentation as you polish it up. Next, I'll show you how to move a page.

Do It:

To move a page while in Page Sorter view:

1. Select the **Major Chips 1995 Sales** page.

2. Drag the page until it's on top of the "Incorporating Your 'Mu'" and a gray line appears to the left of the page. The gray line indicates the insertion point.

3. Release the left mouse button. The Major Chips 1995 Sales page now appears immediately after the Introducing Major Chips page. All the pages are automatically renumbered.

Continue moving the presentation pages around until they're all in the following order: *Introducing Major Chips' Chocolate Chips, Agenda, Introducing Major Chips, Major Chips' 1995 Sales, Researching the Market, The Resulting Answers, Incorporating Your "Musts" into Our Product, Refining Our Recipes, Pricing, The Driving Forces Behind the New Division, Major Chips' Mocha Mouse, Filling Your Order, Taking the Next Step.* Figure 12.7 shows all the presentation pages rearranged.

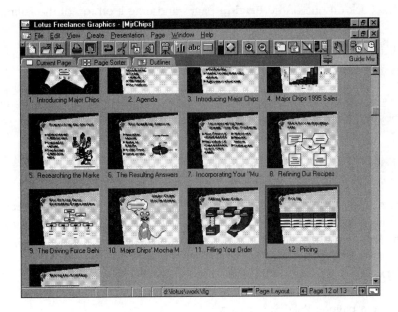

Figure 12.7 *The presentation pages rearranged.*

Duplicating a Page

Sometimes, you may want to have two copies of the same page in the presentation. You could simply recreate the entire page but a quicker and easier way of creating a second page is to duplicate it. The **Duplicate Pages** SmartIcon has been available to you in most of the other Freelance windows that you've been working in but you may get more use out of the feature here in Page Sorter view. Let's duplicate the *Pricing* page and place it after the *Filling Your Order* page.

Do It:

To duplicate a page:

1. Select the **Pricing** page.
2. Click the **Duplicate Pages** SmartIcon. The second Pricing page appears immediately after the first one.

    You see, duplicating is that easy. Now let's move the duplicate page to a position after the Filling Your Order page.
3. Click on one of the **Pricing** pages and drag it on top of the Filling Your Order page.
4. Release the left mouse button when the insertion point appears after the Filling Your Order page.

There's one page in this presentation that just doesn't seem to flow with the rest. It probably should be deleted from the presentation.

Deleting a Page

After reviewing the presentation pictures in Page Sorter view, you may decide that you don't need a page or it just doesn't fit with the rest of the presentation. The Mocha Mouse just doesn't fit the presentation any longer. Let's delete the page now.

Do It:

To delete a page in Page Sorter view:

1. Select the **Major Chips Mocha Mouse** page.

2. Click on the **Delete pages** SmartIcon. The Major Chips Mocha Mouse page is immediately removed from the presentation.

Removing a page is easy. By the way, have I reminded you to save your presentation lately?

Copying Pages from Other Presentations

As you build a collection of presentations, you'll probably find that some pages in one presentation can also be used in another. In Freelance, you can copy a page from one presentation and incorporate it in another. As an example, I'll copy a page from the Bountiful Buttons presentation that we created in the "Jumpstart" chapter and place it in our Major Chips presentation.

Do It:

With the Major Chips presentation open:

1. Select **Copy Pages from Other Files** from the Page menu. The Select Presentation dialog box pops up, as shown in Figure 12.8.

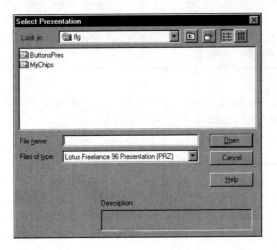

Figure 12.8 *The Select Presentation dialog box.*

2. Select **ButtonsPres** from the list.

3. Click **Open** to continue. The Copy Pages from Other Files dialog box appears, as shown in Figure 12.9, with the selected presentation in the window.

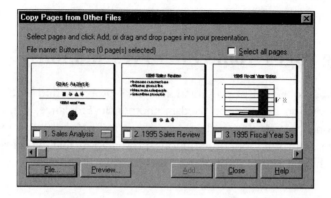

Figure 12.9 *The Copy Pages from Other Files dialog box.*

4. Click in the **1995 Sales Review** check box that appears at the bottom of the page in the left corner.

You can select all the pages of a presentation by clicking in the **Select all pages** check box. To review the contents of the entire page, press the **Preview** button.

5. Click on the **Add** button to add the page to the Major Chips presentation. The Add Pages dialog box appears.

6. Select the **At end of presentation** radio button and click **OK**.

7. Click **Close** to exit the Copy Page from Other Files dialog box.

The page we added appears at the end of the Major Chips presentation now. When you copy a page from another file, Freelance automatically updates the page SmartMaster so that it matches the rest of the pages, as shown in Figure 12.10.

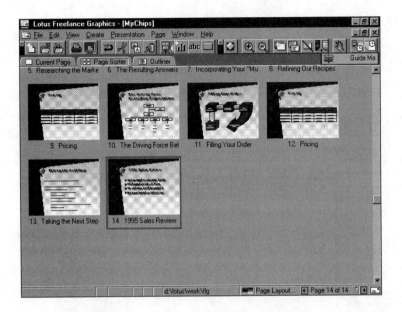

Figure 12.10 *The added page with the spotlite SmartMaster.*

Since that was for demonstration purposes only, you can delete the page.

Creating Speaker Notes

When planning a presentation, you need to learn the content, familiarize yourself with the pages, and try to anticipate any potential problems, among other things. How can you juggle all this information and be lively in front of a group of people at the same time? You can use speaker notes. Speaker notes help you keep track of information you want to pass along, the jokes you want to make, and the people or actions you want to mention during the presentation. You can even leave notes for co-workers who may use this presentation too. You can have speaker notes for every page or just a couple of pages. There is no limit to the amount of information you can add to a speaker note. Your audience can't see the speaker notes. You can only see them when you open the speaker note window or print them out in your presentation (more about that in the next chapter). Let's add a speaker note to the Introducing Major Chips page.

Do It:

To add a speaker note to a page:

1. Select the **Introducing Major Chips** page.
2. Click on the **Add or Edit Speaker Notes** SmartIcon. The Speaker Note - Introducing Major Chips window pops up, as shown in Figure 12.11.

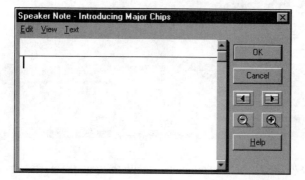

Figure 12.11 The Speaker Note - Introducing Major Chips window.

NOTE The left and right arrows allow you to navigate between pages. Clicking the right arrow opens a speaker note for the next page; clicking the left arrow opens a speaker note for the previous page. You can also zoom in or out of a speaker note by using the magnifying glass icons in the dialog box.

3. In the Index card window, type

    Stress that there are more than 23 years total experience running a quality business:

    Bob Refos - Potato Chip company owner for eight years.

    Ellen Nacey - Computer Chip company owner for 15 years.

    Major Chips profiles have appeared in national magazines as one of the top ten promising companies of the decade.

4. Click **OK** to exit the speaker note. A small index card icon appears next to the page title, as shown in Figure 12.12.

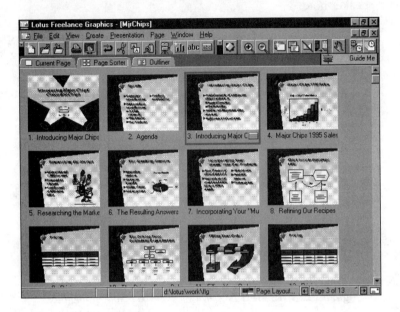

Figure 12.12 *Speaker note icon.*

Also, notice that the Add or Edit Speaker Notes SmartIcon has changed to include an ABC on it. This indicates that the highlighted page has a speaker note. You can add speaker notes at any point during the design process by clicking on the **Add or Edit Speaker Note** SmartIcon that you'll find in every view mode; you don't have to wait until you're cleaning up the presentation.

Editing a Speaker Note

In Freelance, you can edit the speaker notes for content and attributes. While reading these notes, you may find the font difficult to read, or that you missed a crucial piece of information. While you can add as much text to a speaker note as you want, Freelance limits the amount of speaker note text you can print (it's dependent upon the font and size). Let's change the attributes of the text in the speaker note we just created.

Do It:

To edit a speaker note:

1. With the Introducing Major Chips page still selected, click on the speaker note icon beside the page title. The Speaker Note—Introducing Major Chips window, pops up.

2. Select **Text Properties** in the Text menu. The Text Properties for Speaker Note dialog box, shown in Figure 12.13, appears.

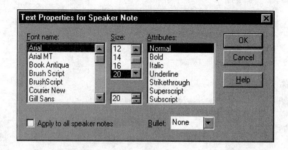

Figure 12.13 *The Text Properties for Speaker Note dialog box.*

3. Scroll down and choose **Times New Roman** from the Font name list.

4. Select **14** from the Size list box.

5. Click on **Apply to all speaker notes** so that you don't have to open each speaker note and change the attributes.

6. Click **OK** to close the Text Properties for Speaker Note dialog box and view the changes. The speaker note window reappears.

7. Click **OK** to exit the Speaker Note - Introducing Major Chips window.

Let me show you how to delete a speaker note next.

Deleting a Speaker Note

Freelance lets you delete speaker notes when you no longer need them, but remember that you cannot restore a deleted speaker note. So if you delete it and then decide you need it, you'll be stuck entering it all again.

Do It:

To delete a speaker note:

1. With the page selected, choose **Delete speaker note** from the Page menu. The Delete Speaker Note dialog box pops up, as shown in Figure 12.14.

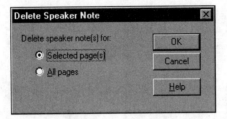

Figure 12.14 *The Delete Speaker Note dialog box.*

2. Click on the **Selected page(s)** radio button to delete the speaker note for only the selected page.

3. Click **OK**. A message box pops up warning you that you cannot undo this action.

4. Click **Continue** to delete the speaker note.

The speaker note icon disappears. Now that we've finished creating our presentation, it's time to rehearse.

Rehearsing a Presentation

Rehearsing a presentation gives you the opportunity to get comfortable talking about the subject matter, lets you time yourself, and allows you to practice so that you don't have any embarrassing moments while doing the actual presentation. Freelance has a special feature that allows you to work your way through a presentation and automatically records how much time you spend on each page and for the entire presentation. You can even add speaker notes while rehearsing.

Do It:

To rehearse the presentation:

1. Click on the **Begin rehearsing screen show** SmartIcon. It's the one with a film camera and stop watch. The title page appears, as shown in Figure 12.15.

Figure 12.15 Rehearsing.

There are two timers (one for the page and one to keep a running total of the entire presentation), a restart button so that you can restart the page timer, a pause button so that you can pause the timers when creating speaker notes, a speaker note button so that you can add a speaker note, left and right arrows so that you can move backward and forward between pages, and a Done button in case you want to exit the screen show before it's completed.

2. Click the **right arrow** to continue moving through the presentation.

3. When you have completed the presentation, a rehearse summary appears (see Figure 12.16). This tells you how long it took you to go through the entire presentation and displays the time you spent on each page.

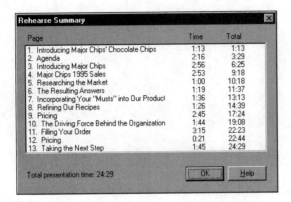

Figure 12.16 *The Rehearse Summary.*

4. Click **OK** to close the rehearse summary and return to Page Sorter.

If you want to refer back to the rehearse summary again, simply click on the **Display Screen Show Rehearsal Summary** SmartIcon. The next time you use the rehearse feature, a warning message box pops up asking if you want to clear the previous rehearsal information or save it. When you make your selection and click **OK**, the presentation appears on full screen again.

From Here...

Our presentation looks really good. We've designed it, polished it up and rehearsed it. Now we're ready to print. In the next chapter, I'll show you how to print speaker notes, outlines, audiences notes, and handouts. You'll also learn how to print borders around items and include such information as the date and time on the printed pages.

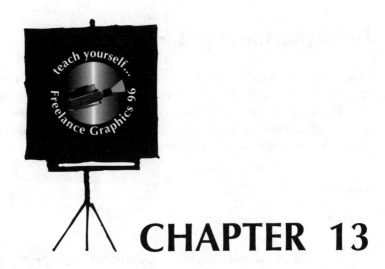

CHAPTER 13

Printing Your Presentation

(Seeing it on paper)

You've created the presentation and cleaned it up. Now it's time to print out the supporting documents you can refer to during your presentation and the materials you want to hand out to members of the audience. Freelance allows you to print the entire presentation as an outline, or print each page with its corresponding speaker notes. You can print multiple pages on a sheet or print pages with blank lines between so that someone else can take notes as you speak. And, you can also print the presentation with some fancy effects such as borders, headers and footers, vertically or horizontally, collate the pages, and even print without the SmartMaster look.

Before we begin to print the presentation, how do we know what the print area even looks like? Are all the items on each page within the print area? The best way to determine this is to use the Show page borders feature.

Displaying the Page Borders

Unless you have access to a printer that allows the printed area to extend to the edge of the paper, you have to deal with what's called an *unprintable zone*, an area around the page border where nothing will print (on most printers, about 3/4" on all sides). The Show page borders option helps you determine if the page items fit within the printable area throughout the presentation.

Do It:

To display the page borders:

1. While in Current Page view, choose **Set View Preferences** from the View menu.

2. Select **Set View Preferences**. The Set View Preferences dialog box shown in Figure 13.1 appears.

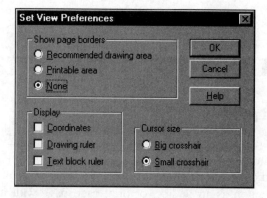

Figure 13.1 *The Set View Preferences dialog box.*

3. Click on the **Printable area** radio button to display the page borders.

4. Click **OK** to exit the dialog box. The presentation pages appear with a dashed rectangle around them as shown in Figure 13.2.

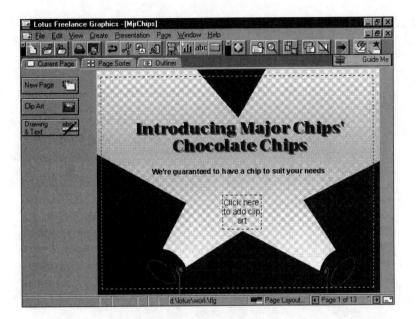

Figure 13.2 *The page borders displayed.*

Everything that appears within the dashed rectangle will be printed; anything outside the rectangle will not be printed. The size of the printable area is determined by the printer (or output device) that's currently selected. You may have to move text or images if they extend outside the print area. Also, if you didn't add a graphic, text or chart to a "Click here" prompt don't fret—"Click here" prompts don't print out. We've adjusted everything that we need to. Now all we have to do it click the print button, right? Well, yes and no—actually, the first thing we need to do is open the print dialog box.

Opening the Print Dialog Box

Whether you're printing a page or an entire presentation, you have to open the print dialog box first. This dialog box allows you to tell Freelance what printer to use, how many copies to make, what pages to print, and everything else that we'll be talking about for the rest of this chapter. Here's how to open it.

Do It:

To open the print dialog box:

❖ Click on the **Print** SmartIcon or choose **Print** from the File menu. The Print dialog box appears, as shown in Figure 13.3.

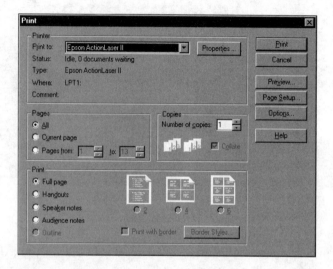

Figure 13.3 *The Print dialog box.*

Let's begin the process by selecting a printer.

Choosing a Printer

The list of printers in the Print dialog box depends upon what you told Windows that you were connected to when installing Windows 95 on the hard disk. Notice that in Figure 13.3, Epson ActionLaser II appears in the Print to area. This is my printer; naturally something else appears in your Print to area. If you're connected to more than one printer, then the last printer you selected appears in the Print to area. Let's select a printer now.

Do It:

To select a printer:

1. Open the **Print to** drop-down list. A list of available printers, including slide drivers, appears.
2. Select the output device you want the presentation to print to.

Don't select **Screen Show** from the Print to list. I'll show you how to make and work with screen shows in the next chapter. We're only concerned with hard copy right now.

NOTE

Until you change the printer selection again, the one you just selected remains the default printer. Next we need to tell Freelance what pages to print.

Selecting the Pages to Print

You may want to print out one particular page that has given you trouble in the design process, or you may decide that only pages 1 through 4 are of importance to you. Freelance gives you the option to print all the pages, some of the pages or just the current page. Let me show you how to make a different selection.

Do It:

To print only pages 3 through 8:

1. Click the **Pages from** radio button. The increment boxes to the right light up.
2. Use the increment buttons to select **3** in the first box and **8** in the second box.

Freelance will now print only pages 3, 4, 5, 6, 7, and 8. If you want to print only the page that appears in the Freelance window, click the **Current page** radio button. For now, click on **All** again since we want to print all our presentation pages—at least this time.

You can also print non-contiguous pages (pages that aren't next to each other—for example, pages 3, 6, and 8). Open Page Sorter view and hold down the **Shift** key while you select each page you want to print. Choose **Print** from the File menu. From the Print dialog box, select the **Pages selected in sorter** radio button in the Pages section. Then proceed by following the steps outlined below.

Selecting the Number of Copies and Collating

You can print one copy of the presentation or up to 99 copies. And, to make things easier for you, Freelance allows you to *collate* the copies as they are printed. Normally when you print, the printer prints the number of copies of each page and then you have to manually put them in order. For example, when you print out four copies of a document, the printer usually prints out four copies of the first page, four copies of the second page and so on. But when you select the collate option, Freelance prints out the first, second, and third pages of the first copy of the document, then it will print the second copy of the document and so on. No more standing at a counter and collating pages by hand! We need to print twelve copies of the presentation for a meeting. Now let's choose the number of copies to print and tell Freelance to collate them.

Do It:

To select the number of copies to print and collate them:

1. In the Print dialog box, use the increment arrows to select **12** in the Number of copies box.

2. Select the **Collate** check box, if it's not already selected, so that the pages are collated as they print.

That's it. Freelance is set to print 12 collated copies of the presentation.

Selecting the Presentation Print Appearance

When printing copies for a meeting, it may be useful to print one presentation page per sheet so meeting attendees can see the presentation as it really appears. In Freelance, you can print the presentation using several layouts. You can print one presentation page per sheet of paper or you can conserve paper and print several presentation pages per sheet. To help you present, and your audience remember the information, you can print the presentation with speaker notes included. Or you can print the presentation with audience notes so your audience can take notes while you present. You can even print the presentation as an outline to help you and your colleagues edit the information contained within the presentation.

Printing One Page Per Sheet

We've chosen a printer, the presentation pages that we want to print and the number of copies. We need to select how the pages should appear when they're printed.

Do It:

To print one presentation page on one sheet of paper:

❖   Click on the **Full page** radio button in the Print section.

When the presentation prints, each page appears on a separate piece of paper.

Printing Handouts

Printing handouts still allows you to display the presentation pages, but now you can fit several presentation pages on one sheet of paper. That saves on the paper and time needed to print it. Let's create handouts with six presentation pages on each sheet now.

Do It:

To create handouts:

1.   Click on **Handouts** in the Print area of the Print dialog box. Thumbnails of the page layouts are now available for selection.

2.   Click on the **6** radio button. Freelance will print 6 presentation pages to a page, as shown in Figure 13.4.

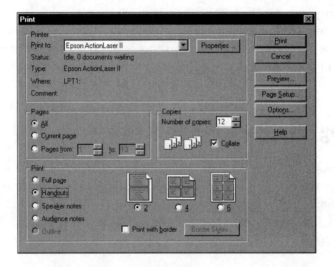

Figure 13.4 *Handouts with six pages to a page.*

To print four presentation pages to a page, you need to change the orientation of the page. I'll show you how to change the orientation from horizontal to vertical later.

N O T E

Now we're set to print twelve copies of the presentation with six presentation pages per sheet. You know what would really be helpful? If you could print the presentation with speaker notes. That way your presentation message will be remembered long after everyone's left the meeting.

Printing with Speaker Notes

Presentation pages don't include everything that you plan on saying during the presentation. Speaker notes help you add supplementary information; only you can see these notes. But if you want everyone to see them, you can print your presentation with speaker notes. Printing with speaker notes allows you to expand upon the points that you've made in the presentation, and individuals who were unable to attend your presentation or lecture will be better able to follow the subject matter. Let's print the presentation with speaker notes with three pages to a sheet.

Do It:

To print the presentation with speaker notes:

1. Click on **Speaker notes**. The thumbnails to the right are lighted up.
2. Select **3** from the speaker note layouts. This lays the presentation out with three pages per sheet and the speaker notes to the right.

If there is more text in a speaker note than can fit on a page, Freelance gives you three scaling options. Freelance can scale down all the speaker notes uniformly to fit the pages; scale down only the oversized speaker notes; or not scale any of the speaker notes. Scaling none of the speaker notes means that some of the text in a speaker note may not print.

Printing Audience Notes

Audience notes are similar to speaker notes or handouts in that smaller versions of the page are printed. You can also select the number of presentation pages you want to appear on a sheet. Unlike speaker notes, when you print audience notes there are blank lines underneath or beside the presentation pages. These lines give the audience the opportunity to add their own notes to the handouts during the presentation. Let's change our setting to Audience Notes and print one presentation page per sheet now.

Do It:

To select audience notes from the Print section of the dialog box:

1. Select the **Audience notes** radio button.
2. Click on **2** to print two presentation pages with audience notes per sheet.

The audience notes are ready to be printed. For editing purposes, it's helpful to print a presentation in the form of an outline. Let me show you how.

Printing an Outline of the Presentation

To check the information flow of a presentation for errors and gaps, it's helpful to print a presentation in outline form.

Do It:

To print an outline of the presentation text:

1. While in Outliner view, open the File menu and select **Print**.
2. Choose **Outline** from the Print section of the dialog box.

When you print in this form, the thumbnails you see in Outliner view are not printed. In addition, the outline may or may not print in the font that you have selected. Don't panic if your text doesn't look right; Freelance prints outlines using a default font. You can't change this default font—the font is built into the program so that you can quickly print an outline. When you print your actual presentation, the fonts you select will print instead.

To continue with our example and print the presentation as handouts, go back and select the handout radio button and just one copy.

Previewing the Presentation

Okay, we've selected the printer, the pages, the quantity, and the print layout. What else is there left to do? Preview it of course—just to make sure the it looks okay.

Do It:

To preview the presentation before printing it:

1. Click on the **Preview** button. The Print Preview dialog box pops up, as shown in Figure 13.5.

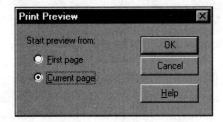

Figure 13.5 *The Print Preview dialog box.*

2. Select **First page** to preview the presentation beginning with the first page.

3. Click **OK** to proceed. The first page of the presentation appears.

4. Click the **Next** button to preview the next page in the presentation's sequence. To move back a page, click **Previous**. You can print a page from Preview by selecting **Print**. To exit Preview, choose **Quit**.

If everything looks okay, the next step is to print it.

Printing the Presentation

Now we're finally ready to print. We've selected the printer, the pages, the print layout and previewed it. We need to make one more selection.

Do It:

To print the presentation:

❖ Click on the **Print** button (but don't forget that we told Freelance to print 12 copies). The Print Status message box pops up, as shown in Figure 13.6.

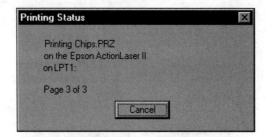

Figure 13.6 *The Print Status message box.*

The output device selected prints the presentation with six pages to a sheet, as you specified. You may not be able to read some of the details because the pages have been scaled down so much. Let me show you some options that you can use when printing the presentation.

Understanding Print Options

Freelance gives you several print options. These options may help your printer print faster or simply make the printed pages look nicer. You can print borders around pages in handouts, speaker notes and audience notes, print the pages vertically or horizontally, print without SmartMaster looks, and change some of the printer settings. I'll show you how to do all these things and more.

Printing Page Borders

As a decorative feature, you can print your presentation pages with a border around the page. Freelance has several border styles from which to choose. The border style is applied to the entire page, not each presentation page on the sheet.

Do It:

After selecting the print layout, here's what you need to do to print the sheets with a border around each page:

1. Click in the **Print with border** check box. The Border Styles button is lit.

2. Click on the **Border Styles** button. The Border Styles dialog box shown in Figure 13.7 appears.

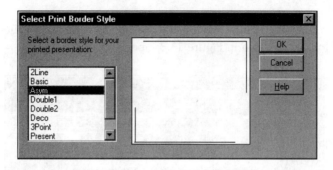

Figure 13.7 *The Border Styles dialog box.*

3. Select **3Point** from the Select a border style list box.
4. Click **OK** to return to the Print dialog box.

When you click the **Print** button, a border appears around the entire image. If you change the page orientation, the border readjusts to fit the image again.

Changing the Page Orientation

Changing the page orientation determines if the page prints horizontally or vertically. Most of the SmartMasters are designed to look best when printed horizontally. But there are a few SmartMasters that are designed to print vertically.

*   ❖ architec
*   ❖ custom2
*   ❖ flags
*   ❖ medical2
*   ❖ verbar

The SmartMaster we've been using is really a horizontally oriented design. When printing it as one page per sheet, you may want to view horizontally. To do this, you need to change the page orientation.

Do It:

To change the page orientation:

1. From the Print dialog box, click the **Page Setup** button. The Page Setup dialog box, shown in Figure 13.8, opens.

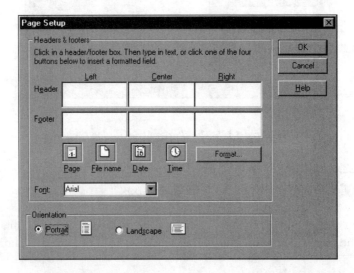

Figure 13.8 *The Page Setup dialog box.*

2. Click on the **Landscape** radio button to change to a horizontal orientation.
3. Click **OK** to return to the Print dialog box.

When you print now, the presentation page appears on the page in a horizontal orientation. Since we're working with the Page Setup dialog box, return to it now and I'll show you how to create headers and footers for the print out.

Creating Headers and Footers

You can add page numbers, the file name, the date, the time that you printed the presentation and even your own information to the top or bottom of the page in the form of headers and footers. Let's create a header and footer displaying the file name, page number and audience information.

Do It:

With the Page Setup dialog box open, here's how to create a header and footer:

1. Click in the **Header Left** text box.

2. Click the **File name** button to add the file name to the text box. [File] appears.

3. Click in the **Header Right** text box.

4. Click the **Page** button. [Page] appears in the text box.

5. Click in the **Footer Center** text box.

6. Type **Potential chocolate industry buyers**.

   ❖ Optionally, you can format the date and time by clicking the **Format** button. You can also change the font by opening the font drop-down list, where you can choose from the same selection of fonts available to you in the presentation text properties page.

7. Click **OK** to exit the Page Setup dialog box and return to the Print dialog box.

Check out your presentation now using the **Preview** button. The presentation will print with two headers and a footer.

Printing Graduated Fills as Solids

Getting a quick printout of the presentation can be more time consuming than you expect if your printer doesn't have enough memory or you have a lot of complicated images in the presentation. Graduated fills are complicated images that can really slow the printer down. If it doesn't make a difference whether the image prints as a fill or as a solid, you may want to consider printing it as a solid. Printers can usually print solids faster.

Do It:

To print a graduated fill as a solid:

1. From the Print dialog box, click **Options**. The Options dialog box pops up, as shown in Figure 13.9.

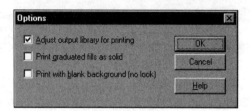

Figure 13.9 *The Options dialog box.*

2. Select the **Print graduated fills as solid** check box.

If you want to print the images as fills again, click on the **Print graduated fills as solid** check box again to deselect it. While we're in this dialog box, let me show you how to really streamline the printing process.

Printing Without the SmartMaster Background

If you really don't want to be slowed down by the printer and all that matters is the text, printing the presentation without the background SmartMaster look may be an option for you.

Do It:

To print without the SmartMaster look background:

1. Click in the **Print with blank background (no look)** check box.
2. To exit the Options dialog box, click **OK**. The Print dialog box reappears.

Now when you print the presentation, you'll only see the text.

Adjusting the Output Library for Printing

Within the Options dialog box, the Adjust output library for printing check box is selected by default. This option allows Freelance to automatically adjust the colors to ensure that the printed copies of the presentation closely match the colors that appear on the screen. You may want to clear this option check box when you like the way the presentation prints when it's not selected, when you're printing to a printer or output device that has its own color optimization scheme, or when you're using custom colors.

Do It:

To clear the Adjust output library for printing check box:

1. With the Print dialog box open, click **Options**.
2. Click on the **Adjust output library for printing** check box. The X in the check box is removed.
3. Click **OK** to return to the Print dialog box.

Now you can adjust the colors yourself.

From Here...

Now you know how to create quality copies that you can hand out to coworkers and your audience. In the next chapter I'll show you how to create a screen show. I'll also show you how to add some visual effects to the presentation pages, objects and text to help make any presentation more interesting. In addition, I'll show you how to add movies and sound to the presentation.

CHAPTER 14

Creating a Screen Show

(Making your own movies)

Screen shows give your presentation a multimedia look that'll make your audience think you spent months working on it. Multimedia is an increasingly popular way of communicating that incorporates sound, video, pictures, drawings and text. Using the screen show features in Freelance, you can create transitions between pages, create a bullet build, have each bulleted item "fly" onto the page, sequence items to appear in a specific order on the page, and add sounds and video to the presentation. When you apply these multimedia effects to the presentation, the result is something similar to an animated movie. Incorporating visual effects like these helps make a presentation more exciting and interesting. Your audience will be mesmerized!

Displaying Screen Show Properties for the Page

By default, everything on a presentation page (all of the text and graphics) is displayed when you open the page. By changing this default, you can create some cool page effects. For example, you can have the page appear on the screen first and then have each bulleted item move onto the page. You can even time the bullet build so that a new bullet appears every 30 or 60 seconds. In addition, you can have audio effects play when an object is clicked on, or a short video can pop up and run. You're limited only by your imagination and your computer's memory capacity.

Every Infobox contains a Screen Show properties page for each page, as well as for each text and graphic on the page. You control screen show effects by making selections in the Screen Show areas.

Do It:

To begin creating our screen show, display the title page of the Major Chips presentation if you haven't done so already. To display the Screen Show properties page:

1. Click on the **Open Infobox** SmartIcon. The Infobox opens with the page properties displayed.

2. Click on the **Screen Show** tab. The screen show properties page appears, as shown in Figure 14.1.

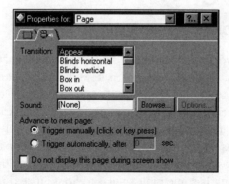

Figure 14.1 *The screen show properties for the page.*

From this properties page, you can select the type of transition you want to have appear between this page and the next, add sounds, determine how to advance to the next page, and even prevent this page from being displayed during the presentation. Let's select a transition next.

Choosing a Page Transition

A *transition* is the effect used to guide you from one page to the next. In the movies, a transition could be a fade out/in, a dissolve, or a wipe. Freelance allows you to create transitions such as these, but you can also choose to have the page "push" across the screen, or have a set of curtains move over the page and then pull back to display a new page, or you can have the page wipe off the screen—there are plenty of selections to choose from. There's a way to set the transitions globally so you don't have to do them for each page. I'll show you how to do this later. But choosing a page transition using the Infobox comes in handy when you want to have different transitions between pages. For example between the first and second pages we can set up a "Wipe right" transition, and then between the second and third pages we can have a "Diagonal right down" transition.

Since we're premiering a new Major Chips product and we're using the spotlite SmartMaster that gives the presentation a movie tone, let's continue with this movie theme. If you select the Curtain transition, the transition appears as a heavy red velvet curtain that closes and then opens (just like in the old movie theaters). Let's select that transition for our presentation.

Do It:

To select a transition:

❖   Using the scroll bar, select **Curtains** from the Transition list.

That's all there is to it. When the presentation moves between the title page and the next page in a screen show, the Curtains transition is used to close the current page and open the new one. You can also have a sound attached to the page, so that when the page opens the sound automatically plays.

Adding a Sound to the Page

Sound files can consist of anything you can think of—for example, you can have a sound file of someone typing, a car driving by, music, or even a burp! Freelance comes with several sound files to get you started—there's a lion's roar, a phone ringing, cheering and applause sounds, and more. As you get into this sound stuff, you'll want to add to your collection—you can find tons of sound files, usually saved as Midi or Wav files, on online services, special effects CD-ROMs or as shareware. We're adding a cheering sound to the entire page, but you can use the same process to add a sound to a bulleted list or an object.

Do It:

To have a sound effect play when the presentation page appears in the screen show:

1. Click the **Browse** button that appears to the right of the Sound text box. The Attaching sounds to: Page dialog box pops up, as shown in Figure 14.2.

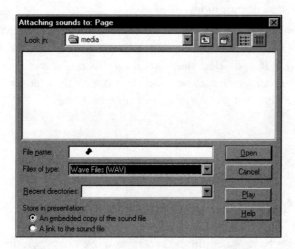

Figure 14.2 *The Attaching sounds to: Page dialog box.*

2. Locate and select **cheering.wav** file on your hard disk. It should be located within a file called Media that you installed when you installed Freelance.

N O T E

Notice the Store in presentation section of the dialog box. From this section you can choose how to attach the sound to the presentation. When you attach a sound, it can be either embedded or linked. If you embed it, the sound file itself becomes a part of your presentation file and, therefore, increases the overall size of the file. Linking the sound and presentation files keeps the size of the file down, but to play that sound, you must always have the sound file available for Freelance to reference it. For example, if you copy your presentation onto a disk, you need to also copy the sound file too, if they are to work together properly. The default is set to embed the sound unless you change it.

3. Select **Open**. The Attaching sound to Page dialog box closes and cheering.wav appears in the Sound text box.

   Notice that the Options button, which was dimmed earlier, is now available. We need to tell Freelance how and when we want the added sound to play.

4. Click the **Options** button to open the Options dialog box shown in Figure 14.3.

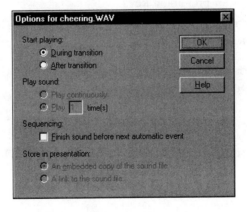

Figure 14.3 *The Options dialog box.*

5. Select the **After transition** radio button from the Start playing section of the dialog box. This tells Freelance not to play the sound until the transition is complete.

6. Enter **3** in the Play 1 time(s) radio button to have the sound file play three times. You can have it repeat up to 99 times, although you'd probably drive your audience crazy if you did.

7. Click on **Finish sound before next automatic event**.

8. Click **OK** to return to the screen show properties page.

When this page appears in the screen show, the sound will be played three times after the transition is complete and before any other items appear on the page. Next, we need to tell Freelance how we want to move to the next page.

Advancing to the Next Page

In a typical presentation, you have to click a button to advance a page. For a screen show, you can have the page advance automatically after a specified time period or you can click to advance. Automatically forwarding to the next page is a nice feature, but be careful. You may underestimate the length of time it takes you to complete a page and then you'll have to play catch-up with the rest of the presentation. Unless you're really confident with the timing (or are using the screen show as a stand-alone presentation), I recommend that you advance to the next page by clicking or pressing a key.

You can move through a screen show using the mouse, or by pressing the **Enter** or **Page Down** key.

❖ To move forward a page, click the left mouse button, press **Enter**, or press the **Page Down** key.

❖ To go back a page, click the right mouse button or press the **Backspace** key.

❖ To restart a paused page that is showing automatically, press the **Spacebar**.

❖ To exit or stop a screen show, press the **Esc** key or click on **Quit Screen Show**.

Do It:

To tell Freelance you want to advance the page manually:

❖ Click **Trigger manually** (click or press key).

If you want to automatically advance, choose **Trigger automatically** and then enter the number of seconds you want to display the page before moving to the next one.

N O T E

If a page isn't appropriate for a particular audience but you don't want to remove it permanently from the presentation, you can click the **Do not display this page during screen show** check box. This prevents the page from being displayed in the screen show but it stills exists in the file.

Now let's tell Freelance what we want to do with the objects or text blocks on the page.

Displaying Screen Show Properties for the Text

The screen show properties page for the text block looks slightly different than the page screen show properties page. From this page, you can control all the effects that you assign to your text. You can create a bullet build, add a sound or video, insert transitions between bullets, and tell Freelance how long to wait between the page's appearance and the bullet's appearance. Let's open it now so we can continue creating the screen show.

Do It:

With the title page of the presentation displayed, and the Infobox open, here's how to display the text screen show properties page:

❖ Click on the **Introducing Major Chips' Chocolate Chips** text block. The Infobox changes and the text screen show properties page is displayed, as shown in Figure 14.4.

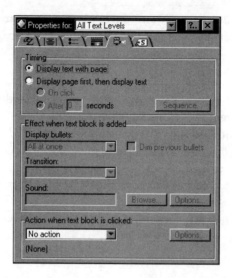

Figure 14.4 *The All Text Levels screen show properties page.*

The default is set to display the text with the page, but we want something more dynamic. Let's make the page title appear after the presentation page appears.

Timing Text and Objects

By default, when you open a page, all the text and objects appear at once. You can change this so that each object appears at a different time. You can have the page appear first, then some text, and then a graphic. The trick is in the timing: you need to tell Freelance how much of a delay there should between objects and text appearing on the screen. What we want to do is display the page first, then have the title appear. To do this, we need to adjust the timing.

Do It:

To adjust the timing so that a page appears before the text:

1. From the screen show properties page, click on the **Display page first, then display text** radio button.
2. Enter **10** in the After 0 seconds text box.

On your own, to adjust the timing for the page subtitle so that it appears 15 seconds after the page is opened. Then open the second presentation page in the Freelance window. Using the steps you've just learned, change the transition to **Curtains**, select **Agenda** (the title of the page) and set the timing so that it appears two seconds after the page. The Agenda page contains a 2-column bulleted list. Let's set it up as a bullet build.

Creating Bullet Builds

Bullet builds are a nice way to introduce the information slowly and add comments as you go along. Each bullet moves onto the page after a specified number of seconds. The previously added bulleted item can be dimmed to make the new bullet the focus of attention. This is an attractive way to add movement to a screen show.

Do It:

To create a bullet build:

1. Select the bulleted list right.
2. Click on **Display page first, then display text**.
3. Enter **5** in the After 0 seconds text box.
4. Open the Display bullets drop-down list and select **One at a time**.
   - ❖ Optionally, you can select the **Dim previous bullets** check box to dim a bulleted item after the next bulleted item appears on the page. Let's select it for this example.
5. Select **Fly up** from the Transition drop-down list. This transition displays the text at the bottom of the page and has it fly upwards to its place in the bulleted list.
   - ❖ You can add a sound to the bulleted list following the steps I showed you earlier. A fun sound for this effect would be a "whooshing" noise as the bullet flies up to the list. Try the **whistle.wave** file, supplied by Freelance.

Next, select the bulleted list to the left and apply the same screen show properties we just assigned to the right bulleted list. Now we have three text blocks on this page that we've assigned screen show properties to. We need to tell Freelance in what order we want the page items to appear.

N O T E

When you create a bullet build, the effect is applied only to the Level 1 text in the list. Any items entered as a sub-bullet to Level 1 text appear at the same time as the Level 1 text. For example, in the left bulleted list on the Agenda page, *Market Research, The Results,* and *Our Product* are all sub-bullets of New Product Information. When the New Product Information text appears, the three sub-bullets appear with it.

Sequencing Objects

Once you've changed Freelance's default behavior of displaying everything on a page at once, you have to instruct it as to the order in which you want the objects to appear. Otherwise, Freelance adds the items to the page in the order in which you changed them.

Do It:

To sequence the objects on the page:

1. Click the **Sequence** button. The Screen Show Sequence Overview dialog box appears in the window, as shown in Figure 14.5.

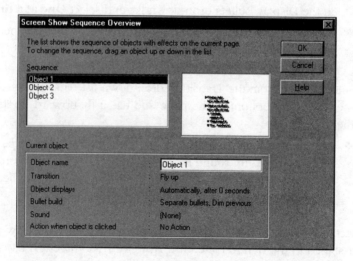

Figure 14.5 *The Screen Show Sequence Overview dialog box.*

In the sequence list window, there are three objects listed. You can click on an object listed and see, in the thumbnail to the right, which item that number represents.

NOTE

2. Click on **Object 2** in the Sequence list. The page title appears in the thumbnail.

3. Drag Object 2 upward and release it when it appears at the top of the list.

4. Click **OK** to return to the Screen Show properties page.

Use the steps I just showed you to put the bulleted lists in the correct sequence. When the page appears in the screen show, the title of the page appears first, then the bulleted list to the left, followed by the bulleted list to the right. And each previously displayed bullet is dimmed when the next bullet appears.

When you have numerous items on a page that you want to sequence, it may help to give each object a name so that you can identify it more easily. To do this, select the object in the Sequence list box. Enter a meaningful name in the Object name text box in the Current object area of the dialog box. Click **OK**. Freelance exits you out of the dialog box. When you click the **Sequence** button again, the dialog box pops up but this time instead of listing Object 1 in the Sequence list, the name you entered appears in the list.

NOTE

You now know most of the basics for creating a screen show. Before I show you something else, turn to page 3 of the presentation, the *Introducing Major Chips* page. Change the title so that it appears 2 seconds after the page. Change the bulleted list into a bullet build with the same properties as we just entered for the previous page's bulleted items. Next, open the *Major Chips' 1995 Sales*, page 4. Change the default so that the page appears first, then the title of the page 2 seconds later. Now I'm going to show you a couple of neat features that you can use.

Assigning an Action to Text or Objects

Freelance allows you to assign an action to a block of text or an object. An action includes jumping to a different area within the presentation, playing a movie or sound, or running a show. When you assign this action to the object, all you have to do is click on the object or text to perform the action. For example, you can draw a rectangle and place it on a page, and assign it the task of showing a movie when selected. During the presentation, the presenter just clicks on the rectangle to run the movie.

Before you proceed to the steps, do the following preparation. With the table on page 4, titled **Major Chips' 1995 Sales**, selected, choose **Display the page then display object**, then enter **2** in the After 0 seconds text box. Select **Fly up** from the transition list and **none** from the sound list.

Do It:

To assign an action to objects or text:

1. Select **Play Movie** from the Action when object is clicked list. The Play Movie dialog box, shown in Figure 14.6, appears.

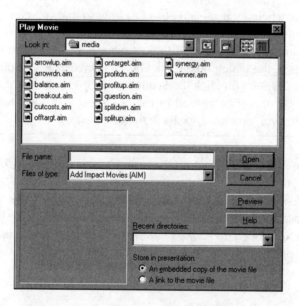

Figure 14.6 *The Play Movie dialog box.*

NOTE There are several mini-movies in the folder already. You installed them when you installed Freelance. To see what each one looks like, click the **Preview** button, but be warned—movies take up a lot of memory, so displaying them can take awhile.

2.   Choose the **profitup.aim** movie.

3.   Click **Open** to assign the action of playing the movie to the chart.

4.   Next, click the **Options** button to tell Freelance how often you want this movie to be played, where on the page it should be displayed and so forth. The Options dialog box, shown in Figure 14.7, appears.

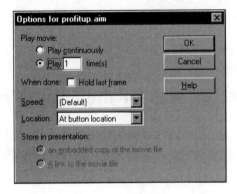

Figure 14.7 *The Options dialog box.*

5.   Click on the **Play 1 time(s)** radio button to play it only once.

6.   Select **Medium** from the Speed list.

7.   Select **At button location** from the Location drop-down list menu.

8.   Click **OK** to return to the Properties page.

9.   Finally, close the Infobox.

When you click on the chart during the screen show presentation, the movie titled *profitup.aim* is displayed. Freelance provides you with a variety of short, animated movies that you can incorporate into your presentation, including moving arrows, profit up and down symbols, question marks, and other short movies clips that get your meaning across. In addition to the movies that Freelance provides you, you can also use movies that you've filmed, digitized and saved as AVI files.

You've learned how to add effects to your pages and the text and objects on the page. All that's left is to show you how to make some global changes to the screen show, and then we'll be ready to view it.

Setting Up the Screen Show

If you want to use different transition styles during the presentation, you have to do it through the screen show properties page we used earlier. But if all of your transitions will be the same, there's an easier way to tell Freelance how to transition between pages, how many seconds to remain on a page, whether you want to be cued to move to the next page, and several other options for the over all screen show effects. This is called *setting up the screen show.*

Selecting Page Effects for the Entire Presentation

Any changes you make in the Set Up Screen Show dialog box affect the entire presentation and override any timing or transitions you already selected.

Do It:

To change the effects for the entire presentation:

1. Select **Set Up Screen Show** from the Presentation menu. The Set Up Screen Show dialog box opens, as shown in Figure 14.8.

2. Select the **Page Effects** tab, if it's not already selected.

3. Select **All existing pages** to make changes to all the pages in the presentation.

 If you don't want the changes you make to affect pages you've already created, select **New Pages Only**.

N O T E

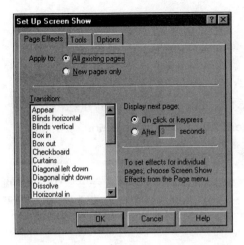

Figure 14.8 *The Set Up Screen Show dialog box.*

4. Choose **Curtains** from the Transition list box. Now the transitions between all the pages appear as curtains.

5. Click on **On click or key_press** to control movement between pages. This manual method allows you control over when the pages open. Otherwise, while presenting a timed presentation, you may have to speed up or slow down to keep up with the set pace. Also, when you enter a number in the After 0 seconds text box, you're affecting not only the page times but the times for the objects and text on the page too.

Good. Now the transition between each page looks the same and you can move forward in the presentation by pressing a key or clicking the mouse.

Displaying the Control Panel

The Control Panel is a set of buttons you can click to move forward, backward, pause, and quit the presentation. If you include it in the presentation, the buttons are designed to be discreet so you'll hardly notice it. The Control Panel can be a helpful feature in controlling how we get to different pages within the screen show.

Do It:

To display the Control Panel in the screen show:

1. Select the **Tools** tab in the Set Up Screen Show dialog box.
2. Click in the **Display control panel** check box.
3. Select **Bottom Right** from the Location section of the dialog box to place the screen show in the window.

When we run the screen show, the control panel will appear at the bottom right in the window. We can use it to go back a page, move forward and even exit the screen show. We need to take care of one more item on this page.

Drawing On-Screen

Using the left mouse button, you can draw on the screen during a presentation to circle and stress information that appears on the page. But if you're clicking to move between pages, you may accidentally draw when you don't mean to. To prevent this, you can turn the Drawing On-screen tool off if you don't plan on drawing during the screen show.

Do It:

To turn Drawing on-screen off:

❖ Click on **Allow drawing on pages** to remove the check mark in the box.

To turn Drawing on-screen back on, click in the check box again.

Signaling a Page Display

Freelance has the ability to signal you when a page is ready to be displayed. You can have Freelance signal you using a tone or with an arrow. To select which method you want to be signaled by, open the Options page of the Set Up Screen Show. Since we don't want the page to be cluttered, let's have Freelance notify us that the next page is ready for display using a tone.

Do It:

To signal that a page is ready to display:

1.   Select the **Options** tab of the Set Up Screen Show dialog box.
2.   Click in the **Sound a tone** check box.

When you hear the tone, you can click the mouse, press **Enter**, or use the **Page Down** key to display the next page.

Running the Screen Show Automatically

The Running the screen show option in Freelance allows you to open a file as a screen show automatically. This can be helpful when you're under time constraints. Let's set this file up so that it runs as a screen show when you open it.

Do It:

To run the screen show automatically:

❖   Click in the **Start screen show automatically when file is opened** check box to be able to open the file as a screen show automatically.

Next time you open the Major Chips file, the screen show will automatically run.

Running a Screen Show in a Continuous Loop

You can set Freelance up so that the screen show returns, or loops back, to the beginning of the screen show again. This is helpful when you want to indicate that you've finished the screen show, you're presenting the same screen show soon after or you simply don't want the Freelance window to be visible.

Do It:

To run a screen show as a continuous loop:

❖   From the Options tab, select the **Run screen show in continuous loop** check box.

Now, when you finish the screen show, the title page reappears on the screen. Well, are you anxious to see the results?

Running a Screen Show

To see the results of all the effects you've added, you need to run the screen show. It's a good idea to occasionally run your screen show while you're working on it to see the results of your selections and make any changes. When the big day comes to show the presentation to an audience, you want to be well prepared.

Do It:

To run a presentation as a screen show:

1. Open the Presentation menu and select **Run Screen Show**. A cascade menu opens.

2. Click on **From Beginning** to see the screen show from the beginning. The first page of the presentation occupies the entire screen.

To exit a screen show before it's finished, press the **Esc** key.

N O T E

As you watch, take notes of the things that you need to adjust once the show is finished. It takes time and practice to get a feel for the timing of a screen show.

From Here...

I've showed you the basics of creating a presentation from start to finish. Now you know how to print it out in various forms and display it as a screen show. The only things left to show you are how to create your own SmartMasters and SmartIcons. Next we'll put together everything you've learned so far as we create a custom SmartMaster that you can save and use for your own presentations.

CHAPTER 15

Customizing SmartMasters
(Putting it all together)

By know you've probably seen most of the SmartMasters that are available to you. There are over a hundred and each one has been designed to work with the color palette assigned to it. Freelance recommends that you not edit the SmartMasters, but you are able to do so if you want. Just be careful, you don't want to screw-up the SmartMaster look for good. If you don't like any of the SmartMasters available you can create SmartMaster looks from scratch using the skills I taught you.

When creating (or editing) a SmartMaster, you can add a backdrop, text blocks, logos and create your own presentation pages. We're going to create a simple SmartMaster look, but keep in mind that what I show you about creating a look can also be used to edit an existing SmartMaster look. And feel free to embellish on what I do. Let's begin by starting a new presentation. Close the Major Chips presentation but stay in Freelance.

Choosing a Blank Look

Freelance has several SmartMaster looks that don't have any designs or images on the backdrop. But they do have "Click here" prompts that you use to add text. Let's choose one of these blank looks now, then we'll add our own design to the background.

Do It:

To choose a blank look:

1. Click on the **Create a new file** SmartIcon. The New Presentation dialog box, shown in Figure 15.1, appears.

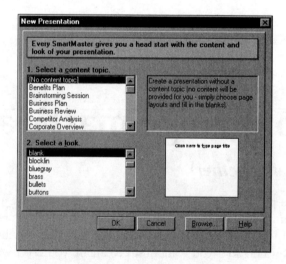

Figure 15.1 *The New Presentation dialog box.*

2. Select **[No look - blank background]** from the Select a look list box.
3. Click **OK**. The New Page dialog box pops up.
4. Select **Title** from the Select a page layout list.
5. Click **OK**. The title page for the blank background appears in the Freelance window, as shown in Figure 15.2.

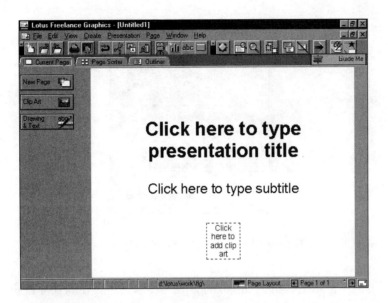

Figure 15.2 *The Freelance window with a title page.*

This is a plain SmartMaster look that you could use for presentations, but it really works better as a place to begin creating.

Selecting a Color Palette

Do you remember that color palette we created in Chapter 11, "Working with Color"? We should really have a palette where the colors work well together. Since we have a palette that we created already, titled *Custom*, let's assign it to our presentation before we continue further. If you didn't create a palette, you can go back and do so now or you can choose from one of the additional palettes that came with Freelance.

Do It:

To select a color palette:

1. From the Presentation menu, select **Edit Backdrop**.
2. Select **Switch Palette** from the Presentation menu. The Switch Palette dialog box appears, as shown in Figure 15.3.

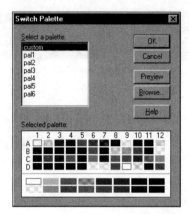

Figure 15.3 *The Switch Palette dialog box.*

3. Select **custom** from the Select a palette list box. The blank SmartMaster title page is visible again, except the title is assigned a color now.

Every color in a palette is there for a specific purpose. Some are for text colors, some for background colors and so forth. That's why the title of the page now has a color assigned to it. Okay, here's where we begin to explore some new territory.

Editing a Backdrop

To change a SmartMaster look, you need to edit the backdrop. The *backdrop* is the design and colors associated with the background of the page. You can't edit the backdrop in the presentation window. We have to first open the backdrop to begin editing it.

Do It:

To access the backdrop:

❖ With the Presentation menu open, select **Edit Backdrop**.

This is where you can add any fixed text or graphics that you want displayed on every page of the presentation. The dashed rectangle represents the space allotted to the text or graphics on every page. Let's reduce the size so that we have room to add a logo later.

Resizing the "Click here" Block Guide

The "Click here" block guide displays the page area where text or graphics normally appear. You may need to resize it if you're adding a logo or graphic to every page. Since we're going to add a logo to our new presentation, let's reduce the size of the block guide. Be aware that when you resize the block guide, you're effecting how the text and graphics will appear on the page.

Do It:

To change the size of the "Click here" block guide:

1. Select the dashed rectangle.
2. Grab the center handle of the left edge and drag it toward the right margin until it looks similar to Figure 15.4.

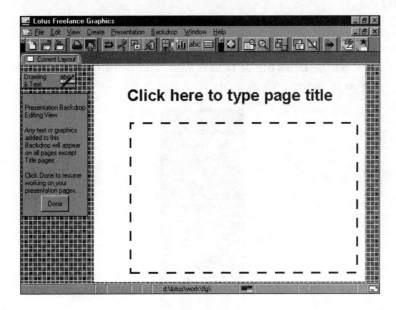

Figure 15.4 *The "Click here" block guide resized.*

Good, now our logo won't interfere with any text or graphics we add. Let's start designing a backdrop for the SmartMaster look.

Creating the Background

Creating a backdrop for a SmartMaster involves displaying text and object properties pages in the Infobox and using the Tools palette. Most of the looks included with Freelance have geometric shapes, patterns and colors that create an attractive backdrop. If you're designing the look with a specific application in mind, think carefully about the colors you're using and the intended audience. Make sure you've completed Chapter 9, which shows you how to use the drawing tools. I'm assuming that you know how to work with these tools.

SmartMasters usually have three colors that dominate the background. The background that we are creating next is the underlying color that will dominate the look. Since this color is so prominent throughout the presentation, it should be a light and subtle shade that will work well with two darker colors. We'll use the darker colors to accent areas of the foreground in the next section.

Do It:

To create a background:

1. Click on the **Drawing & Text** button. The Drawing & Text palette, displayed in Figure 15.5, appears.

Figure 15.5 *The Drawing & Text palette.*

2. Using the Square and Rectangle tool, draw a rectangle around the perimeter of the page.

3. With the rectangle selected, display the **Borders & Colors** properties page.

4. Select **None** from the Border Style list box.

5. Select a pattern from the Interior Pattern list box. I've chosen the pattern in the fifth row down, fourth column across.

6. Select **Scarlet** from the Interior Pattern color list box.

7. Select **Parchment** as the Interior Background color.

8. Open the Drawing menu and select **Send to Back** from the Priority cascade menu. Your Freelance window should look similar to Figure 15.6 now.

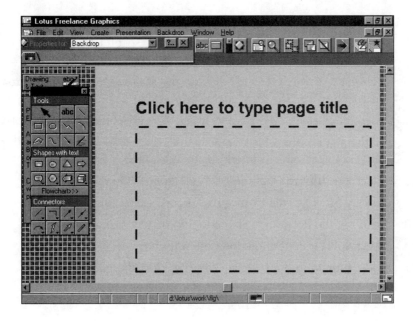

Figure 15.6 *The SmartMaster look changed.*

9. Close the Infobox.

Think of this filled box as the canvas—it's always in the background and will influence the rest of the look. Let's add some shapes to the foreground next.

Creating a Foreground

We could leave the SmartMaster as it is and save the results as a new SmartMaster look, but let's make this pattern a little more complicated and interesting by creating a foreground. If you think of the background as the canvas, the foreground is what we put on top of the canvas.

Do It:

To create a foreground:

1. Select the box you just created.

2. From the Edit menu, select **Replicate**. A second box appears in the window.

3. With the new box selected, click on the **Make selected object smaller** SmartIcon twice. The new box is reduced in size.

4. Open the Infobox. The Borders and Colors properties page is displayed.

5. Fill the second box with a graduated fill (I used the one in the sixth row, third column) from the Interior Pattern list box.

6. Select **Parchment** from the Interior Pattern Color list box.

7. Select **White** from the Interior Background Color list box.

8. Next, use the Polygon & Shape tool to draw a triangle.

9. Select **Solid** from the Interior Pattern list box.

10. Select **Blue** from the Interior Color list. Now the presentation appears as displayed in Figure 15.7.

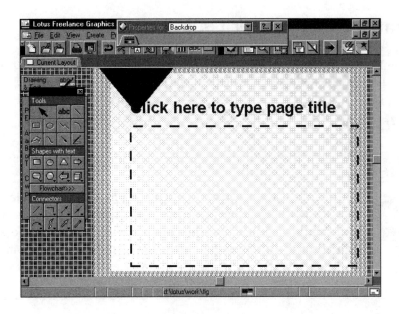

Figure 15.7 *The SmartMaster look with a triangle.*

On your own, add a rectangle to the bottom of the page. Fill it with a graduated fill and select **Scarlet** from the color palette. Don't forget to group the objects you added to the backdrop when you're finished designing it.

Creating a Backdrop was probably easier than you expected. While creating it, you should use the alignment feature to line edges up and center the boxes on top of each other. Remember that you can use your creativity to design some great looking SmartMaster looks. Keep the design simple—you don't want your audience to be more interested in the backdrop than they are in your presentation.

Before you proceed, close the Drawing & Text tools and the Infobox—we don't need them anymore. Let's save our work now.

Saving a SmartMaster Look

Now its time to save the SmartMaster look so it can be used for future presentations. Saving a SmartMaster requires a few more steps than saving a presentation.

Do It:

To save a SmartMaster look:

WARNING

Clicking the **Save** SmartIcon or selecting **Save** from the File menu permanently changes the current SmartMaster. For example, if you click the **Save** SmartIcon, the Blank SmartMaster will be saved with all of the changes you just made to it, leaving you without a Blank SmartMaster. To save a completely new SmartMaster, you must choose **Save As**.

1. From the File menu, select **Save As**. The Warning box may appear if there is only one page in the presentation. Click **OK** to continue. The Save As dialog opens, as shown in Figure 15.8. Notice that the folder called **flg** is open; this is Freelance's default location for your work.

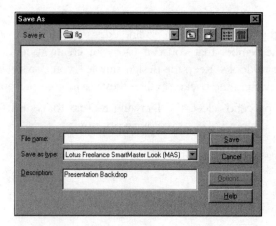

Figure 15.8 *The Save As dialog box.*

To save this SmartMaster look with Freelance's SmartMasters, you must change the flg default.

2. Click the **Up one level** button twice. Your window appears.

3. Double-click on the **smasters** folder.

4. Double-click on **flg**. The SmartMaster files are displayed, as shown in Figure 15.9.

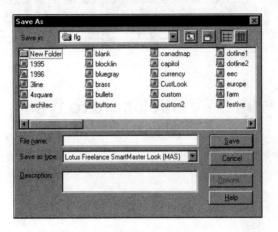

Figure 15.9 *The smasters flg folder.*

 If your window doesn't appear as shown in Figure 15.9, then check to see if **Lotus Freelance SmartMaster Look (MAS)** appears in the Save as type window. If it doesn't, then select it from the Save as type drop-down list. The window should change to display the SmartMaster files now.

5. Enter **CustLook** in the File name text box.

6. Select **Lotus Freelance SmartMaster Look (MAS)** from the Save as type drop-down list. To use this file as a SmartMaster look, you must use this file format.

7. Click **Save** to save the backdrop. You're returned to the Freelance window.

We're done editing the backdrop—at least for now—so click the **Done** button to the left of the SmartMaster Look. If you want to edit the backdrop some more, you can select **Edit Backdrop** again. If you've clicked on the **Done** button and returned to the Freelance presentation window, you're probably panicking right now. Where's the SmartMaster look we just created? Take a look at the title page in Figure 15.10—why didn't its look change?!

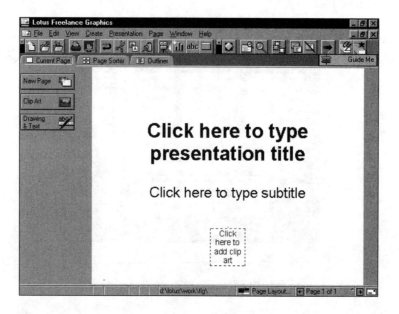

Figure 15.10 *The title page.*

Creating a Title Page with the New Look

When the title page appears, the changes aren't displayed. That's normal. Title pages don't change because Freelance keeps them separate from the twelve standard pages. To create a title page layout, you need to select the Basic Layout page and create your own title page. I'll show you how to do it now.

Do It:

To create a title page using the new look:

1. Click the **New Page** button. The New Page dialog box opens.
2. Select **Basic Layout** from the Select a page layout list. Notice that the CustLook design appears in the thumbnail to the right.
3. Click **OK** to add the page. The page appears in the window.
4. Click on the **Click here to type page title** prompt and type **GlobeTrotter Travel** in the text block.

Let's add a text block so that we can create a subtitle.

Adding a Text Block

Freelance allows you to add text blocks to create bulleted items, titles, notes, labels or callouts. Just make sure you have enough space on the page to add it. Let's add a text block so that we can place a subtitle on the page.

Do It:

To add a text block:

1. Click on the **Create a text block** SmartIcon (it's the one with ABC on it). Notice that nothing happens—your pointer doesn't change.
2. Click and drag the cursor across the page at the location where you want to place the text block.
3. Release the left mouse button. A text block pops up, as shown in Figure 15.11.

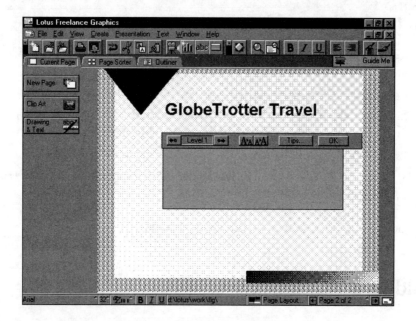

Figure 15.11 *The text block added.*

4. Type **Offering affordable rates to the most popular destinations in the universe**.

You still need to change the text properties, but you have a good base upon which to build. Take a look at some of the other pages and you'll see that the SmartMaster, along with the "Click here" prompts, appears on all the pages (except the title page of course). Close this file. You don't need to save it unless you want to work on it again.

Selecting the Custom SmartMaster Look

If we saved the SmartMaster look correctly, it should appear in the Choose a look list in the Choose a Look for Your Presentation dialog box. Let's open this dialog box and see if it is there.

Do It:

With the presentation open, here's how to select the new look:

1. Select **Choose a different look** from the Presentation menu. The Choose a Look for Your Presentation dialog box, shown in Figure 15.12, opens.

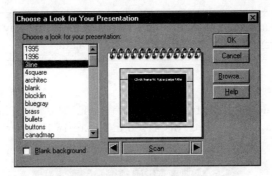

Figure 15.12 *The Choose a Look for Your Presentation dialog box.*

2. Select **custlook** in the Choose a look for your presentation list box. A thumbnail of our SmartMaster look appears to the right.

3. Click **OK** to select the look.

Pretty cool, huh? Now you can use the look any time you want. If you want to use this SmartMaster look exclusively for your company or a client, you may want to add a logo to every page of the presentation. Follow along and I'll show you how.

Adding a Logo to Every Page

Some companies require logos to be placed on every official piece of documentation. It's easy to add a logo to every page of a presentation. In Chapter 10, I showed you how to add a logo to the clip art library and add it to a page. Instead, you can use the selection that allows you to add a logo to every page globally. It's really easy to do. Let's use our Mocha Mouse as the logo.

Do It:

To add a logo to every page:

1. With the presentation open, select **Add a Logo to Every Page** from the Presentation menu.

N O T E

If your logo isn't in the clip art library, then you may need to import it or draw it using the Drawing & Text palette.

2. Select **Add Clip Art** from the Create menu. The Add Clip Art or Diagram to the Page dialog box, displayed in Figure 15.13, opens.

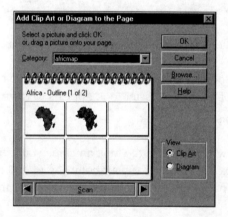

Figure 15.13 *The Add Clip Art or Diagram to the Page dialog box.*

3. Select **Custom** from the Category drop-down list. Mocha Mouse appears in the window.
4. Click on the **Mocha Mouse**.
5. Click **OK** to place it on the page, as shown in Figure 5.14.

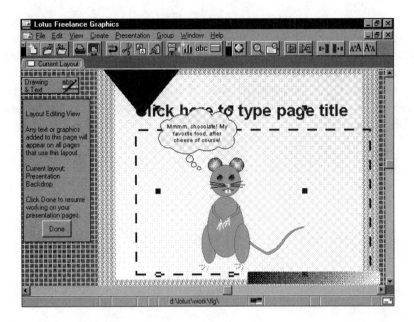

Figure 15.14 *Mocha Mouse on the page.*

Mocha Mouse will need to be scaled down using the handles. When you've scaled down the logo, place it in the lower-left corner outside the dashed rectangle so that it won't interfere with the presentation text.

6. Click **Done** to return to the presentation page.

Mocha Mouse now appears on every page that you add to the presentation—go ahead and give it a try.

From Here...

Freelance gives you the tools needed to create a SmartMaster look that may be more applicable to your presentation topic. You can get really creative and design some artistic SmartMasters using bitmaps and drawings from other programs and import them into Freelance.

Did you ever think, "Hey, it would be nice to have a SmartIcon to do that!" Freelance has a bunch of SmartIcons tucked away that you can use. That's because Freelance lets you customize the SmartIcon bars. You can rearrange or create new SmartIcon bars using the extra SmartIcons that Freelance gives you. And if you don't see a SmartIcon for what you want to do, then create your own! In the final chapter, I'll show you how to customize your SmartIcons to make working with Freelance a little easier.

CHAPTER 16

Customizing
Your Workspace

(Make yourself at home)

I'm sure you know the value of a good SmartIcon by now. By default, Freelance displays two sets of SmartIcons. The first set, which is always available no matter what you're doing, contains SmartIcons that can help you with the basics such as opening and closing files, starting a new file, printing, cutting, copying, and pasting. To the right of these basic SmartIcons is a second set that changes depending on the task you're performing. The appropriate Infobox icon is always available—in addition, you may see icons for zooming in, deleting or duplicating pages, changing text alignment or attributes, etc. You're not stuck with the default SmartIcons that Freelance has chosen for you. You can add different SmartIcons to the existing SmartIcon sets or create new sets of your own.

You can move, hide, display, change or delete SmartIcons individually or as a set. SmartIcon bars and buttons can be customized to include your shortcuts to launch applications, executable files such as .BAT or .EXE, or OLE objects. In addition, you can create your own SmartIcon bars and even your own SmartIcons and then place them on the page as free floating palettes or along the sides of the window. Let's jump in and I'll show you how to make Freelance's SmartIcons work for you.

Moving a SmartIcon Set

You may have worked with other programs where drawing and shortcut tools are placed along the right or left side of the screen or at the bottom. If you'd feel more comfortable with your SmartIcons in a different location, no problem. Have you noticed the narrow space between the SmartIcon sets? This space indicates the start of a new set. A tiny arrow appears in this area too. Click on the arrow—but don't change anything yet. A menu pops up, as shown in Figure 16.1.

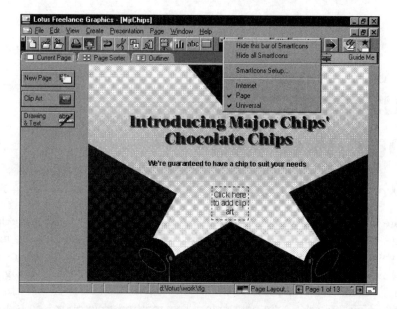

Figure 16.1 *SmartIcon pop-up menu.*

We'll be using this menu to change several SmartIcon settings. Notice the check marks next to Page and Universal—those are the names of the two sets currently displayed. The Universal SmartIcon set, on the left, always appears. This set controls opening, closing, printing, and other actions. The second set is the Page set. This set controls actions such as duplicating, deleting, adding logos to every page, and zooming. The Page set doesn't always appear; it depends on what you're doing. To select a SmartIcon set, you must click on the area immediately below the arrow. This area is referred to as the *bar button*. Let's move the Universal set so that it appears along the left edge of the window.

Do It:

To move a SmartIcon set:

1. Click the area below the arrow (it turns into a hand) of the Universal set and drag it toward the left side of the window.

2. Release the left mouse button. The Universal SmartIcon set now appears along the side of the window, as shown in Figure 16.2.

Figure 16.2 *The Universal SmartIcon set moved.*

That was easy, and the set is discreetly located along the side so that it won't get in your way. Instead of putting a SmartIcon set along an edge, you can float it.

Floating a SmartIcon Set

Floating a set means that the set isn't located along an edge; it's just hanging out in the window and can be freely moved. You may want to float a set when you're frequently using the SmartIcons for a context-specific purpose, the set has a limited number of icons, and you don't want to drag the pointer across the page. For example, you may want to have a set that contains the SmartIcons for alignment, priority, properties, rotating, and flipping closer to an object while you're drawing it. It's just more convenient.

Do It:

To float a SmartIcon set:

❖ Click on the space below the arrow of the Universal set and drag it toward the center of the page. When you release the mouse button, the set looks similar to Figure 16.3.

Figure 16.3 *The Universal set floating.*

As you work on different areas of the page, you can drag the set to the new location. In addition to moving and floating SmartIcons, you can change their size.

Sizing SmartIcons

If you have a high-resolution monitor or your eyesight isn't so hot, you may want to enlarge the SmartIcons.

Do It:

To size SmartIcons:

1. Click the bar button of the Universal set.
2. Select **SmartIcons Setup**. The SmartIcons Setup dialog box, shown in Figure 16.4, appears.

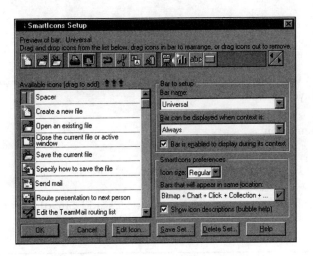

Figure 16.4 *The SmartIcons Setup dialog box.*

3. Open the **Icon Size** drop-down list located in the SmartIcon preferences section.
4. Select **Large**.

5. Click **OK** to exit the dialog box. The SmartIcons appear much larger.

The Universal SmartIcon set is so large now that it can't fit into the window. Go back into the Icon Size drop-down list and select **Regular** to change the sets back to the original size. You may not want to always work with such large buttons because they occupy more space in the Freelance window, leaving you with less space to work on your presentation.

Hiding and Displaying SmartIcon Sets

It can get pretty crowded in the Freelance window when you have multiple sets displayed, so Freelance allows you to hide sets when you aren't using them. They are still available to you, but you can't see them until you decide to display them again. Let's hide the SmartIcon sets currently displayed and then reopen them.

Do It:

To hide all of the currently displayed SmartIcon sets:

❖ Select **Hide all SmartIcons** from the button bar menu. All the SmartIcons displayed disappear.

To display them again:

❖ Select **Show SmartIcons** from the View menu.

The SmartIcons are displayed again. Next, let's add SmartIcons to an already existing set.

N O T E

You can also hide individual sets of SmartIcons. To hide a single set, select **Hide this bar of SmartIcons** from the button bar menu. The SmartIcon set is hidden from view. When you want to display the SmartIcon bar again, open the button bar menu of a visible set and select the SmartIcon set that you want to display.

Adding SmartIcons to a Set

In Chapter 9, we used the priority, alignment, points mode and replicating features a lot. Instead of opening the menus to select these options, it would have been easier and more convenient if these four items had been available as SmartIcons. Freelance has SmartIcons stashed away for almost every action and you can add them to already existing sets, or create new sets.

Do It:

To add to an already existing SmartIcon set:

1. Open the File menu and select **User Setup**.
2. Select **SmartIcons Setup** from the User Setup cascade menu. The SmartIcons Setup dialog box appears.

SHORTCUT

A quick way to open the SmartIcons Setup dialog box is to select **SmartIcons Setup** from the button bar menu.

Let's add SmartIcons for priority, points mode, alignment and replicating features. Take a minute to scroll down the Available icons list to see all the SmartIcons that are available to you.

3. Select **Drawing** from the Bar name list. The Drawing SmartIcon set is displayed when you're using the Drawing & Text palette. Also, the Drawing SmartIcon set appears in the Preview of bar window.
4. Click on the **Replicate** icon in the Available icons list and drag it to the Preview of bar window.
5. Release the mouse key. The Replicate SmartIcon now appears in the Drawing set.

Go ahead and add the following SmartIcons using the steps outlined above:

❖   Align at the bottom
❖   Align at left

❖ Align at right

❖ Align at top

❖ Center in a column

If you start to run out of room in the Preview of bar window, use the increment buttons to the right to view more of the empty section of the window. When you've added all the SmartIcons, your window should appear similar to Figure 16.5.

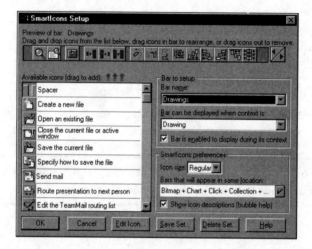

Figure 16.5 *The added SmartIcons.*

NOTE

If you look at the Drawing SmartIcon bar, you can see a space between the Infobox and the **Drag to zoom in on an area** SmartIcons. This helps to visually group SmartIcons that are related to each other and separate them from the other SmartIcons in the set. Add spaces between the SmartIcons that you just added using the Spacer icon located at the very top of the Available icons list. The Spacer icon works that same as the other icons: click and drag it.

There are several SmartIcons in this set that we never used. Let's remove them next.

Removing SmartIcons from a Set

You'll probably find that you don't use some of the buttons in the sets. Freelance's SmartIcon sets contain some buttons that the developers thought that you'd probably use while drawing, creating text, tables and so forth, but you're not required to leave the sets as they are. You can change them by adding to a set as we did, or by removing SmartIcons from a set.

Do It:

To remove SmartIcons from a set:

❖ Click the **Make selected objects larger** icon and drag it off the Preview of bar window. It's removed from the SmartIcon bar.

Remove the **Make selected object smaller** and the **Make selected objects the same size** SmartIcons using the step outlined above. Next, I'm going to show you how to rearrange the icons.

Rearranging the Order of SmartIcons

There are certain SmartIcons that you'll probably use more often than others. These shortcuts can be placed at the beginning of a set for easy access. The alignment buttons are used often when creating objects. Let's move the alignment buttons so that they are positioned before the **Drag to zoom in on an area** SmartIcon.

Do It:

To rearrange the order of a SmartIcon set:

1. Click on the **Align at bottom** SmartIcon and drag it to the left.
2. Position it on top of the **Drag to zoom in on an area** SmartIcon and release the mouse button.

You can rearrange the SmartIcons in the Freelance window too. While holding down the **Ctrl** key, click and drag the SmartIcon you want to move to a different location. For example, to move the Print SmartIcon, press **Ctrl** and click and drag the **Print** SmartIcon to the new location.

The **Align to bottom** SmartIcon now appears before the **Drag to zoom in on an area** SmartIcon. Move the other alignment SmartIcons so they are before the **Drag to zoom in on an area** button, but after the **Align to bottom** SmartIcon.

To separate groups of SmartIcons, use the Spacer icon at the top of the Available icons list.

To save these additions, subtractions, and rearrangement of the Drawing SmartIcon set, click **OK**. The SmartIcon Setup dialog box closes and you're returned to the Freelance window. Next, let's set up an entirely new SmartIcon set.

Creating a New SmartIcon Set

Freelance allows you to create SmartIcon sets that mix and match the SmartIcons available to you. If you're planning to create a lot of screen shows, it's a good idea to create a SmartIcon set that contains all the icons for screen shows. Let's create a set to help in screen show design.

Do It:

To create a new SmartIcon set:

1. Open the SmartIcons Setup dialog box.
2. Select **Movie** from the Bar name list box. The Movie SmartIcon set pops up in the Preview of bar window, as shown in Figure 16.6. I chose this set because it already has some of the elements we need to add to our new set.

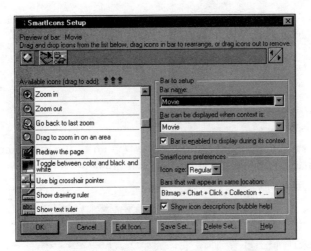

Figure 16.6 *The Movie SmartIcon set.*

3. Add the following SmartIcons to the Preview of bar window:

   ❖ **Open Infobox for selected movie**

   ❖ **Build bullet list page in screen show**

   ❖ **Add a bitmap**

   ❖ **Setup a screen show**

   ❖ **Run screen show from beginning**

   ❖ **Run screen show from here**

   ❖ **Begin rehearsing screen show**

   ❖ **Display screen show rehearsal summary**

   ❖ **Start Lotus Media Manager**

   ❖ **Start Lotus Screen Cam**

I've put my icons in order with spaces included. This looks like a good SmartIcon bar so let's save it as a different set.

Saving a New Set

To be able to use the new SmartIcon set, you need to save it. You could save it as the Movie SmartIcon set, but then the original Movie set is changed. The set we just created isn't only for movies, it's really for screen shows. Instead of saving it as the Movie set, let's save it under a completely different name.

Do It:

To save a new set:

1. Click on the **Save Set** button at the bottom of the dialog box. The Save As SmartIcons File dialog box, shown in Figure 16.7, opens.

Figure 16.7 *The Save As SmartIcons File dialog box.*

2. Enter **Screen Show** in the SmartIcons bar name text box. This is the name that Freelance will always use to refer to this SmartIcon bar.

3. Click the **Browse** button. The Save As dialog box, displayed in Figure 16.8, pops up.

Figure 16.8 *The Save As dialog box.*

4. Enter **Screen Show** in the File name text box.

5. Click **Save** to save the new Screen Show SmartIcon set. Make sure that **SmartIcons** appears in the Save as type text box.

6. Click **OK** to exit the Save As SmartIcons File dialog box.

Now we need to decide when we want this SmartIcon set to appear.

Selecting and Displaying a Set

Displaying all the SmartIcon sets at the same time isn't practical. SmartIcons are context-specific. The Drawing tools don't pop up when you're entering text, for example. Look in the SmartIcons Setup dialog box. The Screen Show SmartIcon set name is selected in the Bar name window, but if you look at the Bar can be displayed when context is window, you can see that *Always* is displayed. This indicates that the Screen Show SmartIcon set that we just created will always appear in the Freelance Window. We don't need it to display that often.

Do It:

To select when a bar can be displayed:

1. Select **Page** from the Bar can be displayed when context is list box.

NOTE

The **Bar is enabled to display during its context** check box should always be checked. This allows the SmartIcon to appear when you need it most.

---

2. Click **OK** to save your changes and exit the dialog box.

To select and display a specific SmartIcon set, you need to choose the name of the set in the Bar name window and then a context in the Bar can be displayed when context is list. The Screen Show SmartIcon set appears with all the pages in Current Page view now, but you can't see it because it's sharing the same location with another SmartIcon set.

Setting the Set Location

SmartIcon sets default to the same location unless you change them. If you have two sets of context SmartIcons that open during the same context, one will appear on top of the other. Look at the SmartIcon bar in the Freelance window now. There are two bar buttons next to each other. That indicates that there are two SmartIcon sets there. One of them is, of course, the screen show set we just created and added. Let's change its default location.

Do It:

To change the location of where a SmartIcon set will appear in the window:

1. Click on the **Screen Show** bar button (it's the bar button where you can't see the set).

2. Select **SmartIcons Setup**. The dialog box opens with Screen Show in the Bar name window.

3. Open the **Bars that will appear in same location** list box.

4. Select **Screen Show** from the drop-down list. Notice that all the SmartIcon sets have a check mark next to them. When you select **Screen Show**, the check disappears. You're telling Freelance that you don't want this set to display in the same location as all the other SmartIcons.

   ❖ Optionally, click on the **Show icon descriptions** check box to disable bubble help.

5. Click **OK**.

When you return to the Current Page view, the SmartIcon set is still hidden. Drag it to the right edge of the window to always display it there. Click on a page title, the Screen Show SmartIcon set disappears. Click on the gray area of the page, the SmartIcon reappears.

Deleting a Set

When you're done with a particular presentation, you may decide that you don't want to keep a special SmartIcon set any longer. To do this, you need to delete it. Let's get rid of Screen Show.

Do It:

To delete a SmartIcon set:

1. Open the SmartIcons Setup dialog box.
2. Click the **Delete Set** button. The Delete Set dialog box, in Figure 16.9, appears.

Figure 16.9 *The Delete Set dialog box.*

3. Select **Screen Show** from the Bar(s) of SmartIcons to list.
4. Click **OK**. A message box pops up asking you if you really want to delete the selected item.
5. Click **Yes**.

Screen Show is now removed from the SmartIcon sets.

The SmartIcons Setup dialog box allows you to access several advanced features. By clicking the **Edit Icon** button at the bottom of the SmartIcons Setup dialog box, you can open the Edit Icon dialog box and change the look of a SmartIcon button, create a new button, or attach a script to a button. These are all advanced features that are beyond the scope of this book. Use Freelance's Help features if you need to change the look of a button or create and add a script.

From Here...

Freelance has several advanced features we haven't discussed in this book. You may never need to use them but you should be aware of what they can do.

❖ **Scripting** Freelance allows you to write your own procedures using a set of tools called the LotusScript Integrated Development Environment (IDE). Using IDE, you can create and debug scripts that let you automate actions such as launching other Lotus SmartSuite applications when clicking on objects within the presentation.

❖ **Publish to the Internet** You can save your presentation as an HTML file (saved as HTM in Freelance) which can be published on the World Wide Web and viewed with web browsers such as Netscape or Mosaic.

This is where I leave you. I've given you all the tools you need to create dynamite presentations. As you work with Freelance, you'll continually discover new tricks and shortcuts. Freelance can be used for many different purposes, and you'll probably come up with new twists we haven't even considered. The more you work with Freelance, the more you'll be able to unleash its vast potential. So have fun, explore, and may the force be with you.

INDEX